SEX
LIFE

ROTATION
~~AN~~

SEX
LIFE

How Our Sexual Experiences
Define Who We Are

Pamela Stephenson-Connolly, PhD

Vermilion
LONDON

1 3 5 7 9 10 8 6 4 2

Published in 2011 by Vermilion, an imprint of Ebury Publishing

Ebury Publishing is a Random House Group Company

The Random House Group Limited Reg. No. 954009

Addresses for companies within the Random House Group can be found at www.randomhouse.co.uk

A CIP catalogue record for this book is available from the British Library

The Random House Group Limited supports The Forest Stewardship Council (FSC), the leading international forest certification organisation. All our titles that are printed on Greenpeace approved FSC certified paper carry the FSC logo. Our paper procurement policy can be found at www.randomhouse.co.uk/environment

Mixed Sources
Product group from well-managed forests and other controlled sources
www.fsc.org Cert no. TT-COC-2139
© 1996 Forest Stewardship Council
FSC

Printed and bound in Great Britain by Clays Ltd, St Ives PLC

ISBN (hardback) 9780091929855
ISBN (trade paperback) 9780091929862

Copies are available at special rates for bulk orders. Contact the sales development team on 020 7840 8487 for more information.

To buy books by your favourite authors and register for offers visit www.randomhouse.co.uk

This book is a work of non-fiction. In some cases identifying characteristics of people interviewed by the author have been changed or obscured to protect the privacy of others.

This book is dedicated to sexologists and campaigners
who fight for sexual rights.

Contents

Introduction

Pleasure is the object, the duty, the goal of all rational creatures.

Voltaire

How many of us had a comfortable, honest and appropriate sex education beyond that embarrassing conversation that usually goes: 'Your father and I think, *erm*, it's about time I talked to you about, *erm*, growing up and ... gosh, is that the time?' Even my students, who were about to become doctors of psychology, would often sidle up to me at the end of a lecture and say things like: 'Dr Connolly, thanks for the directions to my wife's G-spot!' or 'Wow! Until today I never knew it was possible to avoid ejaculating too early!'

Despite the commonly held myth that suggests the opposite, making love does not come easily and spontaneously. Rather, it's something we have to learn. So, isn't it ridiculous that, because of our prudishness, accurate information is so hard to come by? There are many myths about sex, procreation and gender, and it's high time these were busted!

A major research study uncovered some of the following beliefs about conception: 'You won't get pregnant if you douche after sex with Coca-Cola, Sprite or Fanta'; 'You won't get pregnant if you have sex standing up'; and (my favourite), 'You won't get pregnant if your man drinks alcohol before intercourse'. With so much misinformation about, it's a wonder that any of us manages to get it on safely at all. On top of that, we have to ask ourselves, 'Is any sexual information we receive entirely accurate?' 'Can we completely trust all sexuality research?' Do people always tell the truth about their sexual secrets – especially to young research assistants wielding clipboards?

> *I do a lot of research, especially in the apartments of*
> *tall blondes.*
>
> Raymond Chandler

Human sexuality does not just involve physiology. It's heavily influenced by society, race, ethnicity, religion, family background, experience and the messages about sex that each individual gleans from childhood onwards. So, isn't it highly likely that personal stories, truthfully expounded, give us the most valuable insights into the nature of human sexuality in any given society? I happen to think so.

True stories

In telling the sexual story of our lives from conception onwards, I couldn't simply draw upon existing formal research into how things may change from decade to decade, because there's so little of it. Instead, I've recorded the testimonies of men and women of various ages who have actually experienced each particular stage themselves, making this book rich with the direct language of all kinds of people, of different races and religions. Since people of other cultures often have vastly different sexual life-span experiences (and because presenting a world view is beyond the scope of this book), I have concentrated on those living in Western societies.

The language of the testimonies included in this book is often raw. I make no apology for that. Sexuality is often discussed in an extremely down-to-earth fashion, and here it comes straight from the tellers' mouths. I feel it's important that each testimony is presented as faithfully as possible; however, I occasionally changed a few words to ensure that no one could be identified. But if you are easily offended by frank, sometimes even 'coarse', self-expression, it would be unwise to read further.

As people journey through their sex lives they may have common experiences; however, even among those who are culturally similar, no two people are exactly alike in their sexual responses, desires, partner choices or the timing of their sexual discovery and experimentation. So, although I've organised this book according to what is often expectable for each individual's sexual development and experience from one decade to another, I do not mean to imply that there's only one 'normal' pattern of human sexual development from cradle to grave. Rather, there is much variation in all facets of what can be considered 'normal' human sexuality. In fact, I prefer to use the word 'normative' because it seems to allow for broader definitions of what may be commonly accepted – and in my view that is especially necessary when it comes to sexual behaviour.

This not a 'how-to' book. Any learning to be found here takes place through an understanding that we are sexual beings from before we are born, and that – given reasonable health – our sexual lives can continue to be vibrant until the day we die, if we so wish.

Sex is a natural function. You can't make it happen, but you can teach people to let it happen.
                                        Dr William H. Masters

In many instances, I've chosen to avoid commenting on personal testimonies, including some that may seem shocking or inflammatory, because I believe it's more useful to allow individual readers to react to them in their own way and draw their own conclusions. Hopefully this will stimulate more thought – and even discussion – than if the text were encumbered by 'expert opinion'. In any case, there's no one 'right way' to, say, handle dilemmas – such as whether to supply your teenaged girl with condoms, or what to do upon discovering your partner's obsession with internet erotica – because each situation is laden with the specific values, beliefs, agreements, personalities, relationship status, sexual histories and the state of physical or mental health of the people involved. In addition, as a psychologist specialising in sex therapy, it would be wrong for me to pass judgement, especially concerning moral issues; I leave that to others. Instead, as a therapist, I try to help individuals seeking my assistance by engaging with them in a healing protocol that includes putting their struggles into perspective, soothing their fears and offering practical advice. Many are relieved to learn that there is a rich and broad tapestry of human sexual experience – for we are all afraid of being defined as 'abnormal'.

Changing times ... and mores

Not so long ago, a woman filed for divorce because she caught her husband having virtual sex online. This is a striking illustration of the fact that, with every new technological advance or change in societal structure, we may experience sex in new ways. The age of the internet presents us with fresh challenges, and involves a paradigm shift. It begs many questions – not least of which concerns the contemporary conceptions of sexual fidelity. So many people are plagued with private problems such as: 'Is it really cheating if we're not meeting face to face ... if we don't exchange any bodily fluids?'

Throughout history, human beings have had to deal with alterations to the sexual *Zeitgeist*, as well as changes in concrete laws and mores. In Greek times, women were prevented from studying mathematics because it was believed that it would damage their wombs. Once upon a time in England, the Church banned male shepherds because it was believed that having sex with sheep was commonplace – so girls had to do the job instead. And, in the 19th century, doctors had vibrating machines in their offices with which they treated 'hysterical' women by giving them orgasms to 'calm them down'. The history of sex is fascinating and illuminating, and helps us to put our current sexual mores into perspective. We must always remember that how we view sexuality today is transitory; it will change into something quite different in years to come.

Our sexual journeys

Why write a book about the course of human sexuality, as we experience it from the very beginning of our existence until the day we die? I believe it's the best way to illustrate the diversity of human sexual experiences, and thereby engage the reader in a dialogue that stimulates a process of learning more about his or her sexual self. The sexual identity of every mature adult has been achieved through a journey of dynamic development, shaped by many, many influences, including their physical sexual responses, their gender, how they connect with other human beings for partnership and/or sex, how they feel about their bodies and genitals ... and there's much, much more to the story.

Prior to the end of the 19th century – in other words, before Sigmund Freud's writing changed people's thinking on the subject of childhood sexuality – people thought the sex 'monster' came out of the box at puberty. But Freud, who developed important and influential theories about sexual development, insisted that major aspects of human sexual development actually occurred in childhood. More recently, researchers have realised that sexual development is a lifelong process – beginning even before birth and ending as we die – and that our sexual selves change, adapt and develop over the course of our entire life span.

Alfred Kinsey and his colleagues provided a significant amount of data about childhood sexuality, through the extremely detailed surveys that they carried out 70 years ago. And some recent studies have involved asking mothers what they have observed about their own children's eroticism. However, collecting data about childhood sexuality is extremely difficult. Can you imagine the uproar if a bunch of sex researchers turned up at your child's school and parents got a note saying: 'Tomorrow your child will be questioned in detail about her sexual responses'?

Understandably, there has been relatively little formal research on this subject. And, although anthropologists have reported wide variation in sexual mores in different cultures, we really don't know if patterns of early sexual development observed in Western culture apply universally, because we don't have enough cross-cultural studies. So the truth is, we actually have no idea what constitutes 'normal' childhood sexuality. Imagine that … *we just don't know!*

The same goes for sex among elders. In fact, while seeking testimonies for this book, I ran into far more resistance from carers of people in their 80s and beyond than from the elders themselves. The older generations were usually quite happy to talk about their sex lives with someone who was non-judgemental, but even the prospect of such a discussion is distasteful to many younger people. Our society prefers to think granny and grandpa are asexual, but I have news: many are having hot sex, so get over it!

Marketing sex

There has been relatively little research into most areas of sexuality – except, of course, when someone stands to make some serious money out of 'proving' that enough people suffer from some kind of sexual difficulty to warrant government approval for a little pill, in an appealing shade of blue, pink or any other hue. In our culture, sexuality is a cornerstone of market forces; but to make that system viable we have to convince people that great sex is within their grasp, if only they look, smell, taste or sound better. In other words, they'd better arm themselves with 'freshness products' and sign up for teeth-whitening, weight-loss programmes and on-line dating if they want sexual satisfaction. And if none of that works, there are all kinds of substitutes for sex – chocolate, lime-infused vodka, or a safari in India. But first you have to deliver an insidious message that whatever sex they're currently having (if indeed they are) is second-rate, abnormal, unhealthy, or at least less exciting or frequent than 'the norm'. We have an extreme investment in being 'normal', but the truth is (repeat after me!): *there's no such thing as 'normal'*.

I gathered the testimonies for this book through creating a very comprehensive questionnaire that I sent out to 100 people, asking them to complete it and send it back anonymously (I provided specific instructions concerning a privacy protocol). I also asked those people to forward the questionnaire to five others. I didn't have as many replies as I would have liked, especially in the age categories where people were likely to be busier, or maybe lacked typing proficiency, so I began to conduct face-to-face interviews with people whom I found via word of mouth. I am most grateful to everyone who kindly dedicated the time to provide me with such detailed and highly personal material. It was truly a privilege to hear every single sexual story.

I have tried to be as inclusive as possible, and to embrace people of all different sexual orientations, genders and sexual styles. You won't, for example, find separate 'gay' or 'people with disabilities' sections in this book, because I feel it's more appropriate to include testimonies from members of specific communities as side-by-side, undifferentiated examples of normative human sexuality (for, indeed, that's what they are). I have described certain special challenges of various different groups, and these will be apparent from the specific testimonies of individuals who are (subtly) identified as belonging to those groups. However, I do not claim to offer comprehensive information about the sexuality of every community – that would be beyond the scope of this book.

Our inner beasties

Largely due to the myriad of negative messages about sex that we have acquired since childhood, most of us wrestle enormously with the concept of ourselves as sexual beings. It's far easier to embrace more comforting notions that we are, first and foremost, creatures of vocation, spirit, family, style or intelligence – and that we can *think* our way out of any pesky sexual urges that threaten our rationality and decorum. We prefer to ignore the more insightful, nagging voice that recognises our sexuality as some kind of troublesome inner beastie over which we have no control. This powerful chimera interrupts our sleep, tempts us to be intimate with people we ought to avoid, and generally gets us into all kinds of trouble. What's more, he emerges from his cave at the most inopportune of times. Most of us also think of the sex beast as a creature of the adult realm, one who rears his ugly head at key moments in our post-childhood lives – puberty, courtship, when starting a family – and as a prelude to the majority of things that go wrong in human relationships. But he goes back well before our 21st birthdays. One of the aims of this book is to illustrate, through many personal testimonies, that children are highly sexual beings, too.

The concept of embracing our shadow side will be well known to Jungian scholars, and this type of thinking, I believe, can be applied to our lifelong sexuality. Rather than the sex 'demon' being a mysterious entity beyond the grasp of our conscious selves, why couldn't we get to know it as a constant, close companion? Why can't we consider it a beneficial genie who, rather than lurking to pounce when we least expect it, can become a welcome and recognisable part of our conscious selves? After all, he's around our whole lives, and even defies one of the greatest taboos of our time and society – elder sex.

Some people are quite unaware of their sexual beasties, while others just wish they had some sexual feelings with which to contend. Loss or absence of sexual desire, ability or opportunity, and the accompanying feelings one may have about it, are also addressed in this book. Personally, I happen to be a person who loves good sex, and I've thought long and hard about my own sexy 'beastie'. I know he's no cuddly toy, and I must maintain a healthy respect for him. Despite the fact that I'm a knowledgeable sexuality professional, he can leap out unexpectedly. For example, I'm writing this from the tenth floor of a New York building. As I considered the phrasing of the previous paragraph, I looked out of my window and was distracted by movement in a window of the building opposite. An enormously appealing image suddenly formed – a gorgeous, young, tanned man with a naked torso and tiny briefs posing for the photographer who rents that office.

I called to my 22-year-old daughter in the next room: 'Amy! Male-model alert! In tighty-whities! Window opposite!', then immediately felt guilty for displaying a lavish helping of voyeurism to my own daughter – even though she's an adult. I couldn't help staring at the young man, who was flexing his muscles, turning this way and that to show off his beautiful form, as if to arouse me deliberately. Within seconds I felt guilty about looking, even though he was visible to everyone on my side of the entire building. Finally, he bent over to pull on his jeans, offering me a perfect view of his delightful backside.

I was left feeling flushed, excited and lucky – but saddled with an unsettling internal debate: had I behaved appropriately, either in choosing to look at him, or in communicating my interest with my daughter? Was it right to be turned on by a stranger who had no idea what he was doing? More importantly, how would my husband (two rooms away on another side of the building) have felt about it had he known? I decided to ask him.

'What d'you think about that? D'you think I'm a perv?'

'Yeah,' he said, with an approving smile.

I'm glad I have an open-minded husband. I also checked with my daughter. 'Did you think the window thing was pervy of me?'

'No, I thought that was hilarious ... and awesome!' Phew! She had taken it as a woman-to-woman moment. My professional decorum finally returned, and I reminded myself that there's nothing wrong with allowing your children to see that you are a sexual being – as long as the glimpses they catch are appropriate ones, or at least properly explained. Now all I have to worry about is whether I should have let you, the reader, in on my 'dirty little secret' ....

How does your internal dialogue go? Would it be true to say that you, like me, spend a fair amount of time negotiating sexual urges and implementing the necessary controls? I recommend that you take a good look at your own sex beast. What does he look like? When does he emerge? What do you think of him? If you truly get to know this creature, you can control him better – and use him to achieve your pleasurable desires with less risk than if he were a stranger; in other words, it is a good idea to get to know one's sexual self because there's safety in familiarity.

But to get to know the sex beast we have to understand that he's been with us all along. Right from the very start – even before we were born – he's been demanding our attention. He may have changed in style, shape and intensity, but he has never, ever been absent, and nor will he ever be. Our best bet is neither to fear nor mistrust him, but to get to know him as part of our past, present and future sexual journey.

This book is designed to help reconnect the tidy, judgemental, guilty self with the unruly monster forever and ever. He may not be completely tameable, but he can learn to stay off the furniture and do some fabulous tricks.

1

Conception to Five
Boner Babies

Do infants enjoy infancy as much as adults enjoy adultery?

Murray Banks

Our sex life starts before we are born. Yes, it's true. Many people have noticed that baby boys have erections and baby girls experience genital swelling and vaginal lubrication but, in fact, genital arousal can even occur prior to birth, as shown in ultrasound pictures that have captured male foetuses with tiny erections. The sex lives of infants appear to be largely a matter of involuntary genital arousal, but, wait, isn't it just the same for many older humans? I imagine a male infant with an erection might have a large thought balloon above his head saying, 'If only I had the hand-eye coordination to play with that!'

We can't know for sure what infants' sexual feelings really are like, but masturbation to the point of obvious orgasm has been observed in infants of both genders as young as six months old. Even babies of four or five months of age have been observed having experiences that resemble adult orgasm. Some parents are shocked when they notice this in their own children. Over a couple of Cosmopolitans in a city bar, one mother confessed:

I remember when our daughter was less than a year old, my husband and I took her on a long drive to her grandmother's place. Halfway there we suddenly realised that she was masturbating by rocking herself against the divider on her infant car seat. We watched in horror as she brought herself to climax. Then every time we put her in the car we'd hear this hump, hump, hump – all the way to Birmingham.

Both boy and girl infants have been seen to jerk, throb, thrust their pelvises and tense their muscles, leading to a sudden release involving convulsions and rhythmic contractions – followed by noticeable relief and relaxation. Seem familiar? Male babies do not ejaculate, and obviously there'd be no response to the question: 'Was that good for you, baby?', but it's pretty apparent that it was. Most of us do not remember our earliest sexual feelings, so there's no way of knowing exactly what was going on in our baby heads at the time. Fantasising about teddy, perhaps? No, babies are not 'little adults', and we can't attribute the same aspects of sexual feelings and meaning to babies as we do to adults – even though the physical responses are sometimes similar. But babies obviously discover many good feelings that their bodies can provide and, not surprisingly, do their best to recreate them whenever possible. As a matter of fact, that's part of their developmental process.

Given infants' lack of coordination, there are limitations to their ability to manipulate their genitals, but they can usually find ways to stimulate themselves, such as rubbing against a doll or a toy. Many adults observe this, but they may not realise what it is they're witnessing – or perhaps they prefer to remain in denial about the reality of infant sexual responses.

Sex is something the children never discuss in the presence of their elders.

Arthur S. Roche

Sensual touch

At birth, we have a fairly sophisticated sense of touch, smell and taste – the essentials of sexual sensation – and we can certainly experience pleasure. Babies' skin is extremely sensitive to sensual touch; it's as if their entire bodies are one big erogenous zone. As part of their development, they're supposed to make discoveries about how different kinds of touches feel. Most importantly, the early pleasure of being held and caressed helps us to respond positively to sensual and sexual human contact later in life. In fact, the very experiences of being fondled, breastfed, bathed and placed in nappies produce sensual – if not sexual – types of physical responses in babies. In the course of my clinical work I've come across grown men who pay sex workers to put them in nappies and bottle-feed them (just one of the many, many styles of erotic human behaviour). This sexual style is not necessarily pathological, but some of them may be acting out an essential need that was denied to them at the appropriate time – or perhaps they eroticised their infant experiences more than most.

> Some of my clients produce different feelings in me. I mean, all of them think of themselves as 'kinky', and they want me to dominate them because it's a major turn-on for them. But the nappy guys? Well, the way some of them look at me, I get these – I guess you would say – *motherly* feelings.

Being held and caressed is something we all really need at a very early stage of life, and those who don't receive positive sensations from caregivers in infancy may have difficulty bonding with others and being comfortable with adult physical intimacy later on. So the type of attachment (psychological bond) we form with a parent or carer at this early stage will affect our emotional and romantic attachment with future partners.

I was involved with a man who was right for me in many ways, except that he just wasn't the cuddly type, whereas I am. Maybe it was his boarding-school experiences, but he became awkward and uncomfortable about things like hugging. The only time he wanted to be physically close was during sex, and afterwards he'd leap out of bed and into the shower. He was terribly insular and it made me sad.

Adult disapproval

Babies are curious about every aspect of their bodies and the sensations that their various bits and pieces (those yummy thumbs and toes, for example) can provide. Once they develop the ability to touch their genitals, a whole new world of pleasure is available to them. And some infants find they can use genital stroking to soothe themselves when they are feeling anxious. Sound familiar?

I remember lying in bed and thinking it was very pleasant to play with my willy, knocking it around from side to side. It was on a par with chocolate ice cream.

Adults observing early signs of sexual feelings in their children respond in different ways, and in infancy we begin to learn far more about our parents' attitudes towards sexuality than one would think. For example, if a baby hand exploring its own genitals is removed or slapped, the infant begins to learn that certain parts of her body are off-limits. But being cautioned rarely stops the exploration altogether – the child will eventually continue, but will also develop a sense of guilt and shame about it.

At about two years old, I discovered my clitoris, but it wasn't until I was around 13 that I knew for sure that it was 'wrong' to touch it. Then I was fully aware that my mother would have disapproved of what I was doing, and she would have been shocked by my erotic fantasies. But I persevered anyway.

I was sitting in a garden with a number of other adults while a friend's 11-month-old son played happily with his willy in a paddling pool right in front of us. He had a huge grin on his face. His mother was accepting of and comfortable with the situation, but other adults' reactions varied. Some studiously ignored him; some tried unsuccessfully to avoid looking in his direction; and one even suggested the mother should scold and stop him.

I wonder what that disapproving person thought would happen if the child was allowed to continue ... that he'd turn into a 'sex addict'? Become a porn star when he grew up? Or excite an adult who would then abuse him? When I ask such questions I am always quite surprised at the answers, which suggest the most extraordinary leaps of the imagination. People are really quite scared of childhood sexuality.

His grandmother called us in to see what he was doing and we couldn't believe how red-faced and excited he was –

face down, thrusting his hips against the pillow in earnest. We took him to the doctor because we thought it was abnormal at his age – not even four.

Not only is being faced with the reality of infant sexuality shocking to many people, but – despite there being plenty of evidence in support – our society barely acknowledges that it exists. By late childhood most children have picked up cues about needing to keep their sexual behaviour and expression hidden away from the adults around them.

> Don't bother discussing sex with small children. They rarely have anything to add.
>
> Fran Lebowitz

People who draw attention to childhood sexuality – such as those who study it or advocate childhood sex education – are often regarded with suspicion, or even pilloried. This is because many people wish to keep the taboo subject of early sexuality highly secret, preferring to promote childhood as an age of sexless innocence. That's a cosy fantasy, but it's not the reality, and ignoring our children's sexuality, failing to answer their questions satisfactorily or punishing them for experimentation may actually reduce their chances of developing a healthy adult sexuality.

At around three I discovered how fantastic it felt to rub my clitoris. One night I did this under the bed covers while my mother was reading my sister and me a bedtime story. Mother noticed what I was doing and told me to stop, but it felt so good I surreptitiously tried to continue. I suppose my happy face gave the game away. Eventually, she threw down the book and left the room without explaining why. My sister was furious, and blamed me for putting an end to the story. It was all so confusing, and I felt terribly ashamed. I didn't understand why something so pleasant – and experienced entirely by me – should upset my mother. Was it the same kind of crime as picking my nose? Filthy and disgusting? Sex was never ever discussed in our house, but what I learned that night was that sexual feelings were bad and unacceptable, and would cause others to retaliate in an angry way. Even to this day, after I make love, I have this weird sense that something terrible is going to happen.

A healthy response

Once children are old enough to understand, it is important to teach them the importance of privacy; however, also acknowledging that what they are doing is pleasurable and acceptable in private is a parent's best course. The mother in the vignette above might have said: 'I'm glad you've found that your body feels good, but when you want to touch it like that, it's better to be more private, in a room by yourself.'

Of course, it's easy to criticise a parent's response in hindsight. Being confronted with our children's sexuality sometimes takes us by complete surprise, and, without thinking, we can easily over-react. But if we come across a child engaged in self-exploration, masturbation or sex play with other children, it's important that we try not to be punitive.

Mum caught me masturbating once. I was lying on the bed with my dick in my hand. 'Oh God, Brian,' she said. 'Are you coming to dinner?'

I was probably masturbating at four or five. I knew it felt good, but I didn't know why. When I was little, boys sneaked in to play 'you show me yours and I'll show you mine'. I was caught showing my genitals, and I was punished by my mother for that. I was upset because I didn't know I was doing something wrong. I wasn't allowed to see *101 Dalmatians*.

If a parent punishes a child for natural experimentation, she will quickly come to believe that sex and sex organs are bad or dirty. Even a lack of acknowledgement of sexual feelings can lead to children becoming confused.

I don't know if I recognised any sexual feeling *per se*, but at age five I had my first orgasm when riding a kid's bike around on the concrete. I didn't recognise this as 'sexual', but I liked it and kept trying to do it (reach orgasm – even thought at that age I had no vocabulary for it) again and again. I remember wishing that the feeling would last and trying out any number of methods to see if I could get the sensation to keep on going. I would have about five orgasms a day, in quick succession, but could never get a single one to last ...! This makes me laugh to think back on it, but at the time I had the distinct presentiment that this was something I probably shouldn't tell anyone. And I didn't, until a couple of years later, when I felt (after some religious instruction) that maybe I was evil for having had these sensations and was going to go to hell. I convinced myself that if I told someone – like my mum – I would be forgiven by God. That prompted me to tell my mum, but she avoided acknowledging what I was trying to tell her. She told me not to worry about it, but maybe she didn't understand what I was telling her. What I said to her was: 'I have nice feelings down there when I ride the bike over the concrete' and 'I liked it'. Maybe she didn't know how to deal with it and chose avoidance.

An acceptance of a children's exploration and self-pleasuring as a normative part of their development, and helping them to know what is socially acceptable, will help them to become sexually healthy adults.

> The other night my four-year-old daughter was in bed and she said to me: 'I'm touching my privates! Feels great!' I just said, 'Cool!'

> My son was sitting on the toilet with a boner. He looked down and said, 'Whoah! What's going on?' I didn't say anything specific – he was tiny. I just said, 'Yeah, that happens sometimes.'

When children have special needs, teaching them about body privacy can be more difficult.

> I discovered that my son, who has autism, was randomly exposing himself when he first went to school, and also trying to touch his female teachers. We knew it was harder for him than for other children to understand that this was not okay, or to control his impulses, but his behaviour was upsetting a lot of people. The principal suspended him and threatened to expel him if he didn't stop. Fortunately we found a psychologist who managed to teach him about privacy and helped him to control his urges.

Parents and carers of children with special needs are particularly ill-advised to ignore signs of inappropriate or public sexual expression in their sons or daughters. Helping such children engage in appropriate sexual behaviour without making them feel ashamed requires exceptional finesse – and, most likely, professional advice.

What's that 'down there'?

Most children are really budding little scientists, engaged in a vital task to provide themselves with an informed sexual future.

> I have had sexual responses for almost as young as I can remember. I said to my mother one night at bath-time, 'If I play with my willy, it gets hard!' I was not yet at school, so maybe three-and-a-half or four? There was no specific stimulant; I just noticed the physical reaction.
>
> I called it my 'willy', and my sister's was her 'fanny'. I didn't think about them much, except that the hard feeling was sort of nice.

It is helpful for children to be taught the proper names for their genitals so they can feel more comfortable with their bodies throughout their lives. I wish we could teach girls 'vulva', 'vagina', 'labia', and 'clitoris' (not 'pee-pee', and so on!). If we fail to do so we are missing the opportunity to teach them the important functions of different parts of their genitals – or worse, encouraging them to ignore them as 'unspeakable'. Children need to be taught the basic function of their genital parts – what does what. It's best to label vagina, vulva, labia and clitoris as individual parts of the genitals, and to distinguish the urethra and anus as separate entities that are used respectively for urination and defecation. If we don't help them to differentiate between the sex and elimination organs, they may grow up thinking the genitals are smelly and unclean – which will affect their sexual attitudes later in life. Sometimes people reach young adulthood and beyond without ever learning important anatomical details. When I was an associate graduate-school professor in California, a 32-year-old PhD student approached me after my sexual anatomy class and said: 'It's a terrible thing to admit, but until today I thought I peed through my vagina!' She's not the only one.

> When I was a young girl, I picked up the term 'front botty' for my vulva. Front botty? What did that suggest – that female sex organs were just a front-side version of the butt crack?

> I called my genitals 'bottom' – in particular, 'front bottom' or 'fanny'. Vagina was a dirty or embarrassing word.

Studies have shown that girls between one and four are less likely to be given names for their genitals than boys are for their male genitals. Why? Is it because the vagina is considered more shameful, dirty or unspeakable than male genitalia?

> I never seemed to be told by my parents what to call my vagina – although my brother's penis was referred to as a 'stroop', which is an old-fashioned Scots word for 'handle' or 'spout'! I got the impression from my parents

pretty quickly that you did not talk about things that were 'down below'!

Parents label other parts of the body – 'mouth', 'ear' and 'elbow' – so why not 'vagina'? If we don't mention children's genitals, children learn the lesson that 'down there' is bad, dirty and not to be touched. When I am treating a person for a sexual disorder and hear them use the term 'down there' instead of the correct names for their genitals, it gives me a pretty good idea of their attitudes to sex and their genitals – and the kind of environment in which they were raised. It can take a lot of work to help someone like this become comfortable with his or her own body and sexuality.

> Even though I love the feeling of being given cunnilingus, I have to force myself to allow it to happen. I first have to scrub down there until it's clean, clean, clean. I just can't get over the idea that it's a filthy area that tastes bad and I shouldn't really expect my man to go down there. On the other hand, I have no problem going down on him – even if it's not that fresh.

Apparently women do have dirtier genitals than men. Anyone who's ever been to a supermarket knows that! I mean, where are the penile-freshness products? I'm kidding, of course. The female sex organs should not be viewed as intrinsically unclean and there is no need for all those feminine-hygiene products. A healthy vagina does not have an unpleasant odour.

> I was grateful that my mother told me not to douche. She said my vagina was a 'self-cleaning oven'.

There's a discrepancy between the slang terms for female and male genitals. 'Tower of power' versus 'pussy' gives a strong indication about how each has traditionally been viewed. My own students offered the following terms for male genitalia: for the penis, cock, chopper, prick, wang, dong, Peter, John Thomas, meat, tool, stick, drill, pleasure-stick, lollipop and knob; for the testicles, balls and nuts. There are many more. The female list includes: pussy, slit, hole, pee-pee, little man in a boat, peapod and bush.

In Western society, not only are boys' genitals more likely to be named than girls', but girls are rarely given any information about the clitoris. Is that because we think that it might encourage them to enjoy the only organ in the human body that is designed purely for pleasure? Surely we should be teaching them to be proud owners?

> I had no idea I had a clitoris – or at least that it was something distinctive rather than part of the mysterious 'down there' – until I was in my 30s. Learning that it was the focus of my sexual pleasure was a revelation. I always thought there was something wrong with me because I didn't enjoy intercourse as much as oral sex or masturbation.

Is that a gun in his nappy, or is he just pleased to see me? The fact that the penis sticks out – in contrast to the more hidden nature of girls' genitals – is probably the reason why both boys and girls seem to be more fascinated by the penis than boys are by girls' vulvas, vaginas or clitorises. It's smart at least to try to answer a child's anatomical questions the best way we can, and to respect their curiosity.

My son was really into internal anatomy. Around four years old he knew the human body system – he could draw it and wanted to know everything about it. I got him books with lots of pictures, and together we explored this web-information game called 'This is Adam' – based on Adam and Eve – about all the systems of the body, including the reproductive one. At one point there was an option to put a fig leaf over Adam's genitals and I asked, 'Do you want this there or not?' He said, 'I want to see what it's like without the fig leaf.' He was so curious.

Natural curiosity

Young children are certainly interested in the various pleasurable feelings their genitals can provide. When it comes to sexual behaviour, curiosity is the mother of invention, and some children become extremely creative in their pleasure-seeking.

My family had a little 'whirlpool' that sat on the edge of the tub, and I liked to find quiet time by reading in the bath. Once I realised how great it felt to have the jet stream hitting me in the area of my crotch, I took baths more often and paid much more attention. It was secretive, of course. I would play with objects inside me (fingers or the handles of toothbrushes) while in the tub, for added pleasure.

I would put sticky candy on my nipples and have the dog lick it off.

But children don't just focus on their own genitals. From very early on, many are also extremely curious about other children's private parts.

Everyone seemed to like to take a look at me. My six-year-old sister got me on a shelf when I was four and investigated. She always wanted facts. She just wanted a look-see so she put me high up to make it easy.

Children's sexual touching and experimentation are a natural result of their intense curiosity, and in certain other cultures this is expected and encouraged. For example, among certain Australian aboriginal people, there were no taboos against infantile sexuality or intercourse simulation at five or six – until Western ideas started changing that. Nudity is not common in Western culture, so young children who have never seen naked other-gender siblings may have a vague idea that there's a difference, but remain in the dark and curious about the details.

We were five years old and our parents had organised a school run. The first thing one of the boys in the car ever said to me was, 'I'm not your boyfriend, so don't go telling all the girls in your class that I am.' Then he showed me his penis in the back of the Volvo. And I showed him my vulva. We were in traffic, facing the driver of the next car. I remember being really surprised that he didn't have a vagina.

I remember playing the 'show me yours' game with a boy on my front porch. The fact that we were doing this in full view of neighbours and passers-by indicates that we did not think there was anything wrong at all with this game. He showed me his penis, but I suddenly felt shy and only showed him my slip. He laughed at first, but kept insisting I should keep my side of the bargain. Finally he became thoroughly annoyed with me and had a full-on tantrum, causing my babysitter to send him home.

What did that little girl learn? That male tolerance for teasing has limits – they like it only up to a certain point, and if it goes too far they can react with anger. Through such games and experiences children also learn about the social and psychological aspects of sexual interaction – essential learning for everyone.

By the age of six, many children have engaged in some sort of interactive sex play. The 'I'll show you mine if you show me yours' type of play may start as early as three years or so, when toddlers start socialising with other young children, and it's then that they start being especially curious about their friends' bodies – especially the hidden bits. They inspect and sometimes touch each other's genitals, masturbate, or role-play as investigative doctors or nurses. This can occur with members of the same or other gender, and it's all perfectly common and normative.

> When I was six or seven, my mum caught me with Stephen Wong. With our pants down, touching each other's penises. She yelled, 'Stop it!' and 'Don't do it again!' I felt like she wanted me to say something, but she wasn't going to help me with it. She never talked about 'the birds and the bees'; she just signed me up for a sex-education class. We weren't the 'hugs and kisses' kind of family.

A person's sexuality involves biology, physiology and psychology – as well as his or her social, historic and religious background. Likewise, children's sex play and experimentation involve far more than a means by which to satisfy their curiosity about basic anatomy or physiology. For example, their emergent personality traits also influence their sexual expression.

> By four years old I was masturbating every day. And I remember playing 'doctor' with my four- and five-year-old girlfriends. We would find a location in the house that was the last place our parents would come looking for us, then one of us would undress and the other would carry out examinations and our idea of medical procedures. I played this game with both girls and boys, but with boys I was only ever the doctor. I would 'examine' them, but they didn't get to touch me. We used toy doctors' kits that our parents gave us. Each contained a stethoscope, thermometer, blood-pressure gauge and that silver thing with the little light on it that you wore on your head. The only thing I ever stole in my entire life was the thermometer from my girlfriend's kit. You see, I was a perfectionist, and I took my sex-play doctoring very seriously. To have had an incomplete doctors' kit would have been irresponsible.

In their valiant attempts to learn about sex and their bodies, children can display other wonderful qualities – even an entrepreneurial bent.

> My brother charged a quarter or a dime to each of my five-year-old friends, and when he had a good-sized audience he'd take off all his clothes and put on a towel and run across the lawn. At some point he'd flip up the towel so we could see his penis.

Children are also curious about the sexuality of the adults and older siblings around them. Again, we should avoid over-reacting or punishing them for it – even if it is awkward for us.

> My first memory of something sexual was walking in on my parents when I was about two or three. Dad was on top of mother and I looked; it was strange. Mum said, 'Go back to bed, Lavinia', but I knew something was going on. I just thought it was very odd. I didn't consider it an attack because my mother's voice was very calm. After that I was suspicious and a bit of a snoop. Next, I'm about five, when we had a two-storey house and Dad and Mom's bedroom was downstairs. I had chicken pox, so I had to be near their bedroom. One night I heard noises and immediately connected that with sex. I crept down the hall on my hands and knees, and Dad said, 'Get back to bed, Lavinia!' I meekly crawled back to bed.

> *Children are a contraceptive. Every time you go to make love, the toddler toddles in. Try Vaseline. On the doorknob. Sounds painful but they can't get in!*
>
> Kathy Lette

Pleasure and sensuality

The process of teaching children about all kinds of pleasurable feelings and sensuality – not just about sex – is an important job for a parent or carer.

My very earliest sexual memory was really quasi-sexual – having my hair blow-dried by my mum at age four. It was too pleasurable to be anything else, although obviously not understood to be sexual as such at the time.

If we can help engender delight in all lovely sensations – the luscious taste and texture of a ripe peach, the visual beauty found in nature or art, the shivery thrill of running a bird's feather across one's arm – we are setting the stage for children to become sensual beings as adults and to enhance their sexuality beyond the perfunctory 'wham-bam' genital story.

My mother was a dress-maker. I loved going into her work room. She would let me play with the remnants – left-over material from garments she'd made. I adored the feel of silky fabrics and used to run them all over my skin. For contrast, I'd try a bit of heavy tweed, or raw linen.

My sisters and I used to hold each other down and tickle each other in different places all over our bodies. Some of the feelings were exciting, some excruciating, some intolerable. There was a lot of squealing. Looking back, I'm quite sure there were sexual feelings.

Children who grow up comfortable with their genitals and their sexual feelings, and who feel safe enjoying sensuality and pleasure, are extremely lucky.

I was comfortable with all of my sexual feelings. I was a major reader, so I was pretty knowledgeable. I *loved* the sensations. They didn't scare me.

Unfortunately, some kids can end up feeling really afraid of their sexuality. This is most likely to happen if they receive highly negative messages about sex and come to perceive it as dangerous, dirty or evil. Such views may persist through the years and make it difficult for them to enjoy sexuality, even in adulthood.

> They worried, scared and confused me, and made me anxious and guilty. Apart from the physical pleasure, there was nothing gratifying at all about my sexual feelings; they made me feel dirty and horrible – somehow connected to all those 'dirty men' out there, because I thought my feelings resembled theirs.

> I started masturbating at around four, but I always felt guilty and worried, and tried to distract myself or do something else instead. This general feeling around masturbation would accompany me until about three years into my marriage.

In 19th-century Europe and America, parents who believed that masturbation was 'the source of all evil' utilised all kinds of ingeniously cruel chastity devices to prevent their children from becoming aroused via touching or through erotic thoughts. These Victorian methods included spiked cages to prevent their sons' erections, straitjackets, and tying arms to the bedposts. If sexual arousal persisted, they would sometimes resort to leeches and hot irons applied to the genitals – and even castration or clitoridectomy. When we consider that the latter occurred not much more than 100 years ago, it does not seem surprising that the legacy of disapproval regarding childhood sexuality still lingers.

> I really did believe that my short-sightedness was a result of my unstoppable masturbatory efforts. I remember

feeling acute shame and guilt during my appointment with the eye-doctor. I assumed he would know exactly what 'caused' my myopia. After I was given spectacles to wear, I managed to avoid touching myself for a good couple of weeks, but I finally decided that abstinence was actually harder to bear than being called 'four-eyes'.

I think I've only just recently started to acquire a good understanding of how I'm formed – that is, without guilt! I now feel comfortable about my sexuality and my desires, and I think I probably fall right into the 'normal' bracket, if there is such a thing. Even just a few years ago I probably would have tried to suppress even so much as the desire to masturbate – believing it to be deviant behaviour.

Childhood fantasies ...

Sometimes early experiences set the stage for specific erotic interests that may develop in adulthood. The person who had the following experience later developed a strong interest in consensual erotic sadomasochism – just one of the many normative variations in human sexual expression:

> I had a kindergarten teacher who used to act out nursery rhymes with the class. She especially liked 'The Old Woman Who Lived in a Shoe' and used to come round and spank us all as part of the act-out. I liked it and used to ask to do that rhyme.

Young children do have fantasies. Remember?

> My five-year-old sexual fantasies took the form of being a doctor or nurse. I would imagine giving someone an

injection in the ass ... or even a breast. That seemed like an interesting thing, and not something that would hurt. I used to sit in church, pick someone out and daydream.

... and first love connections

Infants may even have their own secret love lives. You know those pictures on greetings cards that some people find adorable – with baby boys and girls apparently making eyes at each other, or even kissing or hugging? Given the opportunity, there can actually be infant-infant encounters in late infancy that resemble sexual love connections, with the two of them gazing dopily at each other, and kissing and stroking just as older lovers do. Young children may even have feelings of love and jealousy – and can become heartbroken.

At around five, I remember loving to kiss and sometimes realising that it did not mean to some of the boys what it meant to me. And they would move on, causing a huge insecure hurt in me.

Boy, girl or not quite sure

In early childhood we also learn which gender role we are expected to play – i.e. what is expected of males and females in our culture. This is reinforced by adults; for example, when they dress up girls in pretty things and give them dolls to play with, versus encouraging sport and 'roughhousing' in boys. By at least three years of age, children have begun to develop a sense of gender identity; they usually know whether they are boys or girls. They start to consider themselves part of their particular group and try to behave the same way as other girls or boys.

This is particularly difficult and confusing for trans-gendered children, who grow up feeling that they are 'trapped in the wrong body'. If a child expresses a strong belief that he or she is gendered differently from what outward physiology displays, it is not useful to make that child feel bad or ashamed, or to use shaming words like 'sissy'. It's important to allow that child to be whatever feels right – boy, girl or something in between.

> Right from the start I thought I was a boy. I dressed like my brothers, behaved like my brothers, and everyone called me a 'tomboy'. I didn't get that. I thought I was just the same – until I realised we had different-shaped genitals. That was shocking to me. Even though I was referred to as a girl, I still didn't believe it. I thought I was a defective boy. No one helped me to understand who I was, or why I hated wearing dresses.

Many people confuse gender and sexuality. Being trans-gendered is about gender, not about sexuality; one's sexual behaviour and sexual orientation are quite different and separate from one's gender identity. In fact, trans-gendered people can be straight, gay or bisexual, just like everyone else. Whether a child's tendency to express gender in an unusual way is transitory or more permanent, it's best to allow that child to make his or her own decisions about it. And if those choices are worrying, I recommend consulting with an accredited counsellor.

Educating tots

Whatever their gender, very few children receive entirely satisfactory sex education, and many receive none at all.

As a young child I was not able to discuss sex with a reliable person, nor get the answers I needed. Sex was entirely taboo in the house. We never ever saw our parents naked. Even much later, when menstruation began, it was not talked about, but a booklet was discreetly left by my bedside. Since I was a late starter – 15-and-a-half years old – this was way after the horse had bolted.

So what should we teach small children about sex and biological development? They should definitely know the correct names for their genitals. Help them accept pleasurable feelings, and to feel that masturbation is okay. Give them permission to enjoy it privately.

I noticed my son's touching of his genitals before he could walk. I had to say, 'I know it feels good, but that's something you do in private.'

So, in summary, the thrust should be to label sexual interest not as 'bad', but only inappropriate for certain times, places or persons. It's also important for children to understand that self-stimulation is normal, pleasurable and acceptable, and that it should take place in private. Then they'll come to understand sexuality as a normal aspect of their development – and that, in turn, will help them to become sexually healthy adults.

If you are asked a question that you can't answer, say, 'I don't know, but I'll find out and tell you.' Kids respect adults who are willing to admit that they don't know something. Accept and respect a child's body and don't over-react if you catch them playing with their own genitals, or those of same-age others. Respect a child's need for privacy (which will encourage them to respect the privacy of others). Don't punish them if they catch you naked or making love. Show them lots of physical affection, listen to them and trust them. In the formative years of development, this type of approach to budding sexuality really matters.

Acknowledging sexuality

Listening to children, trusting them and acknowledging their sexuality in the right way – matter-of-fact and not too intrusively – helps to strengthen positive body feelings and self-esteem. And if we can help them to feel that they are in charge of their own bodies, they will feel empowered to say a loud 'Stop', and then run away and tell if someone tries to touch private body parts in an inappropriate way. But our main message should be that sex is normal, fun and pleasurable – and not something of which they should be generally afraid. It's a delicate but extremely important balance.

It is, however, important to be alert to the potential for abuse and inappropriate touching (particularly in the case of children with certain special needs that may render them vulnerable). Keep in mind that older children can lead a young child into experiences for which they're not quite ready.

I was maybe four years old? I stayed the night at a friend's house (was babysat) and a girl much older than me touched me between my legs with her toes when we were sleeping in the same bed (top and tail), and she told me to do the same to her. I remember feeling really horrible and naughty – and also quite confused. She also made me smell her fingers after she touched herself. It was not very nice.

It's important that all children feel they can talk to a parent or carer about any kind of sexual feelings or experiences, and that those adults will calmly help them to make sense of it all without passing judgement.

> When I was a little kid, I was walking home from school one day when a car pulled up beside me. There was a guy – I thought he was asking directions. I looked in and he was masturbating. I'd never seen a man's penis before. I just ran home mortified. I didn't feel I could tell my mother.

If children do have uncomfortable sexual experiences, it's vital that they feel they can tell someone who will listen without over-reacting – and still love them.

Understanding abuse

Some people consider all early childhood sexuality to be something worrying and negative – linked with impropriety and coercion. In fact, we tend only to hear or read the words 'sex' and 'child' in the same sentence when we are also learning about episodes of abuse. I've already pointed out that becoming aware of young children's sexuality very often engenders concern in their parents – fearing, for example, that overt self-pleasuring displays might stimulate observing adults to acting improperly. I say, 'Relax. Most adults are *not* paedophiles', and we can best protect our children from the few who are by teaching them what kind of touching by adults is okay and what kind is not. Without frightening them, we should outline the fact that no adult has the right to touch them with sexual intent. This involves teaching them about intuition; if they have an uncomfortable sense that an adult is intruding on their physical boundaries, they should trust that feeling.

> The bus was crowded and I had to sit behind my mother and younger sister. A man came and sat down beside me. I knew at once something was weird because he sat so close on my side of the seat and he was squashing me. I looked at him but he was staring straight ahead. He folded his arms and the hand nearest me surreptitiously started trying to touch me. It felt so weird I called out, 'Mum!' He leapt up and jumped off the bus.

Children also need to know that it's not their fault if they are sexually abused.

> My first awareness of sexuality occurred at the age of four, when I used to sit with my 11-year-old brother, watching porn of men and women having sex. My mum worked as a beautician and she relied on my brother to take care of us. He had a plastic milk crate full of sex magazines and VHS porn movies under his bed. When I was six and he was 13 years old, my brother sexually molested me about six times. What I was feeling felt good, but I also felt dirty and knew it was wrong, not right. He also molested my little sister, who was four. He threatened us, but I finally told Mum. They took him away from us and stuck him in juvie. Later he kept it up – did it with others – and he went to jail. He had also molested our cousins and some other people. I found out that when my brother was little, my mother used to leave him at home

by himself, which was very irresponsible. I discovered later that his father (who committed suicide) had molested him. We had counselling, but I think I hid it down deep. I had been very close to my brother. I'm 24 now. In the last couple of years, all this anxiety in me has resurfaced. I'm not sure where it's all coming from. I mean, I know it was not my fault and all that, but I think what happened has really affected me. I have a very high sex drive and use porn a lot.

People who have experienced early coercive sex are often left with complex feelings, such as shame, guilt, anger and a lowered sense of self-worth. They are sometimes sexualised by their abusers, to the point that their future sexuality – including their libido and their sexual connections with others – may remain complicated and unhealthy, until healing takes place.

Into the open

If we acknowledge our young children's sexuality, we are helping to strengthen their self-esteem. We are helping them to have positive feelings about their bodies as well as encouraging their competence and assertiveness. Of course, some people object to any kind of pre-marital sexuality on religious or moral grounds and it is certainly their right to do so. However, ideally parents can set limits and teach a moral code without simultaneously sending a message that sex is intrinsically bad or evil.

I had a very conservative start. Hellfire and damnation – I was going to burn in hell. I was horrified by my cock. I would never even wash my genitals – they were too dirty to touch.

> *I thank God I was raised Catholic, so sex will always be dirty.*
>
> John Waters

In fact, secrecy and hiding information about sexuality actually serves to prepare children for the hypocrisy of our culture of adult sexuality. Paradoxically, in the interests of preserving heightened eroticism, we wouldn't want it all to be open and accepted, now would we?

> I was entirely happy with having sexual feelings in the early innocent phase. They just happened sometimes and they were nice. As I got to know what was happening, they were exciting and forbidden, a very powerful combo.

Yes, if you want to ensure a child's capacity eventually to have really hot sex – and a strong motivation to seek it – you'd think it would be a good idea first to create an environment of steamy guilt. Unfortunately, extreme sexual repression is a powerful negative force in a person's life, and can even lead to unconsciously motivated sexual acting-out of a highly antisocial nature.

> I now understand that my sexual touching of young parishioners was abusive and wrong, but at the time I was tortured by urges that I felt were quite beyond my control. I prayed, punished myself, tried to rationalise my behaviour, but nothing could change that inexorable drive to satisfy my basest needs.

Trying to understand

In the course of my interviews for this book, I spoke to many adults whose very early struggles with sexual understanding have had a profound effect on their later sexuality. In the absence of readily available help or education, some had sought answers wherever they could.

> I had no real understanding of my own sexual physiology when I was a little child – not until I was about 16 or 17, when I got a mirror out and had a good look. Funnily enough, I had a library ticket for the 'adult library' section in George IV Bridge, Edinburgh, and avidly read all the books I could about sex and growing up – *What To Tell Your Teenaged Children*, etc. So I had been exposed to drawings and illustrations, but seen very few actual photos or pictures. I was reading Freud by this stage and found his views on sexuality quite fascinating.

In fact, it was Sigmund Freud who came up with the notion of 'libido'. He suggested that infants were born with a reservoir of undirected sexual energy that eventually – after being focused first on the mouth (oral stage) and then the bowels (anal stage) – finds placement in the genitals by around the age of three. After that, Freud believed, the libido disappears for a while (latency period), only to re-emerge with full genital focus at puberty (genital stage). Freud thought that variations in the course of this process (he called it 'psychosexual development') affected the formation of a person's entire personality. It's an amazing theory – with which many people disagree.

If you can remember having sexual feelings somewhere between the age of four and puberty, you'll be joining the retinue of debunkers! Here's a conversation starter: 'I say, are you a fan of Freud's theory of psychosexual development? I distinctly remember trying to hump my babysitter at age five, so I'd say that old "latency" argument has to be a load of bollocks … don't you agree?'

2

Six to Puberty
The Sexperimenters

From the moment I was six I felt sexy. And let me tell you it was hell, sheer hell, waiting to do something about it.

Bette Davis

Many adults suffer from sexual amnesia. They conveniently 'forget' what horny little beasts they were as children. I've already pointed out that childhood sexuality is an uncomfortable subject these days and many people do not want to believe that children are sexual beings ... and, yet, they are. We only have to think back with an open mind to our own childhoods and our early eroticism, fantasies, explorations and those mysterious 'wet dreams' or secret orgasms.

> I could have an orgasm really easily. For example, I could have one by leaning forward while holding a pencil on my lap strategically placed to connect with my clitoris. Of course, I used the eraser end. All I needed was a tiny bit of pressure. And I could orgasm by leaning against a desk if I was asked to stand up to read or answer questions. Or even just by squeezing my legs together. I could even have an orgasm in front of the nuns while they were talking to me. I think they caught on though, because after a while they wouldn't let us cross our legs.

Middle childhood is a time when profound and influential sexual learning is gleaned from parents, other adults, siblings and friends – and from society at large. These are not necessarily spoken messages. In fact some of the most powerful teachings are picked up by subtle inference. It can be extremely illuminating to delve into one's own background and determine what sexual messages were received from parents or carers – and how that might have influenced our adult sexuality. Girls in particular may receive 'sex is dangerous' messages without the balancing 'it's fun and pleasurable' ones that might eventually help them best to enjoy adult sexuality.

> I never had any proper explanations about sex – there was nothing but what you picked up in the playground. Although once my mum gave me a 'choose your own ending' book designed to give girls insight into how men might prey on them and how sexual abuse can happen. I remember feeling really guilty because I would knowingly choose the foolish answer ('not to tell anyone') because I wanted to see what would happen and kind of liked reading about it. I got a tingly feeling 'down there'. This made me feel *awful*, and I remember actually hating myself for it.

Children between the ages of six and 12 are often even more curious about their bodies and sex than they were in infancy. And they are now acquiring a vocabulary to discuss sex comprehension skills to understand when adults discuss it, and computer skills so they can research it on the internet. Unfortunately, parents who do not help their children to negotiate their sexual journey – and especially those whose attitudes towards sex foster negative and punitive experiences – can engender profound disappointment in the child. This can colour – or even damage – their entire relationship.

> My most vivid childhood memory is of my father coming in from the coal house carrying a coal bucket, and seeing

me scratching myself 'down below'. I was *only* scratching myself! He put me over his knee and gave me a good thrashing. I was totally bewildered and hadn't a clue what was going on. I literally lost all respect for him from that day till the day he died, since I hadn't a clue what I had 'done wrong'. I would have been five or six.

When I was a boy, I knew there were secret things to do with women – their bodies and babies – that I was not supposed to know. My mother would talk in code to other women about things like 'she got into trouble' which, even then, I knew was a *double entendre*.

The unspoken message that this boy gleaned was that sex was worrying, mysterious and dangerous – and that males were excluded from its realities. That may well have been somewhat true of the time, but those sexual beliefs were probably carried into adulthood by that boy, and it's not hard to see how they might have prevented his grown-up sexual experiences from being entirely comfortable. One can only hope that he was directly taught the facts of pregnancy so he could avoid 'getting a girl into trouble' and becoming, himself, the subject of female whispering circles.

At least we don't live in the 19th century, when there was such a fear of sex that a middle-class boy in London might have had to retire to bed with his penis attached to a piece of string hung with bells, designed to attract his parents' punitive attention if he had 'impure' thoughts. As I pointed out earlier, there is still a lingering disapproval of early self-exploration, and it's time we all realised that this attitude can hamper sexual development and may even have an unfortunate effect on later adult lovemaking styles. Thankfully, many liberal adults are becoming more relaxed about their children's sexuality, and some are even models of acceptance.

> One night our seven-year-old son was lying in bed and we were just about to say goodnight when he summoned us excitedly. 'Quick, come here!' We went in and saw that he was lying naked with just a sheet over him. He had an erection and was making the sheet go up and down while he went, '*AROOOOGA!*' – making a sound like a horn from an old-fashioned Model T Ford each time the sheet went up. He was delighted with his new toy. We didn't make a big deal of it. We just said, 'Good trick! Now go to sleep.' But we laughed really hard afterwards.

In contrast to a child whose parents might have reacted with embarrassment or even horror, the unspoken message that this boy received is that his sexual responses are normal, acceptable and fun. Of course, he was not consciously aware of that, but it's not hard to see how this positive sense of his own body, fostered by his parents' acceptance, would help him to experience healthy sexuality later in life, is it? To work out what unspoken messages one received about sex in childhood, I have found the following exercise to be helpful.

Sit quietly and think back to your early days. Put aside what was directly said about sex (if, indeed, it was discussed at all), and instead ask yourself, 'What did my mother/father/carer *really* think about sex?' You intuitively do know the answer to that question, and it will come to you if you allow it to. Was it that sex is shameful? Wonderful? If the subject of sex felt taboo, perhaps the unspoken message was that it was sinful or dangerous. Whatever those messages were for you, they were extremely important influences in the formation of your sexuality. The next step is to ask yourself exactly how those early messages might have affected your adult sexuality. This can be a really illuminating exercise.

Even though our intelligence and adult learning may well have countered negative sexual messages up to a point, the early, deeply held messages can still be highly influential.

The unspoken message I got from my mother was that sex was something women had to endure, and that men were 'only after one thing'. From my father I got the message that sex was something about which women, in particular, should be kept ignorant and pure ... whatever 'pure' was.

My mother always believed sex was a necessary evil, to do with satisfying a 'man's needs'.

The women who received the two messages above both struggled with aspects of their sexuality later on. Although they were both able to function well in the physical sense, each had to work quite hard to give herself permission fully to enjoy making love with her partner, without harbouring resentment or distrust.

Some of my students recall the following:

My mother thought that sex was dangerous.
My mother thought that sex was over-rated.

My mother thought that sex was something girls should never be caught enjoying.

My father thought that sex was okay for his sons, but not for his daughters.

My father thought that sex was best with women you weren't married to.

My father always thought that sex was great – but don't get into trouble.

Sex is a bad thing because it rumples the bedclothes.
                                   Jacqueline Kennedy Onassis

As I pointed out in the last chapter, parents and others who convey messages of disapproval about sex may only be increasing the likelihood that it will continue; the sheer 'naughtiness' – even 'evilness' – of masturbation and sexual contact with others tends to make it even more exciting and guarantee repetition. This is perhaps the most profound lesson in the ambivalence of human nature that we ever receive, but it does not lead to the healthiest form of sexuality.

I discovered masturbation and I loved it, but was constantly told it was sinful, wicked and the way to hell. This actually made it more exciting in truth, and I didn't buy all the hell stuff anyway. But it was a big issue for all of us and many were in agonies of fear about what we couldn't stop ourselves from doing.

One of the ways in which strongly negative attitudes towards sexuality can cause problems in adulthood is that, for some, even universally 'sanctioned' sex (in marriage, for purposes of procreation) cannot be entirely enjoyed. After all, it's hardly likely that someone who has been tortured with guilt about sex for 20 years or so will suddenly be able to let go of all that and summon the necessary positive responses in an instant. And negative sexual attitudes commonly underlie serious relationship problems, as well as full-blown sexual disorders.

> For years I couldn't stay with a woman once I'd slept with her. Once we'd done the 'dirty deed' she changed into a whore before my very eyes.

> My therapist helped me understand that not being able to have an orgasm had a lot to do with how frightened I was of sex. When I was a child, I came to believe (through things that happened to my mother) that you couldn't trust men, and that sex was a destructive force that causes a woman to lose all her power and dignity. Even though I was happily married to a wonderful, kind man I just couldn't allow myself to lose control enough to climax.

So how can we help our children have healthy attitudes towards sexuality? We will obviously teach them moral codes based on our own values, and they will pick up our own attitudes to sexuality even if we do not directly discuss it with them. The trick is to think carefully about the specific sexual messages we impart, and ensure that we are providing them with a balanced view that includes not only our concerns – for example, pregnancy, disease, coercion and morality – but also the positive truths about sex (it is highly pleasurable and can be safe and fun). Obviously, such lessons should to be imparted in an age-appropriate fashion.

Outside influences

Throughout the years from six to puberty, children also need help making sense of all the confusing messages they are bound to receive from peers, other adults and society at large, and ideally we should be the type of parents who can be available to answer questions in a non-judgemental fashion. I know that's not easy for parents who are, themselves, rather conflicted about sexuality – but is parenting ever easy? We may have to do some learning, studying or self-discovery to reach the point where we are comfortable talking about sex with anyone, let alone our children … but it's worth it.

Of course, it's not only our own attitudes and teaching about sexuality that form our children's attitudes towards sex. Religious teaching and societal messages generally, perhaps from school or the media, set rules and blueprints for sexual behaviour. Even the fairy stories we tell our children have a profound influence on their notions of love and sexuality. It is in the telling of Sleeping Beauty, Cinderella and Snow White that girls learn about passivity in sex and love, and boys understand their expected role as saviours, protectors and the architects of a woman's sexual life. The often false and disappointing expectations that follow us into adulthood will continue as long as we continue to expound those fables without balancing them with some realistic information. 'Someday my prince will come' is probably true, but he may come while moving your head on his penis at the school dance when you're just 15. That's not exactly what most girls are led to believe – or wish for.

I used to be Snow White, but I drifted.

Mae West

Boys are encouraged to take on a protective sensibility that conflicts with what they become really enthusiastic about as they strive to gain sexual experience – conquest!

> *Chivalry: going about releasing beautiful maidens from other men's castles and taking them to your own castle.*
>
> Henry W. Nevinson

Again, it's beneficial to help children understand that there are other sides to any story and, as soon as they are capable of it, to encourage critical thought so they can eventually seek, question and find answers for themselves on any topic.

Preparing children for physical changes

Children also need help understanding the sexual development of their own bodies. Somewhere between six and 12 years of age, the first physical signs of puberty become evident, and a sense of privacy about those changes tends to develop as well. But the bodily changes can be disturbing – even frightening – if a child has not been prepared for such events; in fact, these changes can still be hard to deal with when children do understand what's happening to them and why.

> At the age of ten, my friends at school told me girls bleed and I was horrified. I remember hearing them arguing about whether blood comes out the back or the front. When I was finally told about menstruation, my father, who was a vet, related it to cats.

Children are extremely eager to learn about their sexually developing bodies. If denied proper information, they will usually turn to extremely untrustworthy sources of information – other children.

> We thought babies came out of the mother's belly button. I spent a lot of time trying to imagine how that would be possible. A big baby, from such a tiny hole. Actually, I wasn't too far wrong on that one.

> Someone told me you could get pregnant from French kissing.

> My girlfriend told me that if you get a cold when you have your period, you'd get a one every single month thereafter. I was terrified about that. Once a month forever is an awful lot of sneezing.

Without proper information, young people make all kinds of incorrect assumptions about what is going on in their bodies, and end up being far more tortured than they need to be.

> At some point prior to adolescence – probably around 11 – I deliberately stopped masturbating. The guilt was getting to me, and I had a strange notion in my head that it might be interfering with my biological development. I actually thought I might not get my period if I kept going.

In my clinical experience, I've often heard adults express anger and a sense of betrayal at parents and others who failed to help them understand their sexuality and physical development at an early age.

Mother was a nurse. She came to my class and explained to all the kids about menstruation. I didn't love the fact that my mother was talking about that with all the other kids, before she talked to me.

Snooping

Would you expect your child to appear in a play without full preparation? Perhaps it is helpful to think of children as actors on an important stage, and childhood sexuality as a rehearsal for adult sex. I think it's a good idea to acknowledge their curiosity. They're clever, and they notice all kinds of things. Some of them actively snoop!

When I was about five or six, I found a wet condom under my mum and dad's bed. I couldn't quite figure it out and thought it had something to do with a rainy day. Later, when I was 12, I found a box of condoms in my dad's drawer and I put it together.

My sister's bedroom was across the hall. One night I heard noises so I crept out and heard my sister say, 'Be quiet – the children!' She meant my sister and me. I waited forever, but it was quiet. A little later, my father was on the phone sounding very angry, talking to the father of my sister's boyfriend, who was a Dutch man called John. I figure that John had snuck over – this was 1952, when girls weren't supposed to be sexually active. She would have been a teenager then. We never saw John again.

Some children even catch their parents engaging in sexual acts. Now it's a little easier than when they were infants for them to make sense of what they see.

The thing that really got to me was that my mother was lying diagonally, obviously trying hard to hold her head off the side of the bed. She had just had her hair done!

Message: sex can be annoying, inconvenient, and ruin your hair-do. Freud believed that catching one's parents copulating was damaging to the psyche, but others disagree. A number of other writers and researchers (I am one of them) think it depends on what kind of event it is, and what the child makes of it.

My son was terrified because, well, I suppose I was being too loud. Around six he came running in saying, 'Mum, are you all right?' My response was, 'I was just having a bad dream.'

When he was 12 he walked in and saw the covers moving. He said, '*Oh God!*' and walked out, disgusted. The next day, I said, 'I guess you're going to have to learn to knock!' He said, 'I'm not coming in at all anymore – that was gross!'

I saw my parents having sex when I was nine. We all slept together in the same room. I woke up late at night and I saw Mum's legs up and Dad's head was down. I was wondering what was going on. Then I felt my pillow moving like someone was trying to face me on the other side. I was so upset. I knew what they were doing. After that my mum got pregnant and we moved to another house.

Isn't it interesting how the sounds are the same for an awful nightmare and great sex?

Rue McClanahan

What do you do if your older child actually catches you and your partner having sex? Avoid hitting your head on the ceiling when you jump! No, it's the same as when they were toddlers: it's best to avoid over-reacting. Calmly tell the child that it's a grown-up way of showing that you love each other. Say, 'It would be nice if you'd knock next time, because we prefer to do this privately.' Screaming, jumping in the air or shouting at the child can cause far more trauma than the sight of you having sex – no matter what you were doing!

> I shared a bedroom with my mother from the age of nine and when she thought I was fast asleep she obviously masturbated to orgasm ... I had no idea what was happening. I thought she was 'dreaming' and I was afraid to wake her. Once I started reading 'grown-up' books, I had a vague idea of what was really going on ...

Awareness of parental sexuality can be disturbing to children if they have a sense of it being a negative experience.

> I woke in the middle of the night because something was going on in my parents' room. Their bed was squeaking and my dad seemed to be grunting and moving in a rhythmic fashion. But it was my mother's reaction that really bothered me – she was whimpering insistently, begging him to stop whatever he was doing. She was clearly saying 'no', and he was clearly ignoring her. I had not previously thought of them as being sexual together, so it was shocking just to become aware of that. And the style and feeling of it was awful. Even though I didn't know exactly what they were doing, it upset me for a very long time. Next day they seemed to be fine, but I was left with

a sense that my mother – and therefore all married women – must have to suffer something terrible at night-time. I was left with a deep fear of marriage, because I associated it with secret pain and disempowerment.

By late childhood many children have received a clear message that not only is sexual behaviour largely unacceptable or unpleasant, but that conversations about sex have to be severely restricted, if not avoided altogether. And not being able to discuss it only amplifies fear and confusion:

I never had any sex education. I went to Catholic school, and at one point, a nun told us that if you kissed a boy and then he had a car accident and died, he would go to hell because he kissed you. We were beyond accepting that logic.

So how should we go about educating older children about sex? Many parents feel conflicted and don't quite know how, and children who pick this up will intuitively avoid the subject.

My mother was, and still is, very closed to the topic and we would not even talk about 'kissing boys' with her. A piece of relevant information here is that my parents divorced when I was seven.

I can certainly talk to my children about sex, but we don't often. They are more embarrassed than me.

Many parents themselves lack accurate information. And they forget that if we only impart warnings and information that indicates sex is dangerous, that's the main message they'll pick up.

The sexual feelings I remember most vividly from my childhood are all wrapped in guilt – a big, black curtain of guilt and shame.

My mother used to say: 'Delia, if S-E-X ever rears its ugly head, close your eyes before you see the rest of it.'

Alan Ayckbourn, in *Bedroom Farce*

We have to acknowledge the pleasurable aspects of sex or we're not telling the truth about it. The fear and rationale are presumably that being honest about the fact that sex is pleasurable will only encourage children to engage in it. This is mythological and erroneous thinking; children already know from their own solo experimentation that it's pleasurable and powerful. They find it confusing when they are told or shown something to the contrary, and long for honesty, clarification and guidance.

My dad was very open and discussed sex with my sister from a very young age. We were offered condoms to carry in our wallets from the age of about 14. We had very open conversations.

Not all parents will be able to be as accepting as that father, although in my view he is exemplary in offering both information, guidance and practical help to protect his children. Providing accurate information may help prevent pregnancy and avoid disease, as well as helping a child eventually to achieve healthier sexuality as an adult. It's wise to make an effort to be an 'askable parent'. That means that whenever you are asked a question about sex, you answer as honestly and truthfully as you can – in a manner that is age-appropriate for the child (in other words, only giving information that they can handle or digest). If a child asks a question in an inappropriate situation – in the middle of a shopping trip or family party – it's best to say, 'That's an extremely important question and I will answer you fully just as soon as we get home.' Then, hurry home, take a deep breath, and follow up! And if you really can't handle it, find someone suitable who can.

> Kids now are very different from my day. My 12-year-old granddaughter says: 'Hey, look Grandma! I've got two hairs!', as she points to her vulva. She's not so developed for her age and really doesn't want to be a 'tween'. But she's much more open about her development than I was.

Practice makes perfect

As they journey through childhood, boys and girls continue to seek more knowledge about what exactly to do with those developing organs. So they keep practising masturbation (sometimes boys do this in groups). By the ages of six to eight, most boys and girls will have moved on from curious twiddling of their genitals to deliberate and systematic masturbation – provided they are not entirely prevented from doing so by parents who have failed to realise that it's normative behaviour.

My mother knew I was masturbating and she would try to make me stop. She'd come into my bedroom and say, 'Okay, put your hands beside you in the bed, and stop doing that.' There was a weekly paper called *Star Magazine,* in which there would always be a picture of a girl in a 'va-va-voom!' outfit, and I thought that was really sexy. I imagined myself to be her and beat off to that image. It seemed very comforting at that point, like I had control. But it was embarrassing, too.

The girl in the above scenario continued to self-pleasure because, like most children, she was unable to stop. However, she experienced overwhelming guilt about it, and her sense of self-worth was damaged because she felt she was 'bad' and a disappointment to her mother. Like many others, she was also confused by the conflicting messages she was receiving: the socially sanctioned sexy female images in the newspaper versus her mother's disapproval.

First orgasm

By the time they reach puberty, most children seem to have achieved the ability to reach orgasm.

The first time I had an orgasm I was furious. That fabulous feeling I got from touching myself suddenly stopped. I didn't understand where it had gone and I thought I had somehow broken it. It was a huge relief when it came back the next day. I gradually learned to make it last and last. By my ninth birthday I was an expert.

The first time I ejaculated was when I was lying in bed with a broken ankle. At first I was touching myself and I felt so tingly. Then I did it again and it tingled, and then it stopped. I didn't come – I stopped when it felt tingly. I loved that feeling when I came the first time. I realised: there's a feeling that's more exciting than just tingling! But if I relax and hold the tingle in then let it pop – wow! That feeling was so great and then this stuff came out. So I started doing it more and more. I didn't care about the tingle thing, I just kept on doing it. I got really tired and lazy. I got beat up by my mum when I didn't do my chores because I was too 'lazy' – I was jerking off too much. Finally my mum caught me jerking off. She spanked me and she called me a 'loser' and a 'pervert' and 'bad boy'. She didn't want me to go near my sisters.

In fact, learning how their bodies work is an important task for children, in preparation for future partner sex. Having good, satisfying adult sex requires first being knowledgeable and confident about our own sexual responses, and then eventually working out how to communicate them to a partner.

Fantasising

Well before they turn 12, boys and girls usually develop the ability to have sexual fantasies. These may begin when a child is confronted by an image, scenario or experience that becomes sexualised, or woven into his or her sexual imagination.

When I was seven or eight, I used to touch myself and imagine myself as the heroine of a comic strip we had in our local paper. She was extremely glamorous, with an unrequited passion for an elusive man called Basil, who wore an eye patch. In my head I had many sexual adventures – all very happily leading to orgasm – with Basil.

We had a schoolteacher who had a zip on the side of her skirt. It was always open an inch or two and you could see she wore red knickers. I fantasised about her when I was 12. Funnily enough I used to fantasise about licking her pussy, but no one ever told me such a thing was possible. I thought I'd invented it.

Fantasies about, or even actual sexual contact with, relatives – cousins or siblings – are really quite common.

I remember feeling real lust for my older cousin when I was around ten. He was a tease – he used to lie in a hammock in the garden in short shorts with a bulge in the crotch area and say funny, teasing things to me. I was very aware of his body and had fantasies about being kissed by him.

Fun and games

As children grow older, their social opportunities usually increase, and so do the moments when they can enjoy unsupervised play, which often includes sexually charged fun. By around the age of five or six, children often start 'playing house', which provides opportunities for many different kinds of learning.

I didn't play sexual games with other kids until I was about nine. I was with my sister, our next-door neighbour, and two boys – the Johnston brothers. My parents had a huge garden with a chicken coop in the back and we played house out there. One day the Johnston boys said, 'If you show us yours, we'll show you ours!' But even then at that young age I was very conscious of the need to avoid being taken advantage of. I said, 'I'm not pulling my pants down for you!' I felt insulted. I thought, 'You didn't want to be my friend – you just want me to pull my pants down.' I had a sense we were unequal. I had not seen a penis yet. I learned from a very early age that boys just want to get into your pants.

'Playing house' is generally considered to be a game in which girls and boys express traditional gender roles, but it can also provide opportunities for private sexual experimentation – depending on where the house is and how it is constructed! Children who play 'house' have usually managed to form a superficial sense of what marriage – or at least co-habitation – is. Unless they have been exposed to same-sex unions, they will usually think of love partnerships as heterosexual, although at this age there is usually some experimental same-gender sexual contact, regardless of what a person's sexual orientation may turn out to be.

Jim said he knew he was gay when he was six, although he still had little crushes on girls. I had had a huge crush on him when I was maybe seven. We sang numbers from musicals together and went for bike rides (I had no brothers). He said he had a girlfriend called Sally, and I was really jealous. The other boy I was interested in also turned out to be gay.

Many gay adults report that they understood what their sexual orientation was quite early on, and most also gleaned that they had to be secretive about it. Some children who are not gay are confused by their same-gender experimentation, even though it is extremely common at this age. The homophobic messages they will have received from adults and peers in their community can cause severe worry. It is always best to teach children to be accepting of diversity – through both direct instruction and by example – as early as possible. Teaching children to be tolerant of those with sexual and gender differences, and not to use pejorative words for gay or trans-gendered people, is a vital task for us all.

> My friend's dad told him I was a 'sissy' and he shouldn't hang around with me. In retrospect I realise that his father must have been a pathetic, uptight homophobe, but I didn't get that then. It was painful to lose my best friend.

Preferring girl-girl or boy-boy action as a child is very common (in fact, it may be more common than playing such games with members of the opposite gender), and does not usually predict a homosexual or lesbian orientation in later life. It's all part of a child's sexual development.

> A neighbour and I used to go into our garage and shut the door. She and I would play striptease and take it in turn to remove all of our clothes down to little g-strings we made with ribbons and safety pins. It was fantastically erotic, but I felt tremendous guilt about it that lasted for years and years. I also thought it meant that I was really a secret lesbian – even though I had loads of boyfriends and definitely only fancied men.

> I'm straight, but in Catholic secondary school I used to play a kissing game with other girls. We would dive into

the swimming pool and kiss each other at the bottom. I guess it seemed especially exciting to do it down under the water. And the nuns couldn't see.

Crushes

When experimentation is coupled with strong sexual attraction, it can lead to some intense feelings and a change in a child's overall behaviour. Feelings of sexual attraction arise pretty early.

I definitely remember being strongly attracted to boys from kindergarten onwards. I remember dressing up in pretty skirts and pulling my blouse slightly off-shoulder to be as appealing to certain objects of my affection – although where this strategy would lead me I had absolutely no idea. But certainly, the notion of romance had not escaped me. I badly wanted their attention.

Children are capable of experiencing passionate love. Many people think this only starts to occur at puberty but, in fact, children – especially girls – can feel intense interest in another person from an extremely young age. It is usually at school that children begin to develop these 'crushes' on peers or even teachers. This is part of the normal learning process. Children begin to discover how their feelings for someone outside their families can be strong, and can affect their mood and behaviour. They start learning – through trial and error – what kind of approach is appropriate, socially acceptable and likely to be well-received. Many begin to discover the anxiety that accompanies longing, the joy of reciprocated feeling and the pain of rejection. Such feelings can be quite bewildering, and it is beneficial for a child who is experiencing them to have someone to talk to who can help make sense of it all – or at least empathise.

> I remember having huge crushes on boys when I was six or seven. With each one, I felt like I loved him and couldn't wait to see him. It was only ever one boy at a time – I was a child serial monogamist. If he returned my affections and got red-faced when we talked – or even held hands or tried to kiss me – that was super-exciting. But if he rejected me, I felt hurt and sad – especially if he chose another girl over me.

> I began to notice girls flirting with boys at about age 11 or 12. I was quite upset about it and I didn't like the fact that everyone wanted to play 'spin the bottle'. I couldn't take the chance of being turned down, so I couldn't do it. I had huge crushes on some of the boys in my vicinity, but they never knew.

Many people have described having childhood crushes on adults – especially teachers …

> At around 10 or 11, I had a desperate crush on my teacher Mr Learner (excellent name!). Luckily he gave me more attention for my academic achievements than for my pre-teen seductiveness and – unlike many less-fortunate girls – I came to associate displaying braininess with sexiness. Some of my friends were not rewarded for exhibiting intelligence, and preferred to hide it, in favour of 'being sexy'.

Family attractions

As I pointed out earlier in this chapter, it's not easy for children to integrate all the different, often conflicting messages they receive about love and sex from so many – largely unreliable – sources. Some of the most unreliable sources of sexual information are brothers, sisters and cousins:

> When I was six years old, my sister – who was one year my junior – promised she would let me play with her boobs when she got some. Thank Christ that never eventuated.

> My first feelings of sexual attraction were probably for my sister. I was very close her when she was five and I was six. When relatives slept over, we shared a bed, and there was touching, etc. It's weird to think of it now.

Sexual experimentation between similar-aged siblings is quite common, but it is of serious concern if it involves force, or occurs between children of dissimilar age. It can be extremely disturbing for a young person to be coerced into sexual contact by an older one. Being threatened or forced into sexual activity can have a damaging psychological effect on anyone, and a long-term effect on their sexuality. They may be left with deep feelings of shame and guilt, as well as a damaged sense of self-worth, and may suffer from post-traumatic stress. In the aftermath of abuse, long-term sexual effects can include avoiding sex, suffering from lowered sexual desire – or having an increased libido that may be inappropriately expressed – difficulty enjoying certain types of sexual contact, feeling sexualised by others, not being able to trust future partners and being unable to achieve orgasm.

By the time I was six, I was being abused by my 14-year-old older brother. This went on until I was 10 and he was 18. He made me strip and he looked at me, touched me everywhere, put his fingers inside, and came on my stomach. I thought he was peeing on me. I would beg him not to pee on me. I used to say, 'I'm going to tell mum about this!' but he would say, 'Go ahead – but you did it, too.' He also said, 'I'll beat you up' and things were violent enough around the house without that. The confusing bit was that it felt good. I used to struggle and scream, but he would cover my mouth. It was really scary and his 14-year-old penis didn't look like 'kid' equipment. I didn't remember all this for a long time and felt miserable about myself. It happened when he was babysitting me. I never told my mother. It wasn't because I thought it would be too much for her to handle. I later realised I didn't tell her because she was going to blame it on me and her favourite boy would be off the hook. Later on, I was very nervous and hesitant when my husband initiated sex. I wanted to have it, and once I could allow it to happen it was lovely, but getting to that point was horrid.

When my brother, who is four years my junior, was five, he became aroused while I was reading him a story. I didn't discourage him and we touched each other through our pyjamas. I recognised my own sexual feelings and, although I didn't understand paedophilia or bisexuality at this age, I grew to feel that I had taken advantage of my little mate. The concept or mention of paedophilia has made me physically sick ever since this realisation. It has never been discussed and we are still very close. I know we will discuss it eventually ... No such guilt feelings about similar, much earlier stuff with my sis; I guess because we're so close in age and were so young.

Uncomfortable experiences

When it comes to sexual experimentation with peers, some early sexual experiences are enormously exciting and positive, while some are not so.

> The boys were there, wanting to see our genitals. I don't recall seeing theirs – if I did, I wasn't impressed. My sister was four, and I was seven. I made my sister show hers. I said, 'She'll show you. Pull down your pants, Susan!'

> In kindergarten, we had to contend with 'Killer Kisses'. The boys would chase the girls and force them to kiss them. You had to hide behind the handball court to get away from the killer kisses. It was half giggly, half genuinely scary.

Such games have been known to get out of hand. Adults may not notice older children's sexuality as much as they might have done earlier in childhood – mainly because older children have often learned to be quite clever about creating opportunities to be private, either alone or with peers, for sexual fun. But without adults around to discuss, limit and supervise them, they can develop an unhealthy acceptance of coercive behaviour – another reason why it is so important to be able to help children make sense of feelings that arise during early sexual contact. Children are generally better protected if they feel they can trust a parent or carer to be available to discuss worrying feelings of any kind. For example, many children witness exhibitionist or public sexuality in adults and need help making sense of it.

When I was 12 years old, I was upstairs on a bus going home from school. I looked down out of the window and saw a man driving an adjacent car with his cock out, masturbating. I was frozen with fear and never spoke about it to anyone.

Some have to negotiate confusing, inappropriate and surprising advances made by strangers, and really need help, comfort and clarification.

He was just crouching there behind his garden fence. I felt he was sort of waiting for me and my sister to walk by, but I wasn't sure. His genitals were hanging out of the side of his shorts – had he arranged them that way so we would see? It was confusing – and disgusting. The confusing bit was not just that I didn't know if it was deliberate or not (in hindsight I think it was because he was looking at us with a very pointed grin), but also that I'd never seen male genitalia and I gleaned from that image that the whole 'package' resembled not one but several pork sausages. I also felt guilty, as if it was our fault, too, for even looking.

When I was a boy, there always seemed to be people trying to feel you up – on buses, in parks, etc. There were guys pretending to bump into you on trains, and men hanging about park toilets. It was everywhere.

Budding maturity

Even before puberty, many older children are having quite mature experiences for which they are ill-prepared. This can be extremely disturbing for them so, again, they need to be protected as far as possible, and require help in making sense of what occurred.

As a child I saw lot of images of older women having sex with men. Then, at about 11, I started touching myself to the point of ejaculation. All those girls in school, they all loved me, but I didn't feel interested in them because they didn't have boobs. But my mum's friends: when I saw them or they came over I'd run and hide in the toilet and jerk myself off. One night my mum had a friend who was sleeping over. She had sex with her boyfriend at our house. In the morning I walked in and she was asleep naked. I went over and kissed her vagina. Then I ran outside and had to jerk off before I went to school.

When I was young, maybe five years old, I saw a lot of people having sex. Usually this was because the bedroom door in our house was often open and they were drunk. Ladies would be moaning and I thought the guys were hurting or killing them.

I remember my cousin who was babysitting us. She met this guy on the bus and they came to the house. She was drunk and so wild with hickeys all over her. I remember her eyes. She looked like Cher, but her attitude was Tina Turner. She was sucking her boyfriend's neck. I felt something was boiling in my stomach. My heart beat really fast and I was trying to swallow but something was stuck in my throat, seeing naked people. 'Wow!' I thought. 'I wonder what they're doing?'

I saw my aunt having sex with her husband. I asked myself, 'Why are these people doing this?' I didn't know anything about a hole and a penis that had to go inside it. I thought they just laid there and rubbed against each other. Then I saw my aunt sucking her husband's dick. I thought, 'She's so in love, she's kissing it.'

Probably the best sex education I had – not the biological stuff, but getting the idea that sex is fantastically involved and exciting – came in the form of a crumpled, typed treatise called 'How Purity Lost Her Halo' that was passed to me by a school friend when I was around 11. I remember thinking at the time that it was well written, and it described the process of a young woman having sex for the first time, and being taught all kinds of extraordinary (or so I thought at the time) acts by an experienced, older and clearly benevolent man. Even to this day I remember portions of it, such as 'being a clever lover, he mixed sandwiches and drinks first while she sat longing for the moment when he would take her in his arms'. From that I got a delicious sense of sexual tension and longing – and also of her pride in her own body, her knowledge of being ready for sex, and her willing participation in this learning process. There were also things in it that disgusted me, such as when he taught her to 'put his testicles in her mouth and gently suck them', but much of it was extremely positive. Unfortunately, none of the boys or men I subsequently had sex with understood how to create erotic tension, and my teenaged years were filled with disappointment on that score. Perhaps we should be open to include erotic education in what we inform young people about sex – so they actually get a sense of how amazing it can be!

The woman who gave the above quote saw her piece of sex education as a positive learning experience, but another person might not have done. The point is that we cannot be with our children every second of the day, and they are going to come across images, written words and live scenarios that confront them with sexual experiences of varying types. We cannot expect children to put it all together in their heads, and these testimonies illustrate the need for parents to set aside their own awkwardness and try to help them with it.

The sexperimenters!

Sexual learning does not occur separately from other learning – it's all intertwined. For example, childhood play first develops as a solo activity, and then children start playing in the vicinity of others in parallel play, progressing on to sharing. Sexual behaviour develops in the same order; after a period of self-exploration, we eventually progress to a more sharing – hopefully reciprocal – type of sexuality with others.

When I was around eight, there was a girl down the street who would show me her vagina. We called it her 'fanny', and she let me and other boys touch it. In fact, there was usually a line of guys outside the laundry shed waiting to go in and do it. She seemed to enjoy it. She was always laughing.

In the process of childhood experimentation, we learn how our own bodies work – and perhaps a bit about how others' do – which contributes to the process of preparing us to be competent partners in the future. In late childhood, some children even experiment with oral sex and attempt vaginal or anal intercourse. Although parents will naturally have some concerns about this, it is quite normative, except in the case of repeated aggressive or coercive sexual behaviour towards other children. As puberty dawns, the early 'sexperimenters' in our society are becoming more and more sexually aware, as well as anxious, eager, confused and curious about the intriguing prospect of becoming a teenager.

My dad told me, 'Anything worth having is worth waiting for.' I waited until I was 15.

Zsa Zsa Gabor

3

Adolescence
Am I Normal?

The back seat produced the sexual revolution.

Jerry Rubin

n our society, we generally think of the bridge between childhood and adulthood as occurring between the ages of 12 and 20. In some other cultures it's a more narrow passage, but Western people in that category – branded as teenagers – have roughly eight years in which to 'grow up'. This process is expected to include achieving sexual maturity, yet that journey is generally viewed with a good deal of ambivalence. On the one hand it is accepted that physical maturation is a normal and unstoppable process; however, there's much debate and concern over what exactly teenagers are supposed to do with their new, mature sex organs and their hormone-fired libidos.

My problem is that girls are always running through my mind. Considering my thoughts, they wouldn't dare walk.

Andy Gibb

Teenagers are acutely aware of the spectacular changes in their bodies, as the sex hormones that were first produced before they were born are rather suddenly accelerated into mass production, causing their genitals and internal reproduction organs to develop and mature. They are just as interested in the appearance of secondary sex characteristics –

in others, as well as themselves – including facial, pubic and underarm hair, and breasts.

In biology class the teacher said breasts were a secondary sex characteristic, but in my book they were definitely primary. All the guys wanted to get to 'first base'.

Since breasts are featured on page 3, I think we should make things equal and feature male secondary sex characteristics too: testicles!

Jo Brand

Nature is not an 'equal opportunities' entity. Teenagers do not mature at exactly the same rate, and in some instances physical maturation occurs even prior to 12 years old, while some people have to wait a lot longer. This in turn can create some social inequalities. For example, boys who mature early seem to gain the approval of their peers.

Colin Reese was the guy we all went to for advice. He had repeated a year so he was a year older. He had already had sex with three girls in our circle – as well as with a grown-up woman who lived in his street – and we all wanted to know how he did it. He had a fully mature penis and a lot of thick pubic hair, and he used to show us how to have sex using a tub of redcurrant jelly.

For girls, going from baby doll to Barbie in a short space of time is not always an easy adjustment. Noticing others' reactions to their changed bodies can be extremely disconcerting, and lead to all kinds of embarrassment and awkward situations.

I began to realise that men – not just boys – were noticing and admiring me, and sometimes making audible comments about my attractiveness: 'Hey doll face! Show us your tits!' Even my father's friends. Ugh! It was disgusting!

I heard my mother talking with her tennis pals about my breasts, complaining that I'd grown out of three bra sizes. I mean, there were men there and everything. I felt so humiliated.

Boys were snapping our bras. We were all wearing training bras. It really hurt. Finally the teachers stepped in: 'No more snapping bras!'

I enjoyed the changes my body underwent – for example, I couldn't wait to get my period and to become a 'real woman' and I liked wearing a bra for the same reason. But that was just the physical stuff, and it didn't hold much water. In contrast, the emotional stuff was painful; I felt unanchored, lonely, worried and scared – *most* of the time. This is due almost entirely to my parents' divorce and my mum's new boyfriend moving in. My brother was living on the streets at the time as well. It was a nightmare for me.

Adolescents are often dealing with an awful lot and, in addition, they have to get used to their new attractiveness very quickly. Most adolescents struggle with not quite knowing how to send or receive the right kinds of sexual messages. Some even become sexualised – feeling (or being) valued for sexual behaviour or appeal alone. Having the sense that one is viewed as a sex object, or being the brunt of imposed sexuality, can lead to low self-esteem, lowered scholastic achievement or body-image issues. It may even lead to sexual risk-taking and – if young people do not understand how to set limits – it can make them vulnerable to coercion.

Being admired for my cleavage was a big change from the insignificance I felt as a low achiever at school – not very good at sport and so on. Suddenly, I had this new tool to increase my pride in myself and I began playing it up. I bleached my hair, padded out my bra and started wearing makeup and short skirts. It worked. Sometimes, though, I got a bit more attention than I was quite ready for, and a few older guys forced themselves on me around that time.

Some teenagers are tortured by feeling that their bodies are maturing faster, slower or differently from their friends'. This can affect their confidence, their sense of self-worth and even the style of their sexual contact and exploration. They are keen to be attractive to peers, so being rejected or humiliated is appallingly painful.

I remember a boy I liked saying to me, 'Would you wear shoes if you didn't have feet?' I said, 'No.' And he said, 'So why would you wear a bra if you don't have boobs?' I was mortified.

In Girl Scouts we watched a movie about development. Becoming a woman seemed a hugely exciting thing – we were all ecstatic and couldn't wait. The coolest thing was getting a bra, but I developed a little later. As a keen ballet dancer I was thinner, and my mum wouldn't let me shave my legs then, either. My friend got boobs really early –

'double E' – and she mocked me for not having boobs and not shaving my legs.

All my friends grew and developed way before I did. At 16, some of them were real men with facial hair, pubic hair and grown-up genitals. At the same age I was still a boy – short, smooth-skinned and with a penis that seemed smaller than everyone else's. Public undressing – especially after sports – was humiliating for me. It didn't matter that I grew bigger than everyone else over the next two years. That first thoroughly awkward stage was something I never recovered from until long after I left school.

Such discrepancies can be particularly troubling for adolescents who feel they are truly atypical. In some cases this may have a long-term effect on their sense of body image and sexual confidence.

One of my breasts started growing before the other one did. I was terrified that I was going to end up with just one. I was too embarrassed to tell anyone, and suffered for ages and ages. Finally the other one grew, too, but size-wise it never caught up to the other. It wasn't until I was in my 20s that I learned that many women have different-sized breasts.

I was enormously ashamed of my 'man boobs'. Other kids in my soccer team would make jokes about how I needed a bra, and make 'milk' jokes and so on. I didn't understand why my body was doing that. I never heard the term 'gynaecomastia' and didn't know that it was a real medical diagnosis. Actually, I was terrified. I thought there was a good chance I might be turning into a girl.

Without having someone to turn to – a knowledgeable person who will answer questions and address their concerns with respect and a minimum of judgement – teenagers can suffer a great deal. They are acutely sensitive to how others view them and, even if others are giving them admiration and positive feedback, they can become confused and miserable, and lose confidence.

> Older boys at my school were only interested in girls who had boobs. And the girls with boobs seemed to like the attention and thought they were cooler than those of us who didn't have any. They also acted on the attention – having serious petting sessions and even intercourse in some cases – and enjoyed enormous popularity as a result. Most of us caught up eventually, but we tended to feel we'd lost a lot of ground. The nicest-looking boys were already 'going steady'.

Some teenagers even have negative feelings about their normal weight gain at puberty – due to the emphasis our society places on slenderness.

> I remember sitting in the car as my dad drove me to school. I was growing taller, so my school uniform was getting short for me. I suddenly noticed my thighs spread on the seat and was appalled at how wide they had become. I think that might have sparked the beginning of my eating disorder.

Body image is an extremely important factor in sexual health. Teenagers who feel comfortable with their bodies' development and enjoy their new sexual maturity are probably more likely to have a healthy body image as adults, and to feel comfortable being naked with a partner. Those whose bodies make them feel ashamed, anxious or embarrassed may continue to struggle with body image in the future.

Of course, increasing sexual maturity and attractiveness makes it more likely that opportunities for sexual contact with others will arise.

> *Happiness is watching TV at your girlfriend's house during a power failure.*
>
> Bob Hope

Surges of testosterone – in both boys and girls – make adolescents incredibly horny, and it really doesn't seem fair that this is also the period of life when we're expecting them to sit important exams and prepare for the adult world of work. It's like expecting a 40-year-old man to attend a make-or-break job interview at a strip show.

> When I was 14, the 'paper delivery boy' walked me home from the youth-club dance and kissed me goodnight on the lips! It was *the most exciting thing* that had ever happened to me and I loved it. Until then I honestly had no idea what made people 'do that'!

Quite a few people I've helped in therapy have told me that non-penetrative adolescent petting was the most erotic sex they've ever had.

> I still remember that first moment, in my truck, when she let me hold her, and she put her chin up so I could kiss her.

When I pressed my lips against hers, she put her tongue in my mouth … it was unbelievably arousing. I immediately came in my pants.

In order to try to help adults reconnect with sexual desire that has dwindled for one reason or another, I sometimes suggest that they get into the back seat with their spouses and try it again! The return of that sense memory often does the trick.

> *Sex is the Tabasco sauce, which an adolescent national palate sprinkles on every course in the menu.*
>
> Mary Day Winn

Of course, adolescent eroticism is not all rosy. As children enter adolescence, they may have many awkward sexual experiences. Who doesn't wince at certain memories from that age?

On my first big away-from-home adventure at 14 – a 13-hour bus ride with my first real girlfriend – we did constant mutual masturbation. Neither of us climaxed – frustration central. What was I doing wrong? *Urrrghhh.*

I remember lots of kissing – lots of different girls, all friends, and no real 'sex'. This was the best and worst all rolled into one. It was mostly initiated by the girls! I loved all of it, but I was still quite shy. Most of this occurred at dances and parties, etc., and I remember lots of awkwardness.

Self-pleasuring

In fact, masturbation is the main type of sexual activity experienced during adolescence, and teens seem to do it just as often whether they are also separately having sex with a partner or not.

> *Masturbation: the primary sexual activity of mankind. In the 19th century, it was a disease; in the 20th, it's a cure.*
>
> Thomas Szasz

People I interviewed used terms such as 'wank', 'whack off', 'jerk off', 'beat off' or 'beat the meat', and for girls it was 'rubbing off', 'rolling the pill' or 'fingering'. Most people self-pleasure as children, but some do not start until they are in their teens.

> I started masturbating at about 16. I knew that it was 'very, very wrong' and that the wrath of God could strike at any moment. The subject was *never ever* mentioned by mother, or adult relations!

Although masturbation is something that people do throughout their lives, at this point (and earlier) it partly serves the purpose of being a rehearsal for partner sex – a means of discovering how our bodies work, which can later be imparted to another person and thus help achieve proficiency and satisfaction in lovemaking. As a matter of fact, during the course of my work as a sex therapist I have noticed that some people who missed this important stage of self-discovery may have significant problems later, such as an inability to reach orgasm.

But masturbation style is also important. During puberty, boys tend to learn to masturbate to orgasm as fast as they can, before anyone catches them. This pattern can become entrenched, and some theorists believe that this can make it difficult for them to slow down, as required, when they're eventually with a partner. It could, therefore, be a possible contributing factor for some men who struggle with early ejaculation.

> I had to wank in our one bathroom because I shared a room with my younger brother and there was nowhere else in the house private enough. But pretty soon one of my three sisters would be knocking on the door – and calling out to Mum if I was taking too long. Between all the hours they spent in there fixing their makeup and so on, I often thought I was going to die of frustration. I learned to come really fast, usually in the shower. During those years, cleanliness was next to happiness.

As described in the previous chapter, a first orgasm may occur prior to puberty – with or without ejaculation – but, whenever it happens, it is usually quite a surprise.

> My first ejaculation occurred while I was stimulating myself. I remember it very well. I was about 15. Then I tried to make it happen again and again. Soon after that first time I had a wet dream, which was brilliant, so I actually tried to resist wanking so that I would have a dream again. This plan didn't work very well, but it was the nearest thing to cutting back that I ever did.

Many men have also told me they masturbated in the company of fellow teenagers.

> At around 13 or 14, my cousin and a friend and I used to go cycling. When we got out into the countryside, we'd skim a few stones in the river, sit down and have a talk, and then we'd have a wank all together in a circle. It was kind of fun, but some guys were ahead with more mature penises, which put a competitive edge on the whole thing. We were really spying on each other, sizing each other up. People would say things like: 'Have you ever seen the size of so-and-so's cock?' Ejaculated sperm was called 'spunk', and we called orgasm 'having a thrill'. Boys would ask, 'Have you ever had a thrill?' I remember being told that when you have a 'thrill', 'spunk' comes out. At that age I knew what the 'thrill' was, but I wasn't getting any 'spunk'.

Some men look back on such experiences with embarrassment, privately wondering if it was actually a homosexual encounter. Although it is certainly a style of shared eroticism, it would not necessarily be homoerotic. Naturally, most heterosexual men view 'jerk circle' behaviour as 'buddies just having a good time together'.

> When I told my best friend I was gay, he said, 'No you're not.' We had often wanked together. I guess he thought: 'What does that make me?'

Homosexual experimentation is quite common during adolescence but, in fact, 'circle jerks' are qualitatively different experiences for gay youngsters.

I wanked together with a group of guys from around the age of nine. We'd do it in a circle. Being gay, it was different for me. They were looking at porn, but I was looking at them.

Girls are less likely to engage in masturbation with other girls, but they usually discover their capacity for orgasm in some way.

I had my first orgasm when I was 17, in the middle of a yoga class. There was this position where we lay face down and grabbed our ankles behind our butts and rocked backwards and forwards. I don't think I knew what orgasms were but I thought it was fantastic and repeated it every chance I had. I became extremely limber during that time. If only I'd known I could achieve the same thing with my finger.

Fantasy and romance

Most adolescents think about romantic connections, and they also have sexual daydreams and fantasies. This may help them to understand their specific desires and rehearse in their minds how they'd go about having actual sexual experiences with others.

I fantasised about being with an older woman my whole teenaged life. I imagined it would be easy and fun.

Most of your teenaged life you're trying to get a feel of girls' tits, but they say 'no', so you have a fantasy about someone who says 'yes' instead. I used to dream about that. Hard to believe when you're young that there's actually women who like it and look forward to doing it.

You know that look women get when they want sex?
Me neither.

Drew Carey

Fantasies fire the erotic imagination, but for some teenagers the reality of sex is a terrible let-down.

I remember the distinct disappointment of discovering that sex was nothing like the fantasies I'd had up until then. My fantasies always took for granted that the emotional connection with my partner was deep and mutual, and that the sex was an extension of that connection. But, in reality, there was no emotional connection and the sex was painful and shameful. I lost my virginity while drunk and barely conscious, and the second time I had sex it was at the top of a school playground where I had once played as a child. Even after I managed to separate (though never entirely) the emotional from the physical, I still felt dirty and ashamed. This was despite being able to orgasm easily and frequently. But this fact only heightened my belief that I was not normal. I only really began to experience pleasure with total freedom from guilt about five years into my marriage.

A lot of what is happening physiologically to teenagers is mysterious to them and remains unexplained. There are spontaneous erections and ejaculations, and vaginal lubrication occurring in a seemingly random manner.

I don't think I was aware of an association between my vagina and sexual feelings until a young man held my hand and I realised that it made me wet.

I had no understanding of my sexual physiology until I was 18ish. Before that I just thought genitals were for going to the toilet.

Eroticism

With such a dramatically changing body, and emotions to match, how many of us who have safely passed through the other side of the tumultuous teenaged years would willingly go back? Probably those who miss experiencing such heightened eroticism.

I remember how powerful touch was. I was 14 years old. I remember being at the drive-in with a 19-year-old boy and my tag-along brother, all sitting in a row. All this boy and I did was hold hands, but it was very intoxicating. My parents caught on and called his parents, telling him not to come by anymore.

Many people I see in therapy – especially those struggling with lack of desire – say things like 'even just holding hands in a movie was more erotic than any sex in my current life'. And contrary to popular belief, having erotic feelings brought on by holding hands *is* a sexual experience. American President Bill Clinton was not alone in using terminology to his advantage, when he said, 'I did not have sexual relations with that woman.' There are many possible definitions for phrases like 'having sex', 'having sexual relations' or even 'making love', but, essentially, if sexual pleasure is deliberately engendered via almost any kind of contact, including on the phone or via the internet – or inserting a cigar in a woman's vagina as Clinton is said to have done – it can be defined as above.

Forbidden fruit

One sexologist, Dr Jack Morin, came up with a 'sexual equation':

$$Desire + Obstacle = Eroticism$$

This means that if you have sexual desire or arousal (which most teenagers have a lot of the time) and there's some kind of obstacle to satisfying that desire (which teenagers also face most of the time) the erotic charge will be even greater than it would have been without the obstacle. If you think about the most erotic experience you have ever had, I can bet that it involved a major 'obstacle' – for example, someone you shouldn't have been with, a situation you should not have been in, or some kind of taboo act. Am I right? This is the ubiquitous teenage sexual challenge – heightened eroticism at every turn.

> My most exciting sexual experiences were when I was young and there was naughtiness involved … For example, when we were ten feet from my boyfriend's sleeping parents in a cabin, or when I was in a raft floating on a river.

> By the time I was 16, I had my first boyfriend and he would come to my house. We never had penetrative sex,

but he touched my genitals and we kissed. My parents were right upstairs.

I only became aware of the full potential for pleasure in my early teens. Very exciting and also very wicked, we thought; I was at a Catholic boys' school. We talked about little else other than girls and how to get the best wank. Oh, and how not to get caught doing it.

Teenagers tend to progress from hand-holding, to kissing, to tongue-kissing, to breast-touching, to rubbing against each other, to touching each other's genitals through clothing, and then direct genital touching. Young men might ejaculate inside their clothing at any stage. This progressive pattern – often likened to the game of baseball – is taught by siblings, cousins and peers. Of course, it doesn't always occur in exactly that order.

> *The first kiss is magic, the second is intimate, the third is routine. After that you just take the girl's clothes off.*
>
> Raymond Chandler

Girls also acquire arbitrary 'rules' from those who know little – if anything – more than they do.

> We all believed you could kiss on the first date, let him touch your boobs on the second and maybe give him a blow job on the third. Anything else and you were a slut.

> *It takes a lot of experience for a girl to kiss like a beginner.*
>
> *Ladies' Home Journal*, 1948

Kissing is also extremely important, as it is usually an adolescent's first close, intimate experience.

> When I was 14, I was at a Catholic girls' school. I had a very advanced girlfriend, who said, 'There are some cute boys in the public school.' We went over there and there was one especially cute one. I decided to approach him because I wanted to learn how to kiss. I didn't break that kiss for about half an hour. We stayed just locked there – it was kind of painful after a while.

> The first time I had a proper kiss I was both excited in the extreme, and also rather disgusted. He put his tongue so far into my mouth I started to understand the expression 'tonsil tickling'. I didn't quite know how to respond, so I just let it happen.

> *The kiss is a wordless articulation of desire whose object lies in the future, and somewhat to the south.*
> Lance Morrow

Breast-fondling is a major erotic pleasure for both boys and girls. The female underwear industry has capitalised on the fact that the visual appeal of apparently large breasts is pretty well guaranteed to have the desired effect.

> I used to stuff my bikini top with socks. They improved my cleavage, but made my chest extremely heavy when wet. For that reason, I tended to avoid the surf.

> When I was around 15, we used to go to a café and there was a girl there who lived nearby. I walked her home from

the café, and we sneaked into an outhouse and kissed. I felt her tits. She unbuttoned her blouse herself and unhooked her bra, then opened my shirt and pulled me towards her – two bare chests. I thought I'd died and gone to heaven. We did it several times, and eventually she masturbated me as well. She liked being stroked outside her knickers, but she didn't let me put my hand inside.

Whoever named it necking was a poor judge of anatomy.

Groucho Marx

Setting boundaries

Many adolescents – after much trial and error – do their best to set boundaries according to what feels right to them, and to make decisions about how far they will go. Girls are not the only ones who set limits on where they can be touched or in which sexual acts they will engage – but they are more likely to do so than boys. Of course, the 'heat of the moment' can change resolve, and so can the use of alcohol or drugs. Peer pressure is also an important factor; those whose friends are sexually experienced, or who think they'll gain their friends' admiration or respect if they reach certain milestones – such as having intercourse – are more likely to do so.

When you find the place where a woman loves to be fondled, don't you be ashamed to touch it any more than she is.

Ovid

Oral sex

There's quite a bit of evidence to suggest that oral sex is becoming more frequent among teenagers, although that mainly involves girls performing fellatio on boys. Some adolescents I've spoken to said they regarded oral sex as less troublesome, dangerous or meaningful than intercourse and that it was pretty common among their peer group. Many did not define it as 'having sex', and regarded it as a means of increasing one's popularity. Unfortunately, teenagers do not always understand that it carries a risk of acquiring HIV or other sexually transmitted infections.

We openly talked about oral sex. The general idea was that everyone was too young to have intercourse – that was not viewed as an okay kind of sex. So we did oral sex – just girls giving it to boys. There was actually a lot of pressure put on girls to give boys blow jobs. The first one was Gretchen. She gave Stephen a blow job, then she boasted about it. She thought it was cool. She was chubbier than some other girls, and was always doing things to make herself seem sexy, but it backfired. At first all the boys gave her a lot of attention, but then everyone turned on her – especially the girls. After that she only dated guys outside of school, and tried to hide it.

The first time I had oral sex was at 18, in a graveyard. It was after a dance in a nearby village. There were very few places to go so we used to end up in the graveyard. There was a girl from the village who sucked my cock. I'd heard about this, but never believed it – I thought the other guys were lying about it. I thought it was amazing.

Oral sex was big at school – mainly girls giving blow jobs and hand jobs to me and my mates. But me, I was curious, so I was interested in both giving and receiving from about 11 years old. We had school sex education, which was very informative. They told us about STDs and how to put on a condom. Actually, I wasn't that keen on blow jobs, and usually my erection would disappear. But we'd hear rumours about certain girls and how they were 'sure things' and did it a lot. Once, after having sex, a girl told me how many people she'd slept with. It was a lot – 50 men, and she was only 19. I felt extremely dirty and got a check-up. I think she told me this because I gave her her first orgasm. I would rather have a girl be pleased than let her do something to me. I like to cuddle and hold, to be romantic and passionate. You don't have to have sex to have all that.

My classmates would copulate with anything that moved, but I never saw any reason to limit myself.

Emo Philips

Having a 'steady' girlfriend or boyfriend has some advantages. In particular, the women I spoke to tended to think it allowed sexual exploration to progress at a manageable rate, while providing a means to a fair amount of pleasure and excitement.

I had a boyfriend who used to park his car at the top of mountain and we'd pet ourselves silly. It never led to intercourse.

First intercourse

Having the first intercourse is sometimes planned, but it can also occur without forethought. For example, I've heard many testimonies indicating that taking alcohol and drugs had led to sexual 'mistakes', through impaired judgement, risk-taking and temporary black-outs.

> I lost my virginity as a result of getting drunk at a uni party. Afterwards I had no idea what had happened, except I had my underwear in my hand when someone climbed into the dorm window and scared us both. The boy I did it with was also very drunk. I saw some blood, but I didn't remember anything because I was too drunk. Later, the boy – who was my boyfriend at the time – wouldn't admit we had made love, even when I asked him. He went into the army, and about 15 years after he came out, he came to visit me. He told me then that he thought I was the love of his life. I said, 'Just out of curiosity, what did happen that night?' He said, 'Yes', he did have intercourse with me. I guess I already knew because I was bleeding.

There are many possible motivations for deciding to have intercourse – feeling ready, 'being in love', wanting to keep a boyfriend or girlfriend, curiosity and peer pressure. But a number of people to whom I spoke remarked that, even though a person may decide to go ahead, things do not always go according to plan.

> It was her first time. She really wanted to, but she was wincing with pain and it was really hard to get my penis inside her. I lost my erection because I felt bad for her. I

tried to get hard again but it kept failing. At one point she even laughed at me, which didn't help.

At school my friends gave me *Playboy* magazine. I kept pictures of vaginas and took them home, laid them on the floor and jerked off. I didn't like girls of my age. This girl neighbour had a huge crush on me. She came to me and took off her clothes, and told me she didn't want to get pregnant. I didn't know how to have sex and I wasn't really turned on at that time. We just lay there and kissed then she put her pants back on and walked out. That was so embarrassing. I didn't know what to do. I didn't know there was a hole. I thought you just put your penis against her and moved like this. She was looking at me like I was pathetic. It was so embarrassing. Later on I saw a blue movie and that's when I thought 'What's going on here?' – and realised what I should have done.

Chastity is curable, if detected early.
Author unknown

Of course, some teenagers feel that it is important to remain virgins until they marry – and manage to do so. Many who do not share this sentiment nevertheless receive strong pressure from parents, religious groups and society at large. In many cultures, maintaining virginity is essential until marriage, so some girls who've already had intercourse resort to surgical restoration of their virginity.

Quite honestly, for girls in my family it was dangerous to go the whole way. My brothers could do whatever they liked, but we had to be very careful. My sister was raped by our older cousin, but she couldn't tell our parents. She eventually ran away, and we lost contact with her.

The recent well-publicised case of a French Muslim bride who was rejected and delivered back to her parents by her new husband – after he discovered that she was not a virgin as she had claimed – illustrates how clashes can occur between people who develop different values depending on their particular environment. The illusion of virginity can be created via hymenoplasty – a surgical procedure that can restore the vaginal membrane – and more and more of these procedures are being carried out at the request of women who have been unable to provide the required proof of chastity that many potential husbands (and their families) require.

> *There are no good girls gone wrong, just bad girls found out.*
>
> Mae West

Even in more liberal cultures, girls want to avoid appearing too easy; but, at the same time, they want to be liked. They have often been socialised to do their best to please men, so they may find it difficult to know just how to behave. Receiving pleasure themselves may be the last thing on their minds. In fact, many people believe that, during adolescence, boys are far more interested in sexual pleasure than girls, whereas females are more interested in having relationships – proper boyfriends – or being popular. On the other hand, I've come across many teenagers who did not fit this stereotype.

At university, when I was 18, I had my first real sexual experiences and, although at first these were painful, I soon found I liked the whole thing ... it made me much more popular, and attractive, but it was also extremely exciting.

These days the honeymoon is rehearsed much more often than the wedding.

P.J. O'Rourke

In my opinion it is archaic to view 'loss of virginity' as that moment when a penis enters a vagina for the first time – for either partner. Does that mean that gay men and lesbians never lose their virginity? Is it really reasonable to call a person who has done everything but have intercourse 'a virgin'? Nevertheless, the decision to experience that membrane-puncturing moment is certainly seen as a *big deal*.

During my first year of college, a lot of people were really intent on losing their virginity. They would be anxiously thinking, 'I need to have sex immediately.' I think people were nervous about being a virgin coming into university – embarrassed about it, and just wanting to get it over with because there's a stigma attached to not being experienced. You could fast-track it if you had a steady boyfriend or girlfriend. And it was way less acceptable to be a virgin boy. With girls, virginity is seen as endearing, but with boys it was assumed that they should be able to take charge and know what they're doing. Also, because in secondary school boys were openly more sex-obsessed than girls, you'd assume they'd already done it.

However they occur, the first experiences of coitus are always defining moments in a person's sexual development – and, as many people I spoke to attested, it's not always a comfortable experience. Calling it 'loss of virginity' doesn't help; in my opinion it would be best termed 'gaining your cherry' – and the whole ice-cream sundae as well! For a lucky few, it's a magical rite of passage.

I became sexually experienced out of the blue. I was like a butterfly leaving its chrysalis, seemingly fully formed. I had left home at 16. A year and lots of travel later I was seduced by a lovely 35-year-old divorcee, who had been crushed by a horrible man. She took me to her stunning place in the Islands and we lit candles. There was lots of crazy kissing and falling all over each other ... then I went down on her for at least half an hour. We made love until the sun rose (I missed my boat home!). She assured me I was the best she had ever had and I really believed her. I didn't tell her that she had 'taken' my virginity, because I thought she wouldn't believe me – and, if she did, she would freak out over the age difference. I was then – and remain to this day – rather good at the whole business. This is not, I hope, a conceit ... I really care about my part-ners; it's what makes me tick, sexually. I kept seeing her for a time, and we shared much.

It is an infantile superstition of the human spirit that virginity would be thought a virtue and not the barrier that separates ignorance from knowledge.

Voltaire

Many people, both male and female, have told me that their first occasion of intercourse was with a more experienced person. There are a number of reasons for this – some say that they made a pragmatic choice to go with someone who knew what to do, while others said that their more experienced lovers seduced them, or that they found sexual self-assurance in a knowledgeable partner to be a highly attractive quality.

When I had intercourse for the first time, I was 17 and camping with friends. I'd been in town with the other guys and when I came back to my tent there was a strange girl in it. She had run away from home and found my empty tent. Another guy had a girl with him. He had met both of them and was in another tent with that girl. He stuck the other one in my tent. She was already undressed in my sleeping bag, so I just got in beside her. She showed me what to do – grabbed my penis and put it in. She was quite bossy. It was great. I felt I'd joined a very exclusive club and I didn't need to lie anymore. All guys lie and say they've done it – for status.

I think I would have been 16 or 17, certainly in sixth form. I was in Paris, with an older and experienced woman. It was fantastic at the time – although, in retrospect, it lasted about 30 seconds. I later learned that she had been so disappointed she had gone off to find her actual boyfriend – she had only taken me to bed to piss him off. Meanwhile, I had promised my mum that I would visit Notre Dame while I was there, so I went off in the middle of the night to do that. I didn't feel any guilt or anything; I just went to keep a promise to my mum.

The first girl I fucked was way older than me. I was 14 and she was 25, and she was my cousin's friend. We did it in the same room – me, that girl, my cousin and her boyfriend. We had a competition. My cousin did the moves and we copied them. First the girl touched me and I got so hard. Then she got a light and showed me her vagina and that's how I knew where the penis should go. She put it in herself. She sat on me, and I felt so warm and so nice. It was so good to go inside a pussy. I didn't come, but for almost an hour she was riding me. Then she said she was hurting and she got off. I was lying there asking myself, 'What the heck is going on?' I didn't know, but it felt *sooo* good.

Not everyone has a good 'first time'. In fact, many people I spoke to had horrible experiences – often related to immaturity, poor decision-making, ill-preparedness or a lack of education.

My first time was totally planned by me. I just wanted to experience it, and for some reason I chose a really unsuitable person to be my first. I was 15 and he was a 30-year-old man with a drug problem. Not only was it horribly painful, but he gave me gonorrhoea. When I bled, he jumped out of bed and harangued me for not telling him that I 'had a period'. I guess I had such low self-esteem at that time, and no one to talk to, I thought that was all I deserved.

Poor decision-making aside, the fact is that breaking a girl's hymen is usually painful for her. There's just no way around that. It's simply not the same for boys.

There was this girl I dated a bit. I came back from being away with my parents and she said she had missed me and she was so in love with me that she wanted to have sex. We went to a motel. I start to enter her, but she begged me: 'It hurts, please it hurts!' But when I tried to pull out, she held me and said she didn't really want me to stop. So I kept going. After we did it, she told me that she was horny again, and I was like: 'What?' Then I fucked her again. There was a lot of blood, so we got a wet cloth to wipe it up. She said she felt dizzy, and then she just fell asleep. After that, when we had sex again, she wanted to hold on to me and she held a deep breath while I did my thing. She only breathed when I came. She said she felt like I was trying to drown her.

Many people choose to 'lose their virginity' for reasons other than sexual desire.

I knew if I didn't let him do it, he'd break up with me. Other girls in my year were after him.

He told me we were going to get married, so we might as well. I could see the sense of that, and went ahead with it. Unfortunately he didn't keep his promise.

> *Losing my virginity was a career move.*
>
> Madonna

There is certainly a strong argument in favour of avoiding inter-course until one is married or at least in a solid, committed relationship. However, many teenagers do recognise the inherent paradox in exhorting people to avoid intercourse prior to marriage, yet still expecting them to be accomplished partners immediately after.

> My formal sex education was one 20-minute talk, with a group of girls at school, by a 'lady almoner', who was unmarried, elderly, obviously a virgin, and who emphasised the importance of remaining 'untouched until marriage'. When I asked, 'Wouldn't this inevitably lead to disappointment, if you have had no practice or experience?', she looked at me, aghast. I didn't ask anything else!

Our society teaches that intercourse is the main sexual event. If, instead, we could openly recognise that what some people today call 'outercourse' (having highly erotic sexual experiences that do not include penetration) is an equally viable way to have sex, we may see fewer cases of sexually transmitted infections and fewer unwanted pregnancies. But even our language for sexuality generally describes the act of penile-vaginal penetration only – 'shagging', 'banging', 'tooling' and 'giving her one'.

> *Anyone who calls it 'sexual intercourse' can't possibly be interested in doing it. You might as well announce you're ready for lunch by proclaiming, 'I'd like to do some masticating and enzyme secreting.'*
>
> Allan Sherman

So what increases the odds that teenagers will have intercourse? Some evidence suggests that adolescents are more likely to have early coitus when parents are not keeping an eye on them, when they are abusing alcohol or drugs, when they don't think a great deal of themselves and/or don't expect they will amount to much in the future, or when they've been sexually victimised. Depression is also a factor – in particular, studies suggest that depressed girls tend to be more sexual.

> At 16, I remember thinking, 'I know I'm supposed to be home at 11, but nothing in my life is going right so I don't have that much to lose.' That night I had sex in the car with Len. I didn't care what kind of trouble I might get into, I didn't care about protection and I didn't care that he was a married man. I just wanted the good feeling to last. Nine months later I had a little boy – and no man.

Peer pressure

Peer pressure appears to be a strong factor in motivating adolescents to have sex, although they tend to be influenced by what they *think* their friends are doing rather than what their friends are *actually* doing. For males, having a girlfriend can provide status, whereas the realities of having a relationship may be secondary. Teenaged boys – certainly when in the company of their peers – tend to approve of and admire sexual experience, and prioritise sexual conquests. 'Scoring' is just as important as scoring in sports – and that can really add to the pressure of wanting to be perceived as a winner on both fronts.

> I'm a big guy and my friends thought I was hot, sexy guy, but they didn't know that I wasn't having sex. I acted like a guy that fucks a lot of girls, but I was having sex with my own hand.

For girls, however, it's a different story. Many people I spoke to said that girls tend to be called 'sluts' or 'skanks' by both boys and girls if they have sex with a boy with whom they're not in a relationship.

> I went to a small school. The more popular girls were not sexual – not good looking, and nasty about girls who had boyfriends. They had some sort of social power, and were considered 'cool'. None of them lost their virginity until after school. But these were also the very girls who got super-skanky after they left school. They went absolutely wild at university.

> *No one is more carnal than a recent virgin.*
> John Steinbeck

Each societal subset, including different ethnic and religious communities, has its own set of views about whether or not it's okay for a teenager to have sexual intercourse – irrespective of the legal age of consent. But one thing they all tend to have in common is a double standard – more relaxed rules for boys than for girls.

> My husband and I are pretty liberal, but we were definitely challenged when our second child – and first daughter – became a teenager. We felt more protective towards her than we had felt towards our son, and did not want her to have the same level of freedom as he had. When she was invited to a 'sleepover' it worried us far more than when he stayed at a friend's house overnight.

My brother, who is younger than me, was allowed to stay over at friends' houses from about 14. Our parents hardly seemed to check up on him at all. By then I was 16 and all hell would break loose if I went to the movies and wasn't home by ten. Arranging a sleepover was way more trouble than it was worth – first there was the check-up call to my friend's parents, then the check-up call while I was actually there, and finally a full inquisition when I got back home.

A pervasive, negative view of sex – with accompanying double standards – is often internalised by teenagers themselves.

As a teenager I remember we were having a sleepover at my best friend's house. She went into her brother Tom's pocket and pulled out a condom! We knew who he was seeing – Martha Love! We were 15, and none of us had had sex. We were totally disgusted. We thought she was a slut.

The role of religion

Evidence suggests that those with strong religious beliefs or spiritual practices – as well as those who reach puberty later than usual – may be more likely to delay intercourse. However, there are exceptions.

My first experience of intercourse was at 16, but then I went without for three years because I was dating a girl who didn't believe in sex before marriage. After I proposed to her, and she'd agreed to marry me, she went and had sex with a guy at work. I broke up with her because I no longer trusted her.

Strong religious beliefs can also lead to intense guilt and inner conflict.

> My mother didn't know how to handle me. I had adopted the bishop of my church as my first role model and, when I was 11, I told him about my feelings towards other boys. 'It's normal,' he said, 'but it is a sin.' In Bible study we learned that 'man shall not lie down with men'. That was when I knew I was going to hell. The issue became one between me and God. 'How dare you make me this way,' I would pray, 'if I'm destined to go to hell?'

How an adolescent feels about being sexual with another person at this age – morally and in terms of religious beliefs – will often predict the type or extent of his or her sexual experience. Having strong academic goals and being a high achiever may also make it less likely that a young person will engage in adolescent sex. Unfortunately, it works the other way around, too. Girls (usually those in mixed schools) may downplay their academic achievements or allow them to slide in order to make themselves less threatening and more attractive to boys. This, in turn, may make it more likely that they will have sex.

> *Men seldom make passes at a girl who surpasses.*
> Franklin P. Jones

Sex and self-esteem

It's been claimed many times that engaging in sexual activity makes teenagers feel bad about themselves, but there's quite a bit of evidence suggesting that sexually experienced adolescents over the age of 15 actually tend to have better self-esteem than their less-experienced peers. When teens do feel bad about themselves for sexual reasons, it tends to occur when they have been coerced, when they did it before they reached puberty, when they did it as a response to peer pressure or when they became sexual as a result of the effects of alcohol or drugs. Otherwise, there doesn't seem to be too much of a downside in terms of psychological, or even physical, ill-effects.

I had many sexual experiences as a teenager. My first intercourse was with a boyfriend when I was 13. He was 16, and we had a long, loving and intensely sexual relationship. We were both curious. I seemed to have absolutely no fear or self-consciousness. It was a really beautiful time of experiencing my own body as it related to his. I had a three-year relationship with him, and it ended amicably after he went away to college.

By my late teens I was very comfortable with sexuality. I was married and in love at 18, so we were comfortable in each other's skins. She was three years older than me. We were very young when we discovered each other sexually in a tent while on the road. I sucked a bee-sting from her ankle and promised I'd always look after her. Well, ten years together ain't bad going ...

The testimonies I gathered – along with existing research – suggest that there are arguments both for and against teenage intercourse. Understandably, our society insists that there has to be some control, so that problems such as disease, sexual coercion and unwanted teenaged pregnancy can be avoided.

And not all teenagers are ready to take on the responsibilities that go along with participating in mature, partner sex. However, it's not easy to feel that one's parents, teachers, religious leaders and society at large want to suppress one's natural and overwhelming urges.

Communication

Experiencing good-quality relationships with parents may reduce the likelihood that adolescents will have sex with peers – and it also seems to lower the frequency, as well as the number of partners. However, a strong positive relationship with a parent does entail having an ability to talk comfortably together about sexual matters.

> When our son finally moved into a dorm room at college, my husband made me go into the store and buy a large supply of condoms. He's way more conservative and shy than I am. My son calmly took them and put them in a drawer beside his bed. He's in a band, and I'm nervous about that world – with disease and everything – so I just keep buying him condoms. I know they're expensive – it's a shame about that, because the kids really need them.

If parents communicate clear messages about their sexual values (hopefully through both discussion and practical help), and monitor their adolescents without being too harsh or intrusive, their children may delay starting to engage in sexual behaviour.

> We gave our son condoms in eighth grade. We said: 'We don't expect you to be using these because we think you're

too young emotionally; but in case anything happens, here they are.'

Household influences

It's not just relationships with parents that impact on a teenager's sexuality; there are other aspects of their home life that may play a role, too. For example, living with a single parent has been found to have an effect on sexual behaviour. In particular, girls whose mothers are dating may be more likely to have sex. And, in general, as I've pointed out in earlier chapters, mothers' views of sexuality – whether spoken or unspoken – have a significant effect on their children.

My mum has never made any secret of the fact that she sees sex as a bit of a chore – one of the sacrifices you have to make if you are to be married. I don't even know if she's had an orgasm; she's never talked about things like that with me, so looking back I guess it's no surprise that she tried to shut down any attempts I made to discuss it with her. Or maybe it's a generational thing? Whatever she did say about sex was always passed on in a very cautionary manner – continual references to 'saving' one's virginity, being 'aware' of the dangers, not getting pregnant and just generally creating a picture of men as sexual predators who are after only 'one thing'. Sex was something I saw as quite scary as a teenager coming of age.

I was 15 when I first had sex, and I stayed in a relationship of sorts with that person for two years. I say 'of sorts' because he was frequently unfaithful and treated me terribly. But I felt I couldn't end the relationship because I'd lost my virginity to him and therefore had an obligation to stay with him. My mum had always impressed upon me how shameful it was to be considered a promiscuous woman. She had only ever had three sexual partners in her life and each time she'd been in a long-term relationship. I thought that was the example I should follow, regardless of how much suffering I went through.

When one's children become adolescents it's a bit more difficult to hide one's own sexuality – although it's no bad thing for them to be aware that their parents are sexual beings. But at this age they know exactly what's going on!

Being a nosy little shit, aged 13 or so, I was shocked and amused to discover a sexual object under Mum's bed. My second stepdad was into porn. I found a massive war chest (literally – he was a vet) *full* of *Mayfair, Playboy*, etc., under a 60 kg dryer in the back shed. I developed strong arm and back muscles during their tumultuous one-year marriage. This was 'unfortunately' (no real regrets) a formative part of my sexual consciousness and the only adult male input to my sexual identity whatsoever.

I didn't think my mother was too happy about sex, having had seven children. They used to go up to bed on Sunday after dinner. My brothers and I would be washing the dishes. My father would say, 'Are you coming up, Violet?' and she'd say, 'Oh, all right then' in a reluctant kind of way. We'd all look at each other.

I was initially quite shocked to notice signs of sexuality in my parents, but as I read more (via library books) I had a certain amount of sympathy. However, I was still puzzled by all the hypocrisy surrounding the subject.

As parents engage in power struggles with teenagers they may become deeply connected with memories – good and bad – of their adolescence. Unresolved issues of their own can get into the mix and cause even more problems.

My mother had me when she was only 17, and I felt she was so determined that this wouldn't 'happen' to me, she was really over-protective. Having such restrictions on being with friends made me really unhappy, lacking in confidence, unpopular and desperate. It also made me feel more than ever that I had been an unwelcome 'accident'.

Older siblings – their sexual views or examples – can also have a profound effect on a person's sexuality.

Nobody talked about sex. My older sisters went to dances with boys, but they never talked to me about it. One got married during war, then after her new husband went back to his submarine she told me how much she loved sex, but that she wished somebody had told her about it. I was 14 and I wasn't really interested. We lived in little house. My older sisters would go out, walk home with their beaux and kiss goodnight at the garden gate – there was no opportunity to have sex. But one of them – the one who joined the army – was rather promiscuous. I was quite surprised at the number of boyfriends she had. She also had two or three backroom abortions, which horrified me and put me off sex. I was a very naïve 20-year-old, and I didn't want that to happen to me.

I was very aware of the consequences. I learned a bit about it at school. One of my sisters had a baby who wasn't her husband's and I didn't understand. I didn't know why she would want to do that with someone else. I just thought sex was an act – no emotions involved. I guess that's the way they taught us at school.

My sister took me to a party and pushed me on to an older person. Next thing I knew he was lying on top of me. I don't even know how I got home. I was very upset that she would do that to me.

Sibling betrayal is always painful. Several people to whom I spoke had been encouraged by older siblings to participate in sexual events for which they weren't ready. But there are a number of other ways in which brothers and sisters influence one's sexual choices, views and experiences. For example, having older siblings who are engaging in enjoyable sex tends to give a message to younger ones that it's okay to do it – and fun to try.

My 18-year-old sister had the most gorgeous boyfriend and I was really jealous of her. I was not old enough to know exactly what they were doing in the garage, but I had a fair idea. When they re-emerged they seemed really happy and bought me lollies, which meant that I associated sex with lovely feelings and sweet rewards.

Becoming informed

As it is in childhood years, information gleaned by teenagers from their siblings, from friends at school, from neighbours or from the media can be off-putting, incorrect or confusing. In fact, in these bewildering adolescent years it can be downright terrifying.

Horrible language was used; for example 'so-and-so got fingered' at the weekend is one reference I remember clearly at age 13. I remember being so shocked by that phrase and by the imagery of it. I couldn't imagine anyone putting fingers inside me, much less that this could be part of the sex that always looked so beautiful in movies. I knew what 'intercourse' was, but I didn't know that there were all these 'extras' out there as well, and it only served to frighten me more. Much of what I learned about sex came from *Cleo* magazines – the 'sealed sections'. It gives me shivers to think of them now; they were so crass, and were all about how to make yourself appealing to men.

My parents had a library in which there were a few books about sex. I read the *Kinsey Report*, but there were also a few sexy paperbacks. One was about some woman in India who committed adultery, got caught and was punished by having a breast cut off. That wasn't so good to know about then. I was about 12.

Even when sex education is liberal and comprehensive, it can confuse and embarrass students.

I remember people in my class speculating a lot about sexuality – the topic was uppermost on everyone's brain. Our 'human development' classes weren't just about sex; they showed videos about anorexia and drugs as well. The sex bits were mortifying. One day I had to put a condom on a plastic penis in front of the whole class. Everyone was giggling. I suppose I could have said 'no', but that would have been even more embarrassing.

Styles of sex education in schools vary enormously, as does the curriculum.

We did have some sex education but you would have been hard pressed to know that it was that. It involved a lot of coded warnings about temptation and the workings of the Devil. We thought it was funny and tried to wind up the teachers: 'Sir, what exactly is "an irregular motion of the flesh"?'

Sex education? They threw it all in with periods and deodorant – all, one package. We got a box with a mini deodorant, a giant pad and a mini booklet explaining birth control, and dated stuff like the sponge. Actually we received more sex education from the 'Glove Affair', which was a themed dance we had at school. They had contests to put a condom on a dildo with your mouth, and slides of different sex organs. We made a womb room so you could go inside a womb-like space. They promoted masturbation versus abstaining from sex – very different from other schools – and actually we had very little teenaged pregnancy in my school. I only heard of one girl who became pregnant, and she was not shunned at all.

Many adults view teenagers and their red-faced horniness with disapproval and fear, but I believe that if we provide proper education and instil in them a strong sense of self-worth, they'll probably make reasonable decisions about sex

– for example, whether or not they are ready for certain experiences.

> I went out with a Dutch boy whose parents were very liberal. They had no problem allowing us to sleep in the same bed in their flat, and even fudged the issue with my parents so I'd be allowed to stay. Even though we had permission and freedom to be sexual, we did not have intercourse because I didn't feel ready.

At the mercy of hormones

Frequent mood swings – say, from anger and sadness to happiness and euphoria – can lead to great tension between teenagers and adults. I wish we could stop seeing it as 'problem behaviour' and instead have more empathy for what adolescents are going through. Although, granted, that's hard if you are bearing the brunt of it!

> One minute my older sister would be laughing and flirting with the boy who delivered the groceries, and the next minute she'd be crying pitifully in her bedroom. Then she'd start shouting at my parents and slamming the door. I simply didn't get it – until I reached puberty myself.

Our society holds a largely negative view of adolescent sexuality, considering it to be out of control, sinful and, most importantly, dangerous – but is it always such a bad thing? I'm not saying we should condone it all and let teenagers have a free-for-all, but some of us do need to lighten up!

> One boy I went out with had very strict parents. His mother caught us kissing at her house and freaked out. She

kept saying 'That was a very grown-up kiss!' and made her son take me home. God ... we were just kissing!

Presumably, such views are based on moral beliefs that sex is basically dirty, and that any kind of sexual contact between unmarried people – or alone – is wrong or shameful.

> *To hear many religious people talk one would think God created the torso, head, legs and arms, but the Devil slapped on the genitals.*
>
> Don Schrader

> *Life in Lubbock, Texas, taught me two things: one is that God loves you and you're going to burn in hell. The other is that sex is the most awful, filthy thing on earth and you should save it for someone you love.*
>
> Butch Hancock

Establishing sexual identity

Adolescents have an extremely important developmental task: to discover who they really are, which includes who they are as sexual beings. It involves trying out different styles of behaviour in order to discover what feels right. Working out sexual orientation (preference in terms of partner gender, i.e. whether you are straight, gay or bisexual) is part of that task.

I first felt romantic towards boys, and had a number of male friends I called 'boyfriends' at a pretty young age. My older brothers and sisters would tease me about this, saying I was 'boy-crazy' even though I wasn't sure what that was – or if it was good or bad. What was most confusing was that I also had crushes on girls, although I was smart enough to realise that this wasn't something I should let on about. It wasn't until I was in my 20s that I could articulate the fact that I was bisexual, but even prior to the age of 12, I knew at some level I was sexually attracted to people of both genders. Being serious about girls just wasn't considered an option by me or by anyone else in my environment.

A certain percentage of teenagers – whether they are gay or not – have romantic or sexual notions about people of the same gender. Teenagers who are truly gay or lesbian are usually aware of their orientation at quite a young age, but, unfortunately, many of them face ridicule, prejudice and even danger – and are rejected by parents who cannot accept their sexuality. They learn to be secretive, and may go on dates with members of the other gender, although they are aware that they're 'just not into them'.

Some of the girls took off their clothes for me, but I was still not turned on. Lot of girls – even the hottest girls in school – wanted to have sex with me, and hated me because I didn't want to do it. They were trying to turn me on, licking their pencils and sucking their fingers, but I was just like, 'Whatever …'.

When I first had sex with a girl, I was 14. My friends were pressuring me to do it with a girl. But secretly I was in a gay youth outreach programme that I joined when I was 13. In that programme I learned that I was normal. When I came back from one meeting I told everyone I was gay and I was proud to say it. A lot of people were just 'duh'. I was dating a girl at the time, but we only had sex three times in a year. I had told her I was bi.

In the above instance, the young man was having sex with a girl just to prove he wasn't gay. Many teenagers get themselves into sexual situations for reasons other than for sexual pleasure, including wanting to be popular. Even adolescents who engage in mainly same-gender sex may not be sure about their orientation, and remain unaware that they are gay, lesbian or bisexual until early adulthood. Others are well aware of it.

I bought my first *Playgirl* when I was 12 and lived with my grandma. I was the only one out of all my siblings who was made to go to church. I didn't like it – I didn't like getting all dolled up. I felt like I was singled out to go to church because of my sexuality. In retrospect, I think they were trying to stop me going to hell.

Parents can have disapproving or punitive reactions when they notice non-heterosexual interests in their children. This can have a psychologically damaging effect on their children, who subsequently feel that they must hide who they truly are.

When I was 13, my mother found my men's underwear magazine. I had been very secretive about it. I had cut it up and pasted men on the inside of a secret folder. My mother found it and freaked out. 'Brian, what is this? What does this mean?' I said 'What do you think?' I was mortified. See, I just wanted to watch TV and have my privacy. 'What were you doing with that?' she said. I don't think she really wanted the answer.

Of course, it's not easy for parents of gay, lesbian or bisexual teenagers. They will naturally be concerned about prejudice, as well as harbouring worries about coercion and disease that all parents fear for their children.

My 19-year-old daughter is hanging out with a 25-year-old lesbian. I'm trying to be relaxed about it, but in reality the idea scares me to death. We live in a very conservative neighbourhood.

In my mother's day and age, 'fags' were strung up in a tree and dragged behind trucks. She was probably scared for me. A gay boy was killed just outside my home town. That made it scary. These guys actually tied him up with rope and dragged him miles down the road behind a car until he died, and then they strung him from a tree. And AIDS was a big thing, too. If you were gay, it was thought to be just in your world. It was so taboo.

As I've already stated, many adolescents experiment with same-gender peers, but those who actually have a same-gender sexual orientation usually become fully aware of this prior to 17 – and sometimes much earlier.

I had a blow job before from boys, but when a girl went to go down on me, I didn't want her to because it felt weird. I drank loads of beer to get drunk. To get a hard-on I would think of the guy whose room we were in – I saw him in his underwear once. Having her mouth close to me did not seem right.

I never liked the feel of boys. But being close to girls gave me the same sort of 'zing' that girls in my class described when they were with their boyfriends. I realised that I had different types of feelings about my closest girlfriends than they had about me. Even then I knew I had to keep those feelings secret.

After identifying themselves with labels – such as 'gay', 'lesbian', or 'bisexual' – teenagers will often find themselves at odds with their immediate environment, such as families, religious groups, school and any bigoted people around them. They may become psychologically distressed and drop out of school or run away, and they are at risk of suicide.

I felt pressure from my church. I knew what I was supposed to do. In the Mormon Church, they were nice about it, saying, 'It's normal, but it's a sin.' You're supposed to get married in the temple, and they start planning your life out when you're ten.

I was six foot, three inches in school. I regularly heard 'Hey faggot!' – that was a prevalent term at that time. I'd turn and say, 'Are you talking to me big boy? Do you want my number?' Then they'd get drunk at the school dance, and whose bottom did they pinch? Not their girlfriends'. All these drunk football guys would be grabbing my arse.

In more liberal environments, gay and lesbian teenagers seem to be coming out earlier, perhaps because they feel there may be more acceptance.

I originally told my girlfriend I was bi. She was OK about that, and she still wanted me. Girls liked my sensitivity.

When I came out in my last year at school, all the taunting stopped. I didn't lose any friends – I gained them.

Trans-gendered youth

When I was six, and realised that I was not going to be a woman when I grew up, I was devastated. It was even worse when I was 13, and my male organs started developing. I wanted to cut them off. How could God have made such a huge mistake, putting me inside a male body? When I fell for Thomas and we started going together, my dad cottoned on and all hell broke loose. I'd already faced his 'sissy' rage, and now it was 'pouf'. I thought about killing myself many times. Finally, at 17, it was like that song 'Lola' – I put on my best dress and jumped on a train. I haven't been home since.

Many people do not understand that being trans-gendered is something quite different from being gay, and this can be a huge problem for adolescents who fall into this category. As I explained in the last chapter, gender identity (feeling that one is male, female, or something in between) is not the same as sexual orientation, which is about partner choice – feeling attracted to people of the same gender, other gender, or both genders. Trans-gendered people can be heterosexual, homosexual or bisexual – just like everyone else. Unfortunately, not everyone in our society is tolerant of diversity, and many trans-gendered people are pilloried on the basis of assumptions made about their sexuality. Trans-gendered youth have usually become aware of feeling 'trapped in another body' well before puberty.

I liked playing with the girls at school – playing 'Double-Dutch'. I was also the only boy playing hopscotch with girls. While other boys were beating each other up, I was doing crêpe paper. Every girl in school was my best friend. I was walking around in fifth grade with a huge group of girls. They called me 'girl'. In second grade I walked like a girl, talked like a girl – why wasn't I a girl? I cried all the time. They were the worst years of my life. Mum didn't know how to handle it. I was so different and it was so extreme. She was kind of negative – shut it down. I don't remember ever having a one-on-one, sit-down conversation. I guess she was exhausted.

When I was a teenager I heard about a 'tranny' posing as a woman and going with a guy. When he realised this, he killed her. That definitely gave me pause.

Trans-gendered teenagers need understanding, acceptance – and ideally a good counsellor to help them to deal with some of the intolerance and difficult situations they may face in their lives.

Heartbreak, pain and inequality

Many teenagers experience devastating heartbreak. They are usually unskilled at negotiating relationships, expressing feelings and dealing with rejection, and they can undergo considerable emotional pain without knowing how to handle the situation that caused it. It can be particularly difficult for teenagers when parents mandate separation from someone to whom they are strongly connected.

When I was 17, my boyfriend had to break up with me because his mum found an unflushed used condom in the toilet. We had gone to his house during lunch for a quickie.

Frankly, if I was the parent in the above example I would be enormously grateful that my son was being safe and, after a bit of investigation, would probably encourage the relationship. I know it can be shocking to be confronted with evidence of your child's sexuality, but all too often adolescents are left with the feeling that their normal sexual desire and expression are on a par with axe murder – and that can have a negative effect on their later-life sexuality as well.

There's often a huge gulf between what teenagers are feeling and what's expected of them. What's more, a lot of what's expected of them is both unspoken and complex – affected and defined by developments and influences in so many aspects of human experience, including those that are biological, social, cultural, religious, familial, interpersonal, psychological, educational and legal.

It seemed like whatever I was doing, it was always wrong. I could no longer trust my instincts because my instincts were telling me to do things that would invariably get me into trouble.

What many people don't understand is that adolescent sexual expression is not just about sex, and not just responding to urges. It is inexorably bound up with the normal stage of psychological developmental – even the troubled and troubling stuff.

And having a stressful home environment will have a significant effect on every aspect of a teenager's life – including sexuality.

I don't really remember any sexual feelings 'starting' at puberty. If anything, my feelings were dulled during puberty, because of so much stress and disruption at home (impending divorce and lots of fighting). Where sexuality was concerned, I was just doing what I thought I should be doing. It was like trying to navigate my way through a minefield in the dark, with no one to tell me what was okay, or what was 'normal'. I so much wanted to be normal, but I didn't know what that was. I wasn't in touch with my own emotions or desires at all – I was a follower, desperately trying to fit in. Puberty was a total labyrinth to me. It disturbs me to think about it.

When I was 13, I had a slumber party for my birthday. I was the shy girl in school who didn't have a boyfriend. But, one day, the girls in the popular group decided to let me in, and I was so happy. Sexually, they were so advanced. So I invited them to come over for my birthday and they came, but what I didn't know was that those girls told their boyfriends to come too – in the middle of the night. They climbed in the window. My father, who was very strict, came downstairs and caught them. The boys dived under the sleeping bags but my father grabbed each one, pulled him out and called his parents: 'Do you know where your son is right now? In my house – in my daughter's room!' He scolded me, saying, 'I can't trust you anymore!' But I only wanted to be popular. I think it scared him so much, but it was terrible. I never had another party, and the popular girls never wanted to hang around with me because I had this furious father. That was an awful, awful thing at the time. To this day, my father has never been interested in any of my boyfriends.

Events such as these can leave massive scars on a person's psyche. The young woman in question learned that being involved in sexual behaviour – even if it was not her own – could cause her to be shunned, mistrusted and punished. But learning aside, some young people start off at a disadvantage. Unfortunately, teenagers are not all equal in terms of gender, sexual orientation, psychology, character, physique, intelligence, privilege, background, race, ethnicity and many other salient factors that can affect the choices they make – or don't – when it comes to sex.

There was this boy – he was 13 and I was 15 – and we would go to the woods and give each other full-on blow jobs to the point of ejaculation. But when I came out, the fooling around stopped because he was black and his family was not at all liberal. I didn't see him for three years but, when I was 19, I went into a gay bar and there he was. He was 17. Gorgeous. Holy shit – he looked older than me, really mature. I could drink; I went through my puking phase at 15. We started making out, then went back to his sister's house. But he still wasn't 'out' and had a very religious family, so we had to see each other secretly. We fell in love. I asked him to marry me and he said 'yes'. Two years later he was shot and killed. At his funeral I looked like I was on meth. People were like: 'Who the hell is that white boy rocking back and forth crying?'

This tragic story, like many I have heard, really illustrates how deeply our sexuality is entwined with the values of our family, religion, race and many other aspects of our society and background – and how terribly difficult it can be when love and sexual passion are at odds with all of that. Certain teenagers face seemingly insurmountable barriers against their sexual self-expression, especially gay, lesbian, bisexual and trans-gendered youth, young people with special needs and anyone whose family objects to their partner choices for one reason or another. Such difficulties can become so intense that many adolescents become hopeless, and at risk of suicide.

Some teenagers and their families struggle with poverty and lack of equal opportunities for education and a hopeful future. Many adolescents are at risk of experiencing negative sexual consequences, such as becoming homeless, pregnant or abused. Some may run away from home, turn to prostitution or abuse alcohol or drugs. Jean Piaget described the 'personal fable' – the idea teenagers have that they are special and invulnerable. Their notion of 'it couldn't happen to me' makes them particularly at risk of unsafe sex practices and contracting HIV or other STDs. Teenagers at risk need help in the form of realistic sexuality education, counselling and support services.

> After my mum went to prison I more or less lived on the street from the age of 14 until I was almost 17. Sometimes I'd get some cash working as a rent boy but my addiction meant that I could never get stable in any way. I'm 19 now and I've been HIV positive for four years now, but at least I'm clean.

Extra challenges

Adolescents who have developmental disabilities and members of certain other groups, such as those with mobility impairments, experience unique challenges that are often not met by social services. For example, a sexually active teenager with poor fine motor skills will have considerable difficulty just putting on a condom. Youth with special needs have to be extremely creative in finding a way to express their sexuality. They need help and special sex education that addresses their specific concerns.

> I have Asperger's. I really like girls and I think they should be attracted to me because I'm a good-looking guy, but I think it may the way I approach them. Sometimes I try to talk to them about music or I just ask if they want to go out with me. Sometimes they're nice, but they often treat me like I shouldn't have asked.

Adolescents with special needs may not always be able to get certain types of help – especially to do with dating and sexuality – from their parents.

> I feel very conflicted about how to help my daughter (who has special needs) with her sexual feelings. When she was a young child, we had to figure out how to stop her touching herself in public – and she still does that sometimes. Now she's a teenager, we're terrified someone might try to take advantage of her. We have done our best to try to explain things in a language she would understand, but she is very impulsive and might just let someone touch her. She might do something inappropriate – or worse. If I'm honest, although this is something I hardly dare voice, I worry that she might become pregnant. Honestly, that's a bigger worry than if my other daughter (who does not have special needs) became pregnant.

Adolescents with special needs certainly deserve to enjoy pleasure and safe sexual expression. But those at risk should be identified and helped by teachers, community leaders and others to manage their sexual feelings safely and make decisions that will help rather than harm them in the long run. Doing this involves open, honest sexuality education and finding ways to help foster healthy sexuality, a positive self-image and a healthy body.

Staying safe

All adolescents have to find a way to negotiate the safety aspects of sexuality – the responsibilities and values that go along with their decisions about sex. This is hard when their judgement is skewed by natural adolescent mood swings, and the pressure of feeling misunderstood and 'wrong'.

> When I was still at school, I made the mistake of going out with a man who was much older than me. At the end of the evening I stupidly went to his apartment, where he forced me to have sex with him. It was terribly traumatic. I couldn't tell anyone – I had no one to tell. I finally told my boyfriend, which was a big mistake because he confronted the man, who then said that I had willingly gone down on him. In fact, the man had threatened to kill me if I didn't do as he said. But my boyfriend didn't believe me, and called me a 'slut'. I've never really gotten over that.

Teenagers can find themselves in very serious situations, trying to use their limited insight to deal with scenarios that would challenge people twice their age. The parents of the girl who provided the above testimony would never have imagined that she might be dealing with such difficulties. Teaching platitudes such as 'sex is something you should enjoy with someone you love in a committed relationship' is all very well, but in real life a huge range of opportunities will present themselves to the average teenager, and it is impossible to provide specific guidance for every one.

> *Never accept rides from strange men, and remember*
> *that all men are as strange as hell.*
>
> Robin Morgan

After instilling values, the best that parents can do is to stress the need to trust one's intuition – to know when things do not feel right and to act accordingly. Teenagers should be taught to protect themselves from unwanted pregnancy, as well as from HIV and other diseases – which means getting very specific with them about the use of birth control and condoms, and the relative safety of the various sexual acts. They need to understand the role of alcohol and drugs when it comes to risk-taking, and to be clear about what constitutes sexual coercion – for example, that it is impossible to give consent for sex if they are intoxicated.

Sexually charged images are everywhere – especially on the internet – so any parents who believe that they are aware of what their teenager is seeing online is rather delusional! How can a parent control where his teen goes in cyberspace when, in order to do that, he'd first have to beg him for some tech support? What's important is to establish lines of communication so a teenager feels safe and comfortable turning to a parent for clarity, advice and help. However, this is easier said than done. We are kidding ourselves if we think by merely putting blocking software on the family computer we've discharged our responsibility as effective sex educators.

My husband gave our son a good description of sex, condoms, relationships and intercourse when he was 15, but he acted as though he already knew it all. He was already active on the internet with porn.

The mere fact that teenagers do have internet access and are way ahead in computer skills puts an even greater onus on parents to make sure they instil appropriate values, and are available to help their teenagers to make sense of all the confusing images and information that bombard them. This may mean familiarising oneself with what actually *is* available on the internet, to get a flavour of the influences to which one's teenager may be subject.

The girls at my school and I were embarrassed that the boys had more 'knowledge' about sex, especially the weird stuff – whether that was realistic or otherwise. It was more socially acceptable for boys to look at porn than for us to do so. Boys would know all these terms – names for certain activities, such as the 'Cleveland Steamer' (I've forgotten what that was) or the 'Houdini' (where the guy would pretend to come and pull out, then surprise her by coming on her face) or 'Donkey Punching' (striking a woman on her back, apparently to heighten orgasm) or 'Tossing the Salad' which was some anal thing. Another one was the 'Rodeo', where the guy does something mean during sex, and when she tries to buck him off, he hangs on as long as possible. I mean, all of these things were probably invented by 14-year-old boys, but at the time we were impressed – not to mention scared. Formal classroom sex education was taught to us at an awkward age, and only really covered the safety aspects.

This testimony is in sharp contrast to what people who are now 70 – and older – told me about their teenaged years.

> I wasn't comfortable with boys. I never saw a male naked until I was 20. We were working very hard all the time, just to keep going during the war and afterwards. There was no thought that you could have sex with anyone – you couldn't get pregnant. I didn't know how not to get pregnant, but I knew I mustn't because we had no money.

People who are in their 50s and 60s today also found their own way to be sexual as teenagers – in keeping with the opportunities available at the time.

> We had to do it standing up, when I was ostensibly taking her home at night. There were lanes with doorways and railways stations that were closed for the night – these places were known as 'knee-tremblers'. We had to do it fast and furious. We couldn't possibly be good lovers – the object was to come as fast as possible, and before you got caught by a passer-by or the police. Female orgasm didn't even enter the equation. We didn't even know there was such a thing.

The messages about sex that adolescents receive today are highly contradictory – on the one hand sexual content pervades the internet, TV and film, and on the other hand many try to educate teenagers to refrain from sexual activity completely. But, as I've already pointed out, sex is often more exciting if it is forbidden or taboo – even dangerous. So, in trying to stop them from engaging in any kind of sexual experiences (as those who advocate the 'abstinence-only' approach to sex education do), we may actually be making it more likely that it will be repeated!

Just saying, 'No' prevents teenaged pregnancy the way 'Have a nice day' cures chronic depression.

Faye Wattleton

Becoming an adult

As the adolescent years progress, young men and women start to acquire more adult erotic feelings and continue their experiments in earnest. In our culture, this bridge between childhood and adulthood lasts from around 12 to 20 years of age, although it's much shorter in some other cultures. And some cultures have a more clearly defined transition – rites of passage into adulthood with special ceremonies and initiation, to mark and celebrate entering a new stage of life.

I was invited to a friend's bar mitzvah. I had never been to one before. I found it very moving, and in the middle of it I felt like crying. I realised that it was because my own coming of age was far from celebrated. In fact, my whole adolescence was a painful time of confusion, sadness, trouble at school and fighting with my parents. I felt they wanted to quash my grown-up feelings – especially the sexual ones. But my friend's parents and her whole network of friends and family seemed proud of her growing into a woman. I remember wishing I'd been born Jewish.

Unfortunately, many of us spend so much time and effort trying to restrict teenaged sexuality that celebrating adolescence is the last thing on our minds. I happen to agree with anthropologist Margaret Mead, who found that in societies like Samoa – where adolescents had prescribed tasks and rites of passage – there was a lot less 'storm and strife'. I have observed that Western adults' own hang-ups about sexuality and their lack of resolution with themselves as sexual beings can make this a miserable and enormously stressful time for everyone in the family – and a period where we can reach the peak of our capacity for hypocrisy.

I felt worried and totally confused about the way people around me viewed sex as evil – because I *liked* it … masturbating, etc. But, if sex is evil, how did I get here?

Many parents are struggling to understand the nuances of the fast-evolving teenage culture.

I heard my daughter using the term 'friends with benefits'. She was speaking about a boy who comes round to our place, and it worried me because I imagined she was having sex with him – probably without any emotional connection. I wasn't even sure what worried me the most – having sex or doing it without feelings. In my day there was usually some kind of romantic connection that preceded having sex.

I kept hearing the expression 'hooking up'. My son would come home and I'd say 'Where were you?' and he'd say 'I hooked up with this girl' or I'd hear him on the phone saying 'You want to hook up later?' But that meant nothing to me – did he just meet up with her or did they pet? Did they have sex? I finally asked, and he said, 'It means, like if you say, "We used to hook up" that means we used to date, but not seriously. But also it could mean we made out or kissed. It usually doesn't mean sex, but it could. High-school kids use it a lot.' 'Okay,' I said, 'glad I got that sorted out!'

Many parents just have no idea how very sexual some of their teenagers are becoming. Sometimes this happens right under their noses.

One night when a lot of people were at our house after a party and my parents were asleep in the next room, she slept on the bed while all us boys slept on the floor. But she woke me up, sucked my dick and then sat on me and fucked me. Then we went back to sleep. People were snoring all round us.

Adults are often keen to try to instil values dictating that sex should only occur in the context of a loving, committed relationship. That's great in principle, but it's not an easy task for the average teenager. They are capable of love, but the power of their hormones – plus their relative psychological maturity – means that sex often occurs in a casual relationship. Discovering how to connect loving feelings and sex may take quite a long time. In fact, many people do not learn this until they are at least in their 20s – or even much later. It takes considerable maturity to achieve the capacity for true adult intimacy.

The first time I was really sexually attracted to someone was long after I'd already lost my virginity. I'd had crushes on guys – and I'd had a horrible boyfriend with whom I'd had lots of sex over two years – but the first time another person really stirred some kind of longing in me (as in a heated sensation between my legs) was at age 17, my second real boyfriend. It was intense, and very lovely to have emotion and attraction attached to sexual feelings for the very first time. Before that I can't say that what I felt for any boyfriend was sexual attraction. It was more obligation and duty, with a bit of self-pleasure thrown in there as a bonus. I guess that's the key difference for me; my first experiences with sex felt very much like mutual masturbation (using someone, and being used), whereas when I first felt some kind of stirring or what I can identify as a true sexual attraction, it was strongly connected to my emotions about that person.

The wonder years

Many older adults look back on the positive sides of their adolescent years with longing and nostalgia. After all, that soaring eroticism and excitement in the company of attractive peers seemed boundless.

The first time I had an orgasm I thought: 'These adults have got it all wrong ... this is really good fun!'

When I think about my adolescence, I just don't know how I survived it. I look at pictures of myself from that time and I was walking jailbait. My school uniform was hiked up to my thighs, my budding breasts bursting out of a blouse I'd outgrown, my bottom lip in a permanent pout! But I loved the sense of sexual potential and what was happening in my body. The intensity in my erogenous zones was shocking at first – it was all so interesting and, at the same time, frightening and extremely powerful.

How idiotic civilization is! Why be given a body if you have to keep it shut up in a case like a rare, rare fiddle.

Katherine Mansfield

Early Adulthood
Who *Am* I Sexually?

When grown-ups do it it's kind of dirty.
That's because there is no one to punish them.

Tuesday Weld

exually speaking, when we become legal adults, there's good news and bad news. The good news is that we are legally allowed to do in private pretty much whatever we want – as long as it's consensual. The bad news is that at this particular developmental stage of our life span, we may have quite a few other priorities. Many young adults are trying to make their way in the world of work. Some are still studying, while others are taking care of families, children or elders. For many, sex has to take a bit of a back seat. They have to concentrating on 'getting on', rather than 'getting it on'!

We met when we were both studying in Edinburgh and in those days we'd have sex all the time – three, four times a day. But after we graduated, reality set in. There was massive competition in my law firm. I was working 14 hours a day to prove that I was ready for promotion. My partner was also working long and stressful hours in the fashion industry. All either of us wanted to do when we came home was have a couple of bevvies and fall asleep.

I had my first child at 19 and two more babies before I was 25. Finding time for sex was almost impossible; in fact, in all honesty, I wasn't even motivated to make love in case it led to yet another set of nappies to change.

Having children had a very negative effect on my sex life … I was sore down below, and had no time for it. Even when there was time, I was usually too exhausted.

Giving birth is traumatic enough, but no sooner have the lactation leakage circles dried on your shirt front than your husband wants nookie. Needless to say, the woman with the recently stitched perineum does not.

Kathy Lette

The rules of attraction

While stress, overwork, fatigue, city-dwelling and relationship problems can all have a devastating effect on our sexuality, for those who are lucky enough to achieve the necessary balance in their lives, this decade can be a time to become more sexually mature, experienced and able to explore eroticism. Some even achieve the ability to establish deep, truly intimate connections with others.

In my 20s, I finally got to understand how amazing love-making could be. Instead of all the quick, guilty fumbling I'd experienced as a teenager, my boyfriend and I could just hide ourselves away for days and really explore the whole thing. We were so in love and we learned to take each other to new heights.

Many young adults are motivated to seek the kinds of sanctioned relationships that were not possible as teenagers – longer-term, loving, sexual connections, perhaps with the option to start a family. Dating takes on a new urgency, the style of which is often dictated by societal changes and technology.

> I met this guy on 'Grinder'. We'd been texting each other for weeks and all of a sudden, right when I had a naked picture of him on my phone, there he was standing right outside my hotel. I used to pick up guys in gay bars, but now that just seems like far too much work.

> I met Jim through an internet dating site. My girlfriends warned I might find myself an axe murderer, and that even speed dating would be a better bet, but Jim and I chatted online for several weeks before we met up and it worked out really well. We've been married for nearly two years now, and so far so good!

New technology that enables people to find like-minded potential partners within a short radius of one's home is said to have made the search for sex and relationships easier for some people, especially those living in large cities. Nevertheless, in the process of attraction, biology is still playing a large part.

Biological processes also help people feel bonded to each other after sex. 'The afterglow' is one way of describing the actions of oxytocin, the same powerful hormone that is secreted to help breastfeeding mothers bond with their infants.

> *The only time human beings are sane is the ten minutes after intercourse.*
> Eric Berne

Once they reach adulthood, many people are relieved that society finally sanctions their sexual expression – at least in certain prescribed situations. But now that they're allowed to 'do it', the pressure's on to do it right. The trouble is, suddenly having licence to do something that's been forbidden for so many years can lead us to go overboard.

The post-grad campus is its own incestuous bubble. I had a steady boyfriend in the first two years, but many people within friendship groups just swap around. One group I'm friends with – a group of about 15 males and females – tend to date each other, and cheat on each other, so they've all pretty much slept with each other by now.

The only difference between friends and lovers is about four minutes.

Scott Roeben

It's not surprising that people in their 20s are scrambling to understand their sexuality. The whole of the previous decade was about 'Don't do it!', and now all of a sudden the cry (in liberal circles) becomes 'Become experienced as soon as possible (to avoid the embarrassment of still being a virgin), and immediately be "good in bed"!' In less liberal circles, it's 'Continue to abstain until you're married, then (overnight) become proficient and create children.' Both are extremely tall orders.

It got to the point where I was in a double bind: I dared not confess that I was still a virgin, but I knew that if I took the plunge and had sex with one of my peers they would know – and I really had no idea what to do. The whole thing terrified me. Dating became enormously stressful because there was always a point where I had to decide, 'Should I trust this person with my secret and get on with it?' I was 34 when I finally threw caution to the wind. It involved a holiday in Spain, a local shopkeeper and a bottle of tequila.

What is adult sex?

Many people believe that adult lovemaking should involve being able to have really good sex with a partner that we care for. But as I've pointed out before, satisfying sex is something we have to learn – it doesn't just happen. There is, potentially, the freedom to perfect lovemaking skills in our 20s, but many young adults are still confused. Many find it difficult to please a partner, while others simply cannot find one. All the while, there remains a gap between sex as a widely promoted marketing tool, and what people are really feeling and doing.

> *What is peculiar to modern societies is not that they have consigned sex to a shadow existence, but that they dedicated themselves to speaking of it* ad infinitum, *while exploiting it as a secret.*
>
> Michel Foucault

Some still find it extremely hard to communicate their needs to their partners, or to understand their own sexual responses.

Many are downright uncomfortable with their normative bodily responses, and may actually be unaware of what exactly happens in their bodies during sex. Well, it's no wonder, is it? After all the censuring of sexual expression up until now, the need to hide their desires and the lack of education, it's quite unreasonable to expect that a person would become entirely sexually healthy or proficient without a lot more work! Some people believe that embracing spontaneity is the way to go.

> When I was in my 20s, sex just ... happened. I barely thought about it – just let my desire and my body lead the way.

Spontaneity is all very well – and lovely when it occurs without a hitch – but simply acting spontaneously without considering the consequences of sex can cause more trouble than it's worth.

> *See, the problem is God gives men a brain and a*
> *penis, and only enough blood to run one at a time.*
> Robin Williams

What exactly does happen in our bodies during a sexual experience? First of all, the term 'sexual experience' can really mean anything from having a flirty verbal encounter with a stranger on an aeroplane, to full-on lovemaking session – i.e. sex is anything that involves arousal of a sexual nature.

My son's best friend from university and I were standing alone in our kitchen after the birthday party. He was ostensibly helping me with the dishes, but his presence made me nervous. I had been aware of his interest in me, but had tried to ignore it. He suddenly picked up the largest strawberry in my fruit basket and offered it close to my lips with such a look of boyish lust in his eyes that I felt compelled to open my mouth wide and receive. He smiled triumphantly as I swallowed it, while I was stricken with guilt. It was the hottest, wickedest experience of sexual penetration I've ever had while fully dressed.

Sex with the right man is a beautiful and moving and lovely thing ... sex with a stranger on a train in the dead of night is even better.

Kathy Lette

Even just desiring to have sexual contact with someone is a human experience of a sexual nature. Sexologists and sexuality researchers have tried to analyse and formally describe a 'human response cycle', or the stages a body undergoes while progressing from anticipating a sexual act through to the finale. The famous researchers William Masters and Virginia Johnson came up with a model of the human sexual response in four distinct stages – excitement, plateau (a kind of levelling off they thought occurred just prior to the rush to orgasm), orgasm and resolution (where the body returns to its previous state).

Since my penis has a mind of its own, it really informs me not only that I'm in the mood, but that I have to do it right away. It won't take no for an answer, so if the woman in question brushes me off, my right hand has to do the honours. Afterwards, when it's having a break, I'll often look at the woman I've just shagged and say to myself: 'What were you thinking?' My penis is less discriminating than me.

Our biological drives are three million years older than our intelligence.

Arthur E. Morgan

Sex therapist Helen Singer Kaplan came up with another sexual response model, in three stages – desire (mentally wishing for a particular sexual experience), excitement (the body responds to the mental desire) and orgasm.

I definitely like to imagine having sex with someone and to have that divine period of longing for him. Then it's extra-exciting when it actually happens. There have been times when I've had sex with men in a really sudden, spontaneous way, but essentially I think I'm programmed to need time to want a guy. If we hook up too quickly, I feel cheated.

The longer they wait, the better they like it.

Marlene Dietrich

These human sexual response models have been relatively useful to many students of sexuality, and have been the basis upon which categories of sexual dysfunction have been formed. However, critics of these models have pointed out that not everyone follows such progressions every time they have sex, so why should we consider any of them to be the standard 'norm'? For example, many people do not achieve orgasm during a particular sexual experience – either by choice or otherwise. Some may return to a state of simple excitement – or even their non-aroused state – once, twice or more before they move to an orgasmic phase.

Last night I was having delicious sex with my girlfriend. She was pleasuring me using a thigh dildo to enter me, while she played expertly (as usual!) with my clit. Just when I was about to come, my mobile phone rang. I had forgotten to turn it off. It was a work call that I needed to take, so I played with my partner's breasts and clit while I dealt with the late shipment issue. She came pretty quickly, even though I could tell she was unhappy that I'd answered the phone in the first place. The customer was yelling at me, so I became completely turned off and upset. As punishment, my girlfriend wouldn't let me come until the next morning. But the way she made me wait – teasing and torturing me – was utterly delicious.

The above is just one example of what was clearly a sexual experience that did not (for the mobile-phone user) follow a three- or four-part sexual-response pattern. But it was nonetheless a valid sexual response/experience. In fact, many people have sex that's not even preceded by desire.

Sometimes I'm just not in the mood, and turn over to try to sleep, but my man knows that if he spoons behind me and plays with my nipples and strokes me in the right place between my legs I'll be ready for him in no time at all. Then we have sex with him doing all the work. Sometimes it pays to be a tired, lazy bitch!

My favourite way to wake up is when my girlfriend goes down on me while I'm still asleep. I wake with a hard-on, thinking I've been having a hot dream – that turns out to be real.

How our bodies respond

When researchers analysed what happens in our bodies between the first inkling that a sexual act is going to occur and the end of the whole experience (assuming for now that there are no interruptions and things proceed smoothly to orgasm), they discovered that it amounted to a highly complex operation involving many of the body's systems. When we get excited (whether or not we are mentally aware of wanting sex) our heart rate and blood pressure start to rise, and the muscle tension in our bodies increases. We might start getting redder in our chest area – a process known as 'sex flush' – and nipples (in both women and men) often become erect. Vasocongestion begins to occur, which involves body tissues becoming engorged with blood, causing the swelling and reddening of the clitoris, labia and nipples in women – and the testes and nipples in men. Most noticeably, vasocongestion triggers the erection of the penis, and it is also the process that leads to lubrication being secreted through the walls of the vagina.

I love that warm feeling when my body reacts to her touch. She usually plays with my nipples first and there's an incredible connection between them and my clitoris. The strength of it surprised me at first and made me feel out of control, but now I look forward to it. My breasts seem to get bigger and I get that pleasant squelchy feeling in my vagina. Since there's no word to describe the female equivalent of a male 'hard-on', I call mine a 'wide-on'.

God, I love it when I get turned on. That incredible rush – it all happens so fast – zero to 60 in about three seconds, it seems like. I get really off-balance mentally – really heady, even dizzy sometimes. The buzziness seems to bounce around my body – ping! ping! – wherever she touches me. My scrotum tightens up and my penis just waves at her: 'Come on, babe, get down here!'

In the period leading to orgasm, our heart rate, blood pressure, breathing rate and muscle tension all increase (even though there can be a subjective sense of levelling out). In men, the testes become even more raised and swollen, while in women the outer part of the vagina becomes increasingly open and engorged, the ringed area around the nipples (areola) swells more, and the clitoris (which has peeked out from under its hood during the initial excitement period) withdraws.

It was weird. I was touching her clitoris, and she was giving me signs that she was about to come, when all of a sudden it disappeared. I simply couldn't figure out where her clitoris had gone, and she was thrashing about so much I just couldn't feel it. Then she stopped and looked at me. 'Show me what to do,' I pleaded. She took my hand and repositioned it a little higher. It felt different, but it was still there. The change to slightly more circular pressure finally took her over the edge.

The idea of the 'plateau' – the period between arousal and the final rush to orgasm – is debated among sexologists, but I think it's a useful concept for pleasure-seekers because, if you can prolong that ecstatic period before orgasm occurs, the orgasmic sensation can be even better. Anyone can learn to do this – you just have to be less goal-orientated, focus on the sensations of the moment and learn to stop for a bit if you get too close to the 'edge'. When you eventually decide to climax, the orgasm will be more intense, and you may be ready to orgasm again even more quickly. There are sexual traditions in other cultures (Indian *Tantra*, for example) where the goal is sometimes to postpone orgasm altogether and deliberately maintain the highly pleasurable plateau period indefinitely. It certainly takes practice to achieve prolonged plateau pleasure, but it can be very rewarding.

My girlfriend got this book about Tantric sex, and it had instructions for a 'Tantric weekend', in which the first 40 hours were all about foreplay with no coming. This sounded excruciating to me, but actually we ended up having the best sex ever. The entire weekend was one amazing session of playing, teasing, stroking and massaging. I almost ejaculated several times, but just managed to stop. Actually, she had learned about this spot to press between my anus and my balls that slowed me down and that helped a lot. When we finally got to Sunday night, we started coming like it was the end of the world – again and again. I've got to say, it was a real eye-opener.

At orgasm, both men and women reach peak levels of breathing rate, blood pressure and heart rate, and have muscular spasms throughout their bodies. Many people are unaware of this, but our rectal sphincters also contract. A number of contractions occur in the outer third of a woman's vagina (orgasmic platform) and also in her uterus. Not all men ejaculate at orgasm (and some even have a condition where semen is expelled internally into the bladder rather than externally), but for most there is a pooling of seminal fluid (in the urethral bulb), followed by muscular contractions around the base of the penis that cause the semen to shoot out of the tip.

I guess God made orgasm so unbelievably nice because that increases the likelihood that we'll want to do it again and again – and keep the human race going. But where does female orgasm fit in? It's not exactly necessary for procreation, is it? I guess they have to come so they'll be in a good mood and look kindly on the idea of letting you in again next time. Yeah, that must be it!

It may be discovered someday that an orgasm actually lasts for hours and only seems like a few seconds.
Dolly Parton

Ejaculation

Men – and their partners – have varying views about the length of time it takes to reach orgasm. Some men are so excited to be inside a woman's vagina (or anywhere else they fancy!) that they ejaculate rather rapidly. If this occurs more quickly than they or their partner wish, either or both of them may perceive this to be a problem.

> *In sex as in banking there is a penalty for early with-drawal.*
>
> Cynthia Nelms

> *His finest hour lasted a minute and a half.*
>
> Phyllis Diller

Early ejaculation is more common when men are very young – which is one of the reasons why their partners often consider them to be better lovers when they're older. Having said that, intercourse that goes on and on forever is highly over-rated, and can make a woman bored and sore.

> *Men, they either come too quickly, or take too long. Premature ejaculators or Oh-my-God-the-ceiling-needs-painting ejaculators.*
>
> Kathy Lette

Our biological responses are certainly major instigators of our sexual responses, but there are enormous benefits for those who also manage to employ their intelligence to improve their lovemaking skills.

My brain is my second favourite organ.

Woody Allen

In fact, the brain can control Woody's 'favourite' organ to some extent. For example, men who tend to ejaculate earlier than they or their partners wish can actually learn ejaculatory control and sustain a longer period of thrusting. Once again, longer thrusting is sometimes desirable for a partner – and sometimes it is not – but many men regard it as a sign of having sexual prowess if they can 'last'.

I once made love for an hour and 15 minutes. But it was the night the clocks were set ahead.

Garry Shandling

I don't think a man is automatically great in bed if he goes on and on for ages. In fact, some of the most exciting times are when you just do it in five minutes.

Cheryl Tiegs

Some men have the opposite problem – their moment of ejaculation with a partner is delayed or even non-existent. This becomes a particular issue in the case of a man who is in a partnership where they are trying to achieve a pregnancy; however, most men can learn to ejaculate with or in a partner if they wish.

The big 'O'

The moment of orgasm is experienced in different ways by different people.

I'm afraid I'm really noisy when I come. I just love to let go and I don't care who hears. If I try to restrain myself, that awareness stops me from having quite so much pleasure. I do try to avoid having sex when we stay with my parents.

Once orgasm has occurred, our muscle tension, heart rate, blood pressure and breathing rate all subside and return to normal, sooner or later. Nipples lose their erectness, and any sex flush disappears. After orgasm/ejaculation men's erections subside – faster if they are older – while their testes and scrotum return to their previous states. In women, the labia and clitoris lose their engorgement and the latter returns to its original position. If a woman does not have an orgasm, her aroused state lasts for quite a while. Unfortunately, for some women the reason for failing to experience orgasm during lovemaking is that they or their partners do not understand that intercourse alone does not necessarily provide sufficient arousal to enable women to reach climax; they tend to need more direct clitoral stimulation.

When I was younger I used to put up with lack of orgasm, and it's amazing how many guys just didn't get it. But now I've learned to be more assertive. I'll probably say something like, 'That was wonderful ... but haven't you forgotten something?' If they look at me blankly, I take their hand and place it on my clitoris and start showing them how to move it the way I like it.

Really that little dealy-bob is too far away from the hole. It should be built right in.

Loretta Lynn

Some women who do not achieve orgasm during a particular lovemaking session are happy to wait until their partners are ready for another round, while others masturbate themselves to orgasm.

> *I consider sex a misdemeanour – the more I miss, de meaner I get.*
>
> Mae West

If he comes before me, I get worried that he may not realise how frustrated I am. I usually give him a few minutes of afterglow and snuggle for a while … all the while praying he's not going to fall asleep on me. But sooner or later I'll give him some kind of hint, like, 'Nobody leaves the room till I come!' or something subtle like that …!

I like to give her one or two orgasms before I enter her, and I find that really pays off. She's usually so glowing, slippery, open … and grateful … she'll give me a great ride!

My partner still doesn't quite get the idea that I really need to have my orgasm just like he does. His previous girl-friends didn't insist upon it, but I have every bit as strong a sex drive as he has, and in my book it's just not accept-able for him to do the old-fashioned male thing and roll over once he's finished. Actually, I've found the best thing is to make sure I come first – then there's no argument at the end!

Warren Beatty could handle women as smoothly as operating an elevator. He knew exactly where to locate the top button. One flick and we were on our way.

Britt Ekland

However, many women never have orgasms and claim to be content about that, too.

I don't really care about having an orgasm. For me, other things about having sex are far more important – the closeness, touching, feeling that he's focusing wholly on me, and the act of feeling complete when he's inside me. It's a different feeling of fulfilment. I also feel wonderful when he climaxes – proud that my body can make him do that ...

Sometimes it just seems like too much work to have an orgasm. My boyfriend seems to think it's a matter of male pride to give me at least one – and preferably more – orgasm each time we make love, and I've had to explain to him it's just not necessary. For some reason he seems to have bought into that idea that there has to be some kind of *quid pro quo* in the orgasm balance. I appreciate that he wants to please me, but I've tried to explain that women are different. We don't necessarily need it every time.

Sometimes I think that my having an orgasm is more important to him than it is to me. I mean, I think it's good that he's thinking of me, but I'd rather come because I really want to rather than trying to squeeze one out to make him feel good about himself as a lover ...

In the case of some women, orgasms take quite a bit of time. Before signing on with such a partner, make sure you are willing to lay aside, say, the month of June, with sandwiches having to be brought in.

Bruce Jay Friedman

Faking it

On the topic of faked orgasms, if sex fraud were a crime, I'd be in jail for life.

Merrill Markoe

It's embarrassing to admit, but I usually fake orgasms during intercourse. I do it because I don't want to disappoint my partner. I try to time my (hopefully) excellent acting, so he thinks I am coming at the same time as him. Truthfully, I can only have real orgasms when he goes down on me.

It's unfortunate that this woman felt so pressured to have exactly the type of sex her partner wants her to have, but he – like many men – has obviously been falsely educated to believe that that 'coming together' is the ideal. Sadly, she had not found a way to take responsibility for her own orgasm; e.g. by asking her partner to touch her clitoris at the same time – or doing it herself – or by insisting on a specific type of position where her clitoris is directly stimulated.

Certain products are now being sold to increase female pleasure during intercourse, such as vibrating rings that encircle the penis and connect to the clitoris during thrusting. Experimentation is required – but it's worth it! When I suggested these methods to the woman in the above testimony, she immediately tried them out – with success. This particular woman happens to be a person with liberal attitudes towards sexuality; however, some people – like the woman who provided the following testimony – have been taught values that make it hard for her to be accepting of even the most natural of processes.

> With one partner, I kept orgasming very easily and I found this to be very embarrassing.

It doesn't seem fair, does it? The previous woman would have loved to be in her shoes. As women mature sexually, many of them regret getting into a rut of sexual pretence and wish they'd been able to ask for what they needed in the first place. Once started, it's not easy to reverse the trend, and many women are secretly remorseful and angry. As I said, we do not need to be goal-orientated or to feel pressure about orgasm.

> *The truth is that sexual liberation really can be very oppressive. Vaginal, clitoral, multiple ... it's a genital dictatorship.*
>
> Kathy Lette

Body image

The way we feel about our bodies generally has a significant effect on our sexuality. If we feel embarrassed by or ashamed of our physical selves, it will change the way we have sex, and may even stop us wanting to have it all together.

I have extra-large labia. I think they're larger than normal. I had a pain in my crotch when I was a teenager, and I asked my mother to look and tell me what might be the matter. When she saw my labia, she reacted like I was an alien, and brought the whole bridge club in to take a look, too. It was so humiliating. Later on, I had a boyfriend with an unusually large penis. When we broke up, he said he thought he'd never find someone who matched him so well genitally. He called me his 'Hottentot'.

I have struggled with my body image for as long as I can remember. Early 2007, I was diagnosed with anorexia and my BMI was less than 15 at that time. My BMI is now 19 and I am still in the treatment phase. I hate the shape of my body and I hope someday this may change. My feelings about my body have affected my sexuality a lot. In my past relationships, I have struggled to have any form of sexual activity.

But women aren't the only ones who may experience poor body image.

I have an unusually thin penis. When I was a teenager, this got round my school and the name 'pencil dick' plagued me for many years. I compensated by building my body, so I attracted lots of women, but I never wanted to have sex with them as that would mean they'd learn about my tiny little secret. I found a woman who seemed kind and understanding, and married her. I eventually learned to please my wife and keep her perfectly happy sexually, but I wonder how my sexuality would have been if I hadn't been born that way.

Men's insecurities about their penises – especially size – often start in childhood, and it's not too difficult to sell an insecure man a bottle of snake oil if you can convince him that it will make him larger than the next guy.

> *Mobile phones are the only subject on which men boast about who's got the smallest.*
>
> Neil Kinnock

Men resort to creams, potions, herbs, sprays and even surgery in the hope of achieving larger penises. In several other cultures, men modify their penises through (often dangerous) processes, such as splitting them, and infibulation – inserting pearls or other objects under the penile skin to achieve a ridge-like effect. If only men could understand that the vagina is a very accommodating organ – it can be happy with most sizes (in fact, an overly large penis can be more of a problem than a small one) and that, in any case, many women are far more interested in how a man pleases them in non-penetrative ways.

Getting things going

Many people would like to be able to act on their sexual urges the minute they arise, but that's not always possible. They must consider how best to approach a partner, and that's tricky because they risk rejection if they get it wrong. Learning through trial and error, people initiate sex with others in a myriad of different ways.

> I hate the way my boyfriend snaps his fingers and points at his crotch when he wants a blow job. He thinks it's

funny, because he's really not that uncouth, but it thoroughly annoys me.

I always know when my husband wants sex. He doesn't say anything;, he just sits there watching my every move as if to say, 'Can you just hurry up and finish what you're doing?' You'd think after all this time together he'd be able to say, 'Let's make love!' He's just shy that way.

I was on holiday in Jamaica. I was lying on the beach with a gorgeous hunk of a man I'd met the night before. He had fallen asleep, but he suddenly woke up and caught me looking at him – I suppose with a high degree of lust. He knelt up, scooped me off the sand and slowly carried me into the water. It wasn't playful; it was serious hubba hubba. I was gone!

I was in a restaurant and the couple at the table beside me were looking at the menu. The man winked at his partner and asked, 'Are you right for tonight?' She gave an embarrassed nod, which prompted him to say, 'Good! We'll order wine!'

The pub was closing and he helped me on with my raincoat. He took my scarf and set it around my neck, then put his hands inside it and gently lifted out my hair – every strand – and wound it around his hand, pulling me round to face him. He looked at me so intently! We didn't kiss then, but I knew we were going to.

It was my biggest fantasy coming true – he literally swept me off my feet and carried me to the bedroom. I don't know quite how he managed that because I'm hardly petite – but he made me feel so … 'Me Tarzan, you Jane!'

I think you're running into a lot of trouble if your idea of foreplay is, 'Brace yourself, honey, here I come.'

Dr Phil McGraw

In our society it is more common – and probably considered more acceptable – for a man to initiate sex with a woman, rather than the other way round. Yet many men fantasise about confident women who take the lead.

On our fourth date, we were sitting in a restaurant. It was one of those little intimate Italian places – checked table-cloths and candles in Chianti bottles. In the middle of our main course, she suddenly slipped off her high heel and started running her stockinged foot up inside my trouser leg. I thought I was going to pass out with excitement. I couldn't get out of there fast enough.

It seems to me that more and more women are becoming comfortable with a more sexually dominant role, and this is probably good news for female pleasure. Lesbians tend to be more comfortable taking responsibility for their own pleasure than heterosexual women. If heterosexual women could learn to initiate, to make decisions about particular positions and to be unafraid to show their partners exactly how to please them, they would not be so reliant on men for satisfaction.

After being left in a state of frustration many, many times, I just decided, 'To hell with it! I'm going to play with my own clitoris, while he's busy thrusting away.' As it happens, that turned him on, too! He'd seen it in his porn collection.

Whatever our sexual orientation may be, working out how to attract partners, negotiating the dating stage and initiating sex are challenges that presented themselves in adolescence and continue to face us in our 20s. For many people, it's an ongoing learning task – one that persists through other stages of life as well.

I was talking to a woman all night and I thought she fancied me, but I was wondering how to make the next move. I didn't want to invite her to my room in case she rejected me. A mate came up and said, 'Are you going to fuck her?' I said, 'Behave yourself!' Then I turned to her and said, 'I dunno – am I going to fuck you?' and she said, 'Yes'. It was one of the biggest turn-ons I'd had my whole life.

We didn't need to discuss it. He was sitting behind me and I was sitting on the floor in front of him. The room was full of people, but he laid just one finger on my shoulder and I knew. It was electric. Half an hour later we were naked in his room.

Her need is a huge issue. If she wants it, I am already well on the way. I have had sex with women who would not remotely interest me otherwise – just because they clearly wanted me to do it. After that, to be attractive to me, certain physical characteristics are more appealing. It's much better if she is fun to be with and talk to – if she laughs easily. Also, a bit of basic hygiene is pretty critical.

That's *embarrassing!*

Of course, sex is not always pretty. Everyone experiences some kind of embarrassing moment during sex at one time or another.

Once I had sex with this young man as a kind of gift. He had been so admiring of me and I knew that he had put me on such a high pedestal for some reason – I guess I was feeling a bit unworthy of it or something. Anyway, it was a kind of charity fuck that I later regretted. Next morning I woke up to the sound of my own unbelievably loud fart and an ensuing terrible odour. He looked at me in horror and I realised my queenly image had been irrevocably tarnished. He even told people about it, which wasn't nice, but probably served me right.

Sometimes when I'm having intercourse, particularly when it's rear entry, there's this fart-like sound coming from my vagina as he thrusts. I imagine it's air being trapped and released, but it's loud, embarrassing and distracting. I've heard it called a 'vart' and I wish I could figure out how to avoid it happening. It's not very lady-like.

When I come, I kind of wet the bed. A lot of fluid comes out. It can be embarrassing, especially with new partners, and I sometimes feel like a circus freak, although some men I've been with really like it. I used to think I was really abnormal, but I went online and did some research and found that I'm not the only woman who ejaculates. With me, it doesn't spurt out like some women you see in porn movies (are they rigged?), but a lot of creamy liquid does gush out – enough so that I need a towel to soak it up. Now I try to warn potential partners ahead of time. That can work in either one of two ways – either they are really curious (sometimes uncomfortably so) or else they run a mile.

I got breast cancer when I was only 23. I have a lot of scarring from my mastectomy and only one breast. At first I used to dress it up with lingerie and a padded bra that I never took off, but one day I just decided I was going to show my partners who I was. They can either take it or leave it. It's a fast way to learn what kind of man you're with.

Genital care

Attractiveness is not just about looks. Hygiene certainly seems to be important to most people I've spoken to, although people can sometimes be a bit too obsessed with cleanliness, not realising that most genitals are naturally quite clean and should not be confused with the anus.

> He needs to have a good sense of humour, and above all he needs to be *clean*! Some men are not very hygienic!

> I don't mind a bit of sweat at all. As a matter of fact, I love the smell that comes from a man's armpits. But if I'm going down on him and he's too grotty and cheesy there – I've noticed that can be an issue with some uncircumcised men – I'm not that keen on continuing.

Whether a man has been circumcised or not, he needs to take care of his penile health and cleanliness, although it can sometimes be more of a challenge if there is a lot of foreskin. Circumcision and other kinds of genital modification are becoming more controversial and more openly debated issues – for both men and women – and the many cultural and human rights considerations surrounding some of those practices are extremely complex.

> I fell for a beautiful girl whom I met in London. She was from Nigeria, and seemed to be an independent woman

with few family ties. We became very close, and eventually slept together. But I discovered that something had been done to her genitals – in a rather primitive way, i.e. it was not a medical procedure. She didn't want to talk about it, but I found it very disturbing and felt extremely sorry for her. Along with most of the outer part of her genitals, her clitoris had been removed. She said she enjoyed having sex, but I couldn't work out how.

Deliberate body modification aside, the genitals require some care and attention; for example, infections that occur from time to time need to be treated. The common (incorrect) notion that vaginas smell 'fishy' comes from the fact that a certain type of bacterial infection can indeed cause an unpleasant odour (treatment is necessary). But healthy vaginas do not smell unpleasant at all.

The pursuit of pleasure

Most of us do it way too fast. For both men and women, sex is usually much better and stress-free if our goal is simply to give and receive pleasure – taking our time about it – rather than to race to orgasm.

> *Remember, if you smoke after sex you're doing it too fast.*
>
> Woody Allen

And despite common beliefs, intercourse is not necessarily the best or most important part of heterosexual lovemaking. The term 'foreplay' invites the idea that intercourse is the 'main event', and that anything else is just a secondary build-up.

> Don't get me wrong, I definitely love the feeling of having him inside me. Feeling filled up by his body and feeling the full, lusty force of his passion is fantastic and really drives me wild. I feel close, bonded, totally in love with him – and totally validated as a woman. But still, that part of our lovemaking is all about his orgasm, not mine. When I want to come, it can't be while he's moving inside me; it has to be a time when the focus is all on me.

Not everyone relies simply on the manipulation of their genitals for orgasm. The simple fact that people can have orgasms in their sleep illustrates this. And a number of people with physical disabilities have found extraordinary ways to climax, even managing to relocate their erogenous zones to parts of the body that still retain feeling.

> I have a spinal-cord injury, so I don't have any feeling in my genitals. But I get really turned on in other ways – I love being touched and rubbed on all the parts of my body that I can still feel – especially my nipples – and that, combined with fantasising, gets me to orgasm.

We can also learn a lot from gay and lesbian people, who can have fantastic sex without the 'traditional' pattern – although some are very turned on, in both a sexual and an emotional sense, by penetration.

> Unlike many of my friends, I'm one of those gay men who does like penetration. When my lover is deep in my anus,

of course it's feels amazing on a purely pleasurable level, but it's also ... kind of spiritual. I feel incredibly calm, wanted, loved and complete. For me, there's no feeling like it.

Different sexual acts certainly have different meanings for different individuals, and we should never make assumptions about what those meanings might be for our partners. That's where deep discussion and personal disclosure in an atmosphere of trust and safety can really take our sexual intimacy to a whole other level.

When I first came out and was experimenting with women who were established members of the lesbian community, I made the assumption – probably from visual images, DVDs and so on – that using dildos and such to simulate hetero intercourse would be pretty standard. But with my past girlfriends we had never done that, preferring oral or manual touching to bring each other to orgasm. I actually had a horror of vaginal penetration in any form, because I was raped in my early teens. I was glad to find there was great sensitivity about that among the women I met in the lesbian community – and, in fact, many of them also had a distaste for penetrative sex. For me, being held and stroked – and, above all, feeling safe – really does it for me.

I do enjoy penetration – either with a dildo, my girlfriend's fist (I find that super-erotic) or occasionally by a man. But having something in my vagina is not a necessary part of lovemaking for me, and I'd say it happens only about a third of the time.

If we take the time to teach our partners exactly what we like, instead of expecting them to read our minds or 'just know', we will have much more pleasure – and give it as well.

Julia taught me how to make her come with my tongue. I was brought up with all the usual guy talk about vaginas being weird, unpleasant and so on, but when I got down there, I loved it. I loved her scent, I loved her taste. What an incredible flower – so many delicate folds and so sensitive! She guided me, and I experimented myself with little flicks of my tongue in certain places that drove her wild. Just feeling her excitement was an incredible turn-on for me. She gushed into my mouth – and I mean gushed! Since Julie, I've performed cunnilingus on countless women. Each one has been unique – but ultimately satisfied. I've always been grateful to Julia for showing me how ...

The first time I ever enjoyed oral sex was with a guy who was a real 'sex machine' – he was very good at it. With most guys I never really enjoyed it.

As a bisexual, I find that men are usually better at fellatio. Their touch is less tentative, and that's how I like it. But women know how to tease and slow me down – that's not so much a guy thing – and they tend to drive me crazier as a result. Women also take time to focus on my nipples and other erogenous zones, whereas men just tend to go straight for the money.

Honing your skills

Unfortunately, not everyone is a willing pupil, nor does everyone have the patience to acquire the skills for perfect lovemaking. Some people just aren't very good at touching; as children they may not have been taught to appreciate sensual touch. Some find it difficult to focus on touching long enough to please their partners, simply because they're in too much of a rush.

> *If a man does attempt a little half-hearted foreplay, he invariably prods away at your clit as though it's an elevator button and he's running late for a meeting. It is then a woman might cut to the carnal chase and say, exasperatedly, 'Oh, just take the stairs.'*
>
> Kathy Lette

Some people do not have adequate *proprioception* (the sense of touch that usually occurs via an adequate number of nerve endings in the fingers). They can be helped to achieve better lovemaking skills, but it takes time and concentration – and a patient partner.

> I love my boyfriend but I hate the way he touches me. I'm not kidding, he really is terrible and just doesn't seem to learn. His hands are huge and clumsy, like a bunch of sausages. I've tried to teach him, but the way he handles me – it's more like a painful groping from a disinterested stranger. I don't know what to do, and as a result I find myself avoiding sex.

In my office I keep a beautiful, small nautilus fossil. It is a many-textured object – with shiny parts, round grooves, rough ridges and so on. In asking a patient to close his eyes and sensually explore the nautilus, I can tell a lot about his sense of touch and sensuality – and, when it comes to delicacy, some people simply lack a natural finesse. Getting a partner to touch you the way you want to be touched is not a matter of simple communication. Asking 'please stroke my clitoris' is a start, but women will have better results if they give detailed instructions – 'Just a little lower ... use two fingers not one ... round and round is better' – and frequent feedback, such as, 'more gently please' or 'a little bit lower'. Of course, it is particularly important to praise and reward a partner when he or she gets it right!

Unfortunately, certain people are self-focused, and simply disinterested in anything but their own orgasms. Some are shamelessly honest about this.

There's nothing more interesting in this world than my own orgasm ... and nothing more boring than yours.

Dennis Miller

Men tend to require less sensitive types of touch, and some actually prefer quite forceful penile stroking. As a matter of fact, some of them develop a very rough masturbation style early on – for example, with a textured towel – and that 'programming' can make it quite difficult for them to be satisfied by a partner's hand, mouth or vagina.

I'd never found a sexual partner who could get me to come. The way they touched me was always too soft, and when I went inside them I just didn't feel enough to be able to peak. Women always told me I was 'the best' because, unlike other guys they'd known, I could keep going for hours. But having a reputation as a stallion was in sharp contrast to the amount of enjoyment I was actually getting out of it. Finally, when I met my wife, she took it personally that I never ejaculated inside her and we went to see a sex therapist. Now we're happily pregnant – and no turkey-basters were involved!

What turns you on?

People respond differently to various types of stimuli. Some are more turned on by visual cues – perhaps the sight of breasts, buttocks, legs or muscular arms – while others thrill to sexy words whispered in their ears. Another group of people are so tactile in their programming that nothing beats the sensation of touch itself.

Men love with their eyes; women love with their ears.
Zsa Zsa Gabor

That may be true for many people, but it is not always the case, and it's worth learning exactly about one's lover's responses – whether they be more visual, auditory, kinaesthetic or even olfactory. After all, why waste time dressing for sex if your partner would rather you mastered the fine art of erotic conversation?

I'm too shy to express my sexual needs, except over the phone to people I don't know.
Garry Shandling

Or what if your lover would prefer you to pay more attention to allowing your own natural aroma to invade his or her senses?

> The big turn-on for me is her smell. I never like her to wear perfume because her own scent is so arousing.

> *I'll be back from war in three days, Josephine; don't bathe!*
>
> Napoleon Bonaparte

Sexual style

Our 20s can be a time when people consolidate knowledge of who they are as sexual beings – although that can always change later. Without the restrictions of adolescence, they have more freedom to explore different sexual styles and can properly begin to decide what works for them – and what does not. In adolescence, a personal sexual definition is barely possible, but this becomes clearer during the following decade. Definitions of what constitutes good sex are as diverse as people themselves.

> My own special definition of good sex is that it should be romantic, touching, tender, mutually rhythmical, loving, eye-to-eye – and in enough light to see one another.

> My definition of great sex is that it should be hot, naughty and wild, breaking as many taboos as possible!

> My idea of good sex is that it should be slow, comfy and easy – without too many gymnastics. I don't enjoy it when my partner tries to show off.

Partnered sexuality reflects the relationship style. For some people in our culture, one of the tasks of the 20s is to try out more serious types of partnerships to see if they feel right. This does not immediately work out well for everyone.

> *Getting married for sex is like buying a 747 for the free peanuts.*
>
> Jeff Foxworthy

The end of my first marriage was not brought about by sexual problems. We remained a perfect fit sexually, but other issues led to a separation when I was in my mid- to late 20s. The three years that ensued introduced me to toxic co-dependence with a younger, very beautiful and very messed-up partner. It was an intensely sexual relationship, where I did all the dumb things I forgot to do in my adolescence.

> *Marriage is a wonderful invention; but, then again, so is a bicycle-repair kit.*
>
> Billy Connolly

In their 20s, some people choose to lead a 'single life' of dating, and seek sexual experiences with a range of different people. This may seem random at the time, but it can serve a certain sexual purpose – namely, getting to know more about their sexual identity.

My early 20s involved some of the most exciting sexual encounters I've ever had – and they were just that:

'encounters'! I met one guy at an airport in India. Our plane was delayed so we went to a hotel and spent the time making fantastic love – no names, no personal details. I sometimes wonder where he is now.

My ideas about sex were always 'it's playtime', and I usually had partners who were similarly wired.

Establishing what kind of partnership works best for an individual can involve a great deal of trial and error – and a considerable amount of psychological pain.

I crashed cars for this girl. We were into virtually *everything* – multiple partners excepted. Lots of forest/car/outdoor/hotel/concert/beach/cinema/club sex ... you get the idea. Drugs and alcohol may have been involved. A lot. Psychological warfare was her thing (she told me about her abusive dad, who apparently trained her). I was putty in her hands and, ironically, she in mine. There is something very sick about repeatedly breaking up in order to get back together. She liked to cheat and hurt. It gives me cold shivers. I escaped the madness by moving into a gay household! She would caterwaul outside some nights ....

I wouldn't recommend sex, drugs, or insanity for everyone, but they've always worked for me.
> Hunter S. Thompson

Sex and drugs

There is no doubt that alcohol and drugs play a large part in people's sexuality. Many people think this is a good way to get 'in the mood', but that is not necessarily true at all. Many substances dull or alter the senses to the detriment of sexual experience, and some have physiological side-effects that work against one's desired sexual response:

I use drink as a general loosener and relaxant. Not too much though. At a certain point it affects my ability to get an erection.

I tried marijuana because a friend said it 'heightens the enjoyment' of sex. But I found there was no difference.

I like using marijuana to enhance feelings during love-making. It doesn't so much increase erotic pleasure for me – it just makes me enjoy being more touchy-feely, which is not my usual style.

I have tried various love drugs over the years, from acid in the 60s to Ecstasy – and now I use Vicodin because of my back pain.

I finally realised I was using alcohol to avoid feeling anything when I had sex – which usually makes me feel very anxious. I had some bad experiences when I was a teenager and sex is rather unpleasant for me – but I don't want to lose my boyfriend, so I down a couple of Cosmopolitans and away we go.

Cocaine and crystal can help you have a quick refractory period – you ejaculate without orgasm. It seems to ease my testosterone urge. I have this male monster in me I can't get rid of. But toe-curling orgasm – it's been nine years. Can't wait for it to happen again.

Alcohol and drugs can affect sexual choices, willingness to engage in certain behaviours and risk-taking. They tend to lower inhibitions and alter a person's ability to make rational choices. What's more, a person cannot actually give consent to sex if he or she is intoxicated.

> There have been a few occasions when I went to bed with a man because I was under the influence and it seemed a good idea at the time. Eventually I learned that it just wasn't worth the awkwardness and guilt of waking up in the morning with a hangover and trying to extricate myself from a jerk with an 'I scored!' smirk on his face.

> A number of people I know became HIV-positive because their long-term partners cheated on them and brought the virus home. But I have no one to blame but myself, because I was doing a lot of drugs and taking crazy risks. It wasn't as though I hadn't been warned.

> If you got gonorrhoea in the 70s, you just went to a doctor and got a shot of penicillin and everything was hunky-dory. We were all sport fucking. It was sex as exercise – no emotion. I had three or four intense love affairs, but it was a wild, wild period. I remember that in July 1977 there was a blackout in New York, and that night there was a total orgy on Christopher Street. Both straight and gay people had a tonne of sex in those days. Then there were the bath-houses, too. In the mid-80s was first time I ever experienced someone with full-blown AIDS. I lived with him for a while and helped him die.

There is a pretty clear connection between impaired judgement due to alcohol or drugs and acquiring a sexually transmitted disease, but not all STIs are transmitted in an altered state. No matter how it occurs, feelings of anger and betrayal are likely to ensue.

He gave me herpes and even though I believe him when he said he did not know he had it, it felt like a terrible betrayal. Our relationship never recovered.

Sex and relationships

Some people never achieve monogamy, and many make commitment vows that they find they simply cannot keep. This can result in the creation of 'alternative' styles of live-in relating.

I haven't known any open marriages, although quite a few have been ajar.

Zsa Zsa Gabor

Others prefer to follow more traditional routes, such as accepting marriages arranged for them by their parents, earnestly seeking suitable marriage partners themselves, or trying out co-habitation with a steady girlfriend or boyfriend.

Marriage is popular because it combines the maximum of temptation with the maximum of opportunity.

George Bernard Shaw

I didn't feel ready to settle down with anyone and, frankly, I usually got bored with one person after a pretty short time. So I just tried out a lot of men, hoping to find someone who would make me want to stay with him. People were pretty judgemental about what I was doing – using words like 'promiscuous' – but in my mind I was involved in … research. I learned a lot about myself, a lot about sex and a lot about male behaviour, so that when I finally met a superior man, I was smart enough to know and pin him down. I don't regret the way I went about it – and 20 years later, we're still married!

What is a promiscuous person? It's usually someone who is getting more sex than you are.

Victor Lownes

Some people take the decision to remain celibate until marriage.

Several friends are in exactly the same position as me (currently non-existent sex life), some friends have very active sex lives with their partners, and other friends do not have partners, but still have active sex lives. I do not really make the comparison with my friends. I do feel old (29) to still technically be a virgin (although I have engaged in all other forms of sexual intimacy in the past), but I have several friends who are also virgins and are older than me, too.

The decision whether to co-habit in a sexual relationship prior to marriage – or whether to marry or have a civil union at all – is something that has to be addressed sooner or later, particularly if there is a plan to bear or adopt children.

I suppose it was partly because we're both females brought up to value commitment – to search for 'The One' and settle down – that we decided pretty quickly, when we were both in our late 20s, to be exclusive partners and eventually made vows to each other in a civil ceremony. My partner has borne our children, so our sex life has definitely been influenced – maybe even ruled – by her hormonal changes.

Once any style of relationship is formed, the question of whether it is to be an exclusive one or not arises. The decision can be in the form of some kind of understanding or contract – which can be either spoken or unspoken.

> *I'm married, but I don't wear a wedding ring because I've found that it tends to give women the impression that I'm unavailable.*
>
> Bill Muse

To avoid misunderstandings – and the mistake of leaving too much undefined 'wiggle room' – I believe it is always best to spell things out.

> We agreed that essentially we were going to be monogamous, but that if one of us ever wound up in some situation where amazing, once-in-a-lifetime sexual opportunity presented itself, we could go for it.

> Fidelity is great, again, if it is agreed upon. I'm okay with it, but there seems to be a lot of hypocrisy around it, with one ending up lying about their choice, because they want freedom, but they don't want their partner to have freedom.

We both felt – and made it clear to each other – that if one ever strayed, the other did not want to know about it. We agreed not to ask, too. But it had to be discreet – and safe.

No doubt a committed, long-term relationship is an excellent goal for many people. However, to expect one person to provide all your needs – emotional, intellectual and physical – for a lifetime is often just pie in the sky. Solving that dilemma, even in some part, is the key.

I think committed, long-term relationships are great, but only as long as both choose that. And I've found that one-night stands can be fun, but then one needs to take that for what it is. It always seems that someone wants more.

The awful thing about one-night stands is that it is so difficult to keep things tidy.

Anne Cumming

For many people, monogamy is very difficult. It's easy to blame someone else for breaking trust, but being sexual with just one person can be very difficult to sustain. Many people first discover this in their 20s, as they try out monogamy for the first time.

I'd chosen to be with Gemma, and we were engaged to be married. But, at the same time, I had this nagging feeling that I wasn't ready to settle down. There were all these gorgeous women around – and quite a few of them were coming on to me. I just couldn't take the pressure.

Like many other guys I know, I have struggled with monogamy long and hard – and normally lost. I think it's an ideal to aim for and I think breaking it even by arrangement with a partner is potentially hugely damaging and difficult. I also know that for me monogamy is unachievable.

To be honest, I just don't think I can stay faithful. I've tried hard, but there's always a point where an opportunity presents itself – usually someone else who likes the drug of chance-encounters-turning-sexual-in-an-instant as much as I do – and my resolve is gone again. I don't believe I actively search for it – there're just a lot of horny people out there, and I'm one of them. We seem to find each other – you catch a glance and just *know*.

The love bird is 100 per cent faithful to his mate, as long as they are locked together in the same cage.

Will Cuppy

It's as absurd to say that a man can't love one woman all the time, as it is to say that a violinist needs several violins to play the same piece of music.

Honoré de Balzac

Some people seem to accept the human tendency to be non-monogamous. In fact, gossip would have us believe it's a national sport – and not just in France!

Thou shalt not commit adultery ... unless in the mood.

W.C. Fields

A code of honour: Never approach a friend's girl-friend or wife with mischief as your goal ... unless she's really attractive.

Bruce Jay Friedman

Something on the side

In psychological terms, having extra-marital relationships – with or without physical sex – can be extremely stressful.

Here's to wives and sweethearts ... may they never meet.

John Bunny

Sneaking around can be a huge strain and, if the affair is discovered, it can seriously threaten a marriage. In addition, because human beings tend to mate serially with similar types of people, many find their new 'situation' is no less problematic than their primary one.

The first breath of adultery is the freest; after it, constraints aping marriage develop.

John Updike

A lover teaches a wife all that a husband has concealed from her.

Honoré de Balzac

It is difficult to find reliable statistics relating to the proportion of committed men and women who stray (naturally, people do not want to come clean about their secrets). Many people think that it's men who are most likely to cheat. However, judging from my clinical experience, a very high proportion of women do, too. Women appear to be more socialised to desire monogamy, but they can also feel conflicted about it.

I have a problem really knowing what I want. I tell my girlfriends I want to be like Samantha in *Sex and the City*, and date lots of men – even use them for pleasure the same way they traditionally use women – but it's always the same thing: I meet a cute guy, date him a few times, have fabulous sex, and sooner or later I hear myself asking him a question that includes the word 'exclusive'. Well, that's a sure passion-killer for most guys and they always run a mile. I'm such an idiot – I just can't help myself. Somewhere inside me there's a housewife in an apron trying to break free!

A man's heart may have a secret sanctuary where only one woman may enter, but it is full of little ante-rooms which are still vacant.

Helen Rowland

You know, of course, that the Tasmanians, who never committed adultery, are now extinct.

W. Somerset Maugham

Some people stray because they are bored and can't resist an opportunity for a bit of excitement – perhaps because they've lost the spark of sex in their primary partnership.

Some people just want to feel desired for a change, while others have extra-marital sex because they are angry with their spouses and want revenge. It may be that they feel neglected and require validation as a sexual being, or perhaps they have discovered that their partner is involved with someone else. For some people, ageing is a factor – they want some reassurance that they are still vibrant. Others feel trapped in their marriage due to financial restraints – or not wanting to upset their children – and having an affair is one way to 'escape'. Some want to experience a hidden desire – perhaps some kind of edgy sex – that does not interest their partner.

I could never trust my husband with the knowledge that I sought very different kinds of sex with other men – and women. He was a 'meat and potatoes' type of lover, and I don't blame him for that. However, I had these urges to have the kind of erotic experiences that put me on a whole different pleasure plane. And I was so incredibly curious about sex. Once my lover took me to a professional dominatrix, who ordered me to do all kinds of shocking things. Another time I watched while a woman dressed my lover as a woman, then spanked him and penetrated him with a dildo. I went to 'play parties' where there were several rooms full of people engaged in bondage, candle play, spanking, whipping, all kinds of erotic torture ... it was a crazy, incredible time. Now that I'm older I still don't feel guilty about it. I look back on my secret life and smile happily to myself.

Sexual curiosity is a fairly common reason why some people choose to stray, but there are a great many more reasons, such as being irresistibly attracted to someone else, not having as much sex as they wish to have with a primary partner, or trying to make him or her jealous. Sometimes it's because a partner is unable to have sex for health reasons. Some people even have affairs in order to get out of an unhappy relationship, although this is usually an unconscious reason. Less common is having extra-marital sex in an attempt to become pregnant (if it's not possible with a primary partner).

It was really hard to get my needs met in my marriage. It seemed that he had all the control, and made all the decisions. On top of that, he had very little time for me – although he was quite available for his golfing buddies. Then someone came along who paid me a lot of attention and I just couldn't resist that. I enjoyed the sex, but the best thing was feeling adored and appreciated and wanted. Just having that experience helped me to know exactly what I wanted. I dragged my husband into counselling and expressed my frustration – it did help.

Learning of a partner's affair – or suspecting it – can arouse strong feelings. Sexual jealousy is something we're all wired to feel in certain situations, but some of us feel it more intensely than others. Pain, hurt and deep sadness can be experienced at any age by anyone who is disappointed in love. For a few people, the desperation and hopelessness they feel can lead to suicide or even homicide.

I was barely 20, and he was 11 years older – the first serious lover I lived with. I was working in a nightclub to put myself through university, and usually didn't get home until two am. But one night I finished early and walked in on him in bed with a woman I judged to be older, more beautiful and more sophisticated than me. She saw me first, and sat up and shook him awake: 'George – you've got a visitor!' I felt so betrayed. The pain seemed unbearable. I thought about throwing myself over a nearby cliff.

He was my first, and I suppose that made it worse. After two years together, when I had thought we were best friends in every way, he broke up with me very suddenly and in a very cavalier way. I know he wanted to have the freedom to try other women (I was his first as well), but it was enormously painful. I felt so betrayed, and losing him became a much wider problem because I realised that most of the people in my circle were originally his friends, so I became really lonely as well. People let me know they felt sorry for me – it was embarrassing and humiliating, and it took me over a year to even start to pull myself together. It's been four years now and I still miss him, and haven't been able to have sex with anyone since.

Loss of love can lead to serious depression. Human beings are essentially resilient, and healing will take place eventually, but psychological treatment should be considered if the pain lasts for a long time. It is necessary to seek professional help if there are feelings of hopelessness or thoughts of suicide.

Sexual preferences

An important aspect of becoming sexually mature is working out exactly what kind of sex we prefer. Discovering exactly what kinds of sexual behaviours are most pleasurable and communicating that to a partner – as well as being able to discern what one's partner enjoys – require an advanced level of exploration. It's also a never-ending process, as our sexual tastes evolve and change throughout the life span. Some people embark on the 'tertiary education' stage of sexual discovery with great openness and a truly experimental sensibility, some even seeking new experiences with new partners, just for enlightenment's sake.

I suppose I was just lucky to have quite a number of partners (men and women) – most of them older and more experienced than me – each of whom taught me different things. I just loved how sex made me feel – before, during and after – and was completely open to learning all kinds of naughtiness. Oh my God, when I think back to some of the things I tried – doing it in a public library, doing it with two men at the same time, being a woman's 'sex slave' – it was wild and wonderful and I don't regret any of it for a second.

I came out in my late teens, so I was already comfortable with who I was as a lesbian. In my mid-20s I was keen not to just find out what turned me on, but I really wanted to learn how to make my partners happy. The more partners I had, the more it became clear that every woman is different. That's when I realised that listening to her body was the key.

While some people are keen to seek new experiences deliberately, others prefer to let things develop more organically – by allowing their feelings for special individuals with whom they fall in love to lead them to the type of giving and receiving of pleasure that seems right at the time.

> I never chased women like some of my friends did. They were into 'sport fucking', but I never got the point of that. For me, the greatest pleasure is to really get to know one woman, to savour every inch of her body and learn how to really excite her. That's what really turns me on – making her scream with pleasure.

Sexual style develops slowly, and at some point it may have to be adapted to suit changing circumstances.

> I had a serious car accident when I was 22, so now I have to make love in a very different way. Since I could no longer feel anything below my hips, my partner and I began to experiment with upper-body sensations. At this point, sex for me is about having a close emotional connection with him, giving him oral sex and he can make me come by kissing and stimulating my nipples.

In their 20s, people are expected to become fully mature sexually and ready to take full responsibility for their sexual choices. Some actually manage to achieve this.

> We all drank a lot as teenagers, and I didn't make love in a responsible way until I was 21 years old. Then I had a steady boyfriend who was very diligent about my not getting pregnant. I loved it.

> At 21, I stopped having sex for two years. I said to myself, 'I don't need it'. My sex drive is extremely high. I had slept

with one of my friends, who was going through divorce. I thought it was finalised, but it wasn't, and that tore me up. It felt morally wrong. Prior to that, I had been very sexual with lots of women. But after that, I thought it was best to take a break for a while.

Although many young adults in their 20s do reach the point where they adhere to standards of morality and ethics of which their parents or society would approve, I've met hundreds of 20-something people who were just as conflicted and 'immature' about sex as they were during their teenaged years.

My friends at university tend to assume that everyone they know is sexually active. They complain to me about their sexual partners, saying they're not satisfied or revealing something weird they did. They try to egg others on to talk about it, but I would hate to think of my boyfriend complaining about me to his friends. Girls I know do it a lot. It's considered kind of cool or something to talk about their partner's shortcomings – and a statement that they're sexual beings: 'Look at me, I have an opinion about my sex life!' One friend complained that her boyfriend didn't like performing oral sex – they tend to be really specific. They try to get me to talk about it, too, but I'm really private. It's okay if I don't know the person, but really weird if I do know him or her. There are certain things I just don't want to know about. It all feels very 'high school'.

People in their 20s tend to be experienced up to a point, but there is still so much to discover about themselves as sexual beings. Some of them really struggle with moral aspects of sex, or with decisions about whether certain sexual styles are right for them or not. For example, sometimes people discover that they or their partners have 'edgy' sexual desires. They may reject such ideas or, in the interests of being either experimental or accommodating, they may decide to try them out.

> When she asked me to tie her to the bed, I didn't know what to think. It was definitely a turn-on, but I was raised to treat women respectfully and I wasn't sure it was right. But the whole thing got her so hot I just went along with it. I ended up being quite into it, and it became a core part of our sexual repertoire.

Sometimes the boundaries of consensuality are explored or even pushed.

> I had one friend who was dating someone who was kind of violent. She used to have bruises all over her. She talked about it really openly. I thought it was tacky of her because I'm good friends with him. She seemed proud of her bruises – and wore tank tops and would pretend to be upset if people noticed them. She wore it as a badge. She said he was testing the waters at the beginning – I think she ended up kind of liking it.

Sexual abuse

Sex can be difficult for people who have experienced sexual abuse and coercion. It may alter their sexuality for years to come. They may or may not remember episodes of abuse in their conscious minds, but even deeply buried early abuse can affect a person's sexuality later in life, resurfacing in the form of unexplained feelings or behaviours.

My husband loved to receive oral sex. I never understood why I had a problem with it until one day in therapy I remembered my older brother forcing his penis into my mouth when I was eight – I had completely forgotten that.

Consensuality is an essential element of partnered sexuality, but many people have difficulty understanding all the nuances of that – especially when they are young and inexperienced.

My first sexual experience took place when I was 21. I went to a swanky debutante party, where I met a guy I knew from college. He was a couple of years older than me. He invited me to his house. His parents were out of town and I was really naïve – the dumbest person alive. His thing was that he would start drinking, then insist on playing strip poker. We played, then when we were both in our boxers, he just walked me into his parents' bedroom and went down on me. I never came, though. I felt kind of neutral about it, but probably a bit shamed, too. I was so uptight. I realised later that that's what he did regularly – got guys there, got them drunk, played strip poker to have sex with them. He eventually went off and got married.

What was your upbringing?

Different backgrounds and religious viewpoints certainly create idiosyncratic challenges. I've pointed out – at length – that early negative attitudes towards sexuality can have long-term effects on adult sexuality, and this can begin to emerge in our 20s.

> I have had to 'outgrow' the negative feelings given to me in childhood. My Church of Scotland upbringing certainly did not help in any way. I did read *Cosmopolitan* avidly – for tips!

> I didn't masturbate until I was in my 20s. I was born Catholic in a very straight-laced town – I was horrified about sex. The body was sinful, so I never touched myself at all. I was attracted to other boys, but not sexually. I knew I didn't want to go down on them and I thought that was the only thing they did. The term 'gay' was not in the lexicon until 1962. I didn't think I was 'gay' because I didn't want to put my cock in someone's mouth. Yet, in high school, I was so much in love with this one guy that when he went to another college I cried for two weeks. I was very repressed.

> In some ways, having such a liberal upbringing made it more difficult for me. My parents were so open about their own sexuality that it was uncomfortable for me. Then my father did the cliché thing of taking me to a brothel for my 16th birthday. I was horrified. The women there were nice to me, but I found that experience unpleasant and humiliating, and it halted my desire to have sex again for quite a few years. I was basically celibate throughout my 20s.

Abstinence is the mother of shameless lust.

Pat Califia

Well-entrenched religious beliefs and values dictate many aspects of a person's sexuality. Some people are comfortable with and grateful for this strong guidance, while others find it challenging.

> I am a Christian and have struggled with how sexuality fits in with my faith. This is where my guilt feelings come from when I engage in any sort of sexual intimacy. Unfortunately, many of my relationships ended prematurely and I feel this has been due to my wanting to wait longer for sexual intercourse than my partner has been prepared to wait.

> In my religion sex is only allowed at certain times of the month. I've found that other people judge this to be a problem, but I like it. I like the build-up to those special days, and the peace and longing I experience on the days when it is forbidden. Sex on our designated days is really special.

Sexual orientation

Many people in their 20s are still in the process of defining their sexual identity, including their sexual orientation – although, in fact, that can be somewhat fluid over the course of a person's life. In our society there is a lot of pressure to make firm decisions about who we are sexually, because we like to pigeonhole people. With heterosexuality being the 'norm' in our society, people who discover that is not their particular orientation may struggle with prejudice, stigma and judgement throughout their entire lives.

> *The Bible contains six admonishments to homosexuals and 362 admonishments to heterosexuals. That doesn't mean that God doesn't love heterosexuals. It's just that they need more supervision.*
>
> Lynn Lavner

I was married to a woman, but I've never had sex with one. In 1967, I was dating this girl, although I wasn't attracted to her. My best friend was living in London – he'd just inherited a lot of money and he was running all over the Continent, fucking his girlfriend's brains out all over Europe. He invited me to London for the summer. I had left my girlfriend and she'd started dating another guy. After I arrived in London, I went to a café to get some chips and got set upon by a bunch of Teddy boys. They broke my arm and bashed my face and nearly kicked me to death. I was in hospital for a while. When I got back to London, I got a frantic note saying my ex-girlfriend was pregnant with the other guy's child – but he had disappeared and she wanted me to marry her. See, I didn't even know I was gay. I thought gay men were people who put their cocks in other guys' mouths and I didn't like the idea of that, so I thought I couldn't be gay. The girl came over to London and I married her. My arm was broken and I thought, 'What the hell?' Marriage was nothing to me then – just a piece of paper. What's to lose? I thought I would probably get into the whole sex thing once my arm was better. We stayed together until after the baby was born, and then we split.

Some people who believe they are heterosexual nevertheless have same-gender fantasies, and even experiences – well into their 20s and beyond.

> I spent a summer in France and discovered that a number of married women I met were not just comfortable having affairs with men – they dabbled with other women as well. It seemed to be very acceptable, and so I said to myself, 'When in Rome ...' Only it was Paris, and it was the most erotic time of my life.

Just as they did in adolescence, some heterosexual people have same-gender fantasies and question whether or not that might mean they're actually gay. It's really very common to have same-gender fantasies in adulthood, and doesn't indicate anything in particular about sexual orientation, other than that the demarcations between straight, gay and bisexual are sometimes a little blurred, and that from time to time people float in and out of categories to which they thought they belonged – at least in fantasy. People who are actually gay usually understand who they are sexually much earlier in life.

> Guys had made advances to me from time to time, and I found myself flirting with the idea of doing something about it. It didn't fit with either my prolific hetero behaviour or my pretty well-entrenched homophobia. But I allowed myself to go there in fantasy. The gay images got stronger and stronger in my mind, so much so that at one point I thought I actually was gay. A friend of a friend made a play for me at a party and I decided to give it a try, but after that I pretty much knew that wasn't for me. I

mean, it was okay, but it just wasn't anything like as great as having sex with the right woman. I'm still open to having experiences with men, I still fantasise about them, and I even experimented a couple more times over the years, but I'm quite sure about my orientation as a man who likes women.

So sexual orientation is not necessarily 100 per cent stable or consistent throughout our lives. Gay or lesbian people sometimes have heterosexual fantasies or experiences as well.

A couple of years after I'd come out as a gay man, I met a woman I was attracted to and we ended up having an affair. I eventually told my male partner, and he was pretty uncomfortable about the whole thing. It occurred to me it would probably have been more acceptable to him if I'd been with another man. But I was most worried about my mother. I mean, if she found out, she'd kill me.

Anyone who suspects that he or she is bisexual also faces a struggle with societal views that are not universally accepting of such an orientation.

I happen to feel equally attracted to men and women. There are some men I fancy more than some women, and vice versa, but if you presented me with a man and a woman who were both equally attractive people as far as my ideal sex objects go, I'd be really hard-pressed (literally!) to decide which one to go with (hopefully both!). My gay friends never seem to get this about me. They say I'm just a gay man who's too afraid to come out.

It [bisexuality] immediately doubles your chances for a date on Saturday night.

Woody Allen

The school of life

No matter what your sexual orientation, how you express your sexuality reflects both who you are as a person and how you relate to your partner. And it takes time to learn how to be a good lover.

University, from age 18 to 22, was the most sexually active period of my life. It was the 60s, women were just starting to use the Pill widely and sex (and drugs) was freely available. I went on a binge for three and a half years. I did learn to be more caring and I hope 'better' at the whole thing in this time, but in truth quantity was still very much the driver. This trend continued, subject only to increased time restrictions, as I started work. I was by now in a stable relationship, but not particularly faithful. Towards the end of my 20s, I formed a relationship with a much older woman (mid-40s), a friend of my mother. This changed my life, as she made me aware of what a physical relationship could and should be like. She educated me in every way, including emotionally. I remember being really embarrassed as I thought back to the numerous partners I had had in the past, after realising through this woman how things should be.

I can give women an orgasm while we're having intercourse. I got a book called *The Art of the Female Orgasm*. Now, at 24 years old, there has only been one girl I've not been able to give an orgasm – out of the 15 I've been with.

Sexual communication (which is not easy) should also mature during one's 20s, but it's not easy. Every aspect of partner sex requires learning and practice; some people innately understand that and so they quite deliberately continue to explore and experiment..

I just wanted to know everything there was to know about sex. I tended to gravitate towards sleeping with people a bit older than me, who seemed confident and knowledgeable. I could tell by the way they approached me. If a guy used some corny line or seemed insecure in any way, I'd turn my back on him. But someone who got my attention with a cool approach would have a good chance. One man actually said to me, 'Hey little girl, wanna learn some new tricks?' I was literally putty in his hands. He took me to the restroom and fingered me both anally and vaginally at the same time, while I was sucking his dick (he had really long arms) – that was a new one on me!

My best friend had sex with our history teacher – who was a person with a disability. This teacher was wounded in the Second World War, so he was in a wheelchair. He had a devoted following of girls and boys who just loved him – mostly boys. He was married eventually. He and my friend had an affair, which he only recently told me about. He fondled him and went down on him. I was shocked that he admitted the affair.

I was pretty adventurous. When I was married with two kids I fell in love with a transvestite. I used to take her over to my friend's house to screw her. I thought I was in love with her.

In my early 20s I really understood that women saw me as a sexual object. This gave me a sense of power that, as a little person, I wasn't used to. The thing is, I know a lot of women wanted to try me out of curiosity, but to be quite honest that didn't bother me. Even though I knew they always told their friends or whatever, it didn't matter. I just wanted to get in their pants. The litmus test was whether they came back for a repeat performance, and many of them did – and still do. Part of my appeal is a trick proportion thing – my penis is normal size, but next to my legs it seems gigantic.

Intimate communication

Developing a greater capacity for intimacy is another task of early adulthood. Many people are confused by the term 'intimacy'. Some think it just means 'getting sexually close to someone', but when I use it I am referring to a type of relationship where two people get to know each other on such a deep level that they are able to truly see and be seen by each other – not just sexually, but in every other respect. In such a special, loving type of union, sexuality can be fantastic. Ideally, the uniqueness and individuality of each partner are maintained as well.

We made love with our eyes open, just gazing fully at each other the entire time. It was the most electrifying sex I've ever had, as if our souls were joining as well – yes, that's it – it was a totally spiritual experience as well as being thoroughly erotic. Over the years, the power of our connection waxed and waned as we went through all kinds of life changes, but the memory of that first time truly cemented our bond and helped us to stay together, even when things got really tough.

You don't have to know a person that well to have great sex, but it is important to have the capacity for good sexual communication – whether that is achieved verbally or via strongly expressive body language.

Sometimes talking seems unnecessary. We've learned to read how each other's body responds. But every now and again I feel like I'm getting mixed signals from her and I have to ask, 'Is this working for you, or would you like me to go back to what I was doing before?' It's usually the latter. I've found that finding the path to her orgasm is very like being lost while driving – the best policy is to go back to the last street you recognise and try again.

Some people think that becoming a good lover involves accumulating a series of skills, as though sex were like golf or tennis. But, because every person is sexually unique, the truth is that being a good lover actually involves sophisticated communication, being a sensitive detective and working out what the person you are with really likes – the exact type of touches, and so on. Knowing this can take a lot of pressure off the performance anxiety that plagues many people.

Once they call you a Latin lover, you're in real trouble. Women expect an Oscar performance in bed.

Marcello Mastroianni

If you can develop the ability to ask questions about sexual preferences in a way that makes a partner feel comfortable and ready for open discussion, you are already a fantastic lover. It is advisable to phrase questions in such a way as to invite more than a simple 'yes' or 'no' answer. That way you will receive far more useful information.

> We were sitting in a coffee shop, when he suddenly said, 'How do you feel about the way we made love last night?' I was so surprised, but pleasantly so. He continued, 'Well? What did you most enjoy about it ... and what would you like me to do differently next time?' That opened up a great discussion and I was able to let him know about my lack of experience – and that I'd prefer to find more positions that take the pressure off my back.

Sometimes it's necessary to offer constructive criticism. This is best done by first reassuring your partner about the positive things you enjoy, and then asking for change; for example, 'I have so much fun when we make love. You make me feel wonderful ... although I've been wondering if you'd mind if we spent more time touching each other before you enter me?' Or: 'Would you mind if we leave the light on next time? I love being able to see you properly ...'

If it is necessary to ask for change *during* sex, the same principle applies. For example, 'I love the way you're making me feel – and I especially liked it before, when you were touching me a bit more gently.'

What if you enjoy something generally considered a little 'edgy' and would like to test the waters with your partner without risking too much? Instead of starting off by directly asking a partner to participate, it is often best to ask a general question in an open manner, to gauge their reaction: 'What do you think about threesomes? Does the idea make you hot or not?' Once that is discussed, you could move on to, 'Have you ever fantasised about it? Ever tried it?' and then, 'In what specific circumstances would you be inclined to try it?' That will provide the information to know if you should make a direct approach then and there, wait a while, or give it a miss. Most importantly, if you are comfortable with the sexual style you are suggesting, that will be transmitted; if you feel guilty and worried about introducing the subject, that will be equally apparent, and will probably put the person off.

I do enjoy anal sex and my hunch was that Barry would enjoy it, too, but I didn't know how to suggest it without seeming like a serious slut. So one day (we weren't in bed at the time) I got the conversation round to various types of sex. In the middle of it, I simply said to him, as if it came out of nowhere, 'And how do you feel about anal sex? Ever tried it? Ever wanted to try it?' He smiled, gave me a sly look, and said, 'Why do you ask?' We both giggled and next time we had sex he took the opportunity to give it a go.

I have sought out partners who shared my interests, but proceeded carefully so as not to frighten the horses. I haven't had very many examples of a bad reaction. If it is coming, I will back off very quickly.

Fantastic fantasies

It's one thing to share sexual adventures openly with another person, but what about our internal sex lives? Even people who are quite comfortable with their sexual behaviour may continue to be bothered by their fantasies. They feel guilty about having erotic ideas that may involve being coerced into sex or doing something illegal to someone else. But it is extremely common for people to reach a climax (either alone or with a partner) by imagining something they would never actually do in real life.

I have fantasies about my girlfriend having sex with other men, which is strange because I'm pretty jealous and would never want her to do that in reality. Yet, in my fantasy, I'm the one who introduces her to one or two of my friends and persuades her to give them head. They bang her as well, which really turns me on in that moment.

I've never been sexually abused, and didn't have sex until I was 22, but in some of my fantasies I'm under-aged – say, 15 – and a school teacher is teaching me how to turn him on. He has sex with me. He gets me to remove my knickers and sit in class so he can see my pussy, and halfway through the lesson he takes me to his study to spank me for being so wanton. While spanking me he also fingers me, then makes me suck him, and finally bends me over and fucks me. I have no idea where this scene came from.

Some fantasies can be quite confusing – or even disturbing – for the dreamer. They may be completely at odds with one's actual values, beliefs and behaviour. The important thing to remember is that they are *just* fantasies – the products of our erotic imagination. When the fantasy concerns something thoroughly edgy, the issue is simply whether a person is likely to actually act it out. If you are likely to act out a fantasy that is dangerous, harmful, illegal, non-consensual or anything else that could get you into big trouble, seek the help of a trained, accredited therapist. But, generally, fantasies are really private business and need not be shared with anyone else.

I sometimes feel a bit guilty to be imagining I'm in a more erotic situation with some fantasy man, when in reality I'm in bed with my husband of 15 years. But then I think, 'Well, in his head he's probably having a good time with Jordan.'

You fantasise about two lesbians and a donkey, with the 'Match of the Day' theme running in the background. I fantasise that you run a Hoover over the place once a week.

Jo Brand

Some people fantasise about having sex with people who are unusual, exotic or racially different.

I imagine being approached by one of those men – gigolos – the type you see on holiday in Italy. I would never actually go with one of them, but in my fantasies I allow myself to give myself to one of them every now and again.

I have this thing about black men and I hope this doesn't seem racist, but I do fantasise about them – to me they are the epitome of masculinity, possibly because of their muscular bodies and also the stories you hear about the size of their penises.

Film stars seem to figure in many people's fantasy lives, too.

Johnny Depp (bless him!) and I have had some very exciting times together – in my head! Once I was unfaithful to him with Colin Firth, but I soon went back to Johnny.

If I see a movie with an appealing sex scene, I sometimes replay it in my head and imagine I'm Julia Roberts, Glenn Close or whoever the woman might be.

Of course, for the stars themselves, it's not always easy to be on the receiving end of mass sexual infatuation. This is one of the reasons why fame can be an extremely uncomfortable experience, even for so-called sex symbols who have made a good living out of it.

> *If I've still got my pants on in the second scene, I think they've sent me the wrong script.*
>
> Mel Gibson

Many people imagine scenarios where all responsibility for sex is relinquished. Such fantasies might be rooted in guilty feelings about sexual enjoyment.

I am working at my office desk when my boss comes in and orders me to put my hands behind my back and my legs apart. He ties me to my chair then touches me all over until I am wet, then makes me fellate him. When he's finished, he uses my favourite vibrator on me until I come.

My gym instructor is giving me a session after hours, and at one point he pins me down on a bench, arranges my clothing for full access and has his way with me. He's too strong and muscular for me to resist.

I am driving at night and get pulled over by a female police officer. She gives me a ticket, then orders me to get in the back of her police car. She handcuffs me to the seat and has her way with me. I think I first saw a TV programme that had a scene like that – it always works.

It's extremely common to imagine oneself with multiple partners, too.

My biggest fantasy is having identical twins. They're gorgeous, curvy brunettes and they know exactly how to please me.

Now I fantasise about girls with huge butts and boobs. One girl – I'm sucking her pussy – another I'm fucking, and another is sucking my crack, and we all rotate.

I fantasise about being a call girl with a pimp who makes me have sex with three men at a time. I welcome them wearing just an apron and high heels, and serve them drinks. Then I fellate each one to start them off, and pretty soon one is also in my vagina and the third in my ass. My pimp films the whole thing.

It is not uncommon for people actually to act out some of their sexual fantasies, such as those about having simultaneous, multiple partners – although that's not for everyone.

I hate orgies ... holding your stomach in for hours on end.

John Mortimer

Being able to have one or more partners who make themselves fully available is a fantasy favoured by many people – perhaps as a reaction to the actual unavailability of partners in real life.

> *For most people the fantasy is driving around in a big car, having all the chicks you want and being able to pay for it. It always has been, still is, and always will be. Anyone who says it isn't is talking bullshit.*
>
> Mick Jagger

People are wired differently. For some, their fantasies involve receiving pleasure rather than giving. This may or may not match their actual sexual style.

I guess my best fantasies involve having everything done to me in some sort of sexual spa – by both men and women. I do nothing.

He carries me to the water's edge and gently lays me on the sand. It's warm, with soft breezes, and there's no one around. He touches me all over. As the tide comes in, he gets bolder and bolder, but I am completely passive. He makes love to me when we're almost covered by the waves.

I imagine myself being sorted by two or three of those nasty girls in my porn movies. Not the kind of girls I'd date or take home to mum. They're all working on me at once – and also doing dirty things to each other, which turns me on even more.

If God had meant for us to have group sex, he'd have given us more organs.

Malcolm Bradbury

Many people have told me that they imagine themselves being sexually dominant – even if they are not so in real life.

> I usually fantasise about this one woman, who resembles my fourth-grade teacher. At first she is in charge in the classroom, but I make her kneel down and give me head, then I bend her over my desk and have my way with her.

Many people have told me that they have concerns about the kinds of fantasies they have, especially the very common ones about forcing someone to be sexual or being forced themselves.

> I am especially ashamed of my favourite one, where I'm still at school in a dormitory and one of the priests comes in and starts touching me under my blankets. He takes me to his study and makes me kneel – supposedly in prayer, but he forces me to perform oral sex. Then several other priests take turns entering me from behind – and even a few nuns get in on the act.

> I get in the lift and the lift operator refuses to take me to my floor. Instead he heads to the basement, stops the lift and touches me all over. Then he forces me to fellate him. Next he takes me into the parking garage, where four or five parking attendants play with me as well. They take it in turns to have me in various ways, including double entry. When I'm in the throes of excitement while pleasuring

myself, this scenario seems incredibly erotic, but in reality when I get to my office building I usually take the stairs. If I saw that lift operator again, I just might blush with embarrassment.

Is it taboo?

Highly uncomfortable, unexplained sexual reactions that appear to violate strong societal taboos do occur from time to time. It's best simply to notice the feelings that they arouse in us, and then put them in perspective; in other words: 'That's strange and uncomfortable, but I'm not really going to act on that.'

I did once get a very strong erection while trying to comfort my grown-up younger sister, who was upset about something, and I once had an erotic dream about my brother. I found both totally inexplicable and neither occurred again.

I was standing beside my dad in church singing a hymn – I must have been around 19 – and I suddenly had a really uncomfortable sexual feeling. I felt wet in my crotch and terribly guilty. I mean it was God's house and this was my own father. The feeling did not last very long, and nothing like that ever happened to me again, but it was uncomfortable enough for me to remember over all the years since.

The enormous breadth of the range of sexual patterns and behaviours that exist among humankind illustrates that there is rich, normative variation and we should not be too quick to judge anyone. Certain sections of society have developed different sexual views and behaviours from others because the general rules are different. For example, sexual mores in some areas of the world of rock 'n' roll are probably shocking to many outsiders.

> We'd come off stage and there'd be women waiting for us in the green room. We didn't know who they were and we didn't care. Some guys would do it then and there, while others would fuck in the van. The women had favourites. Some groupies liked guitarists; some preferred singers. They chose you, not the other way around. The groupies were in charge – a lot of people don't understand that. They were always in control. A lot of it was about cock-sucking. I thought there was not a lot in it for them, but apparently there was. And there would be a share system – if there were four guys and three groupies, the one who finished first would send her along to the fourth one's room, like room service.

Sex as a weapon

Sex is normally a healthy activity, but there are some instances when it is not. Some people use sex in various unhealthy or even damaging ways for all kinds of reasons. It can be used to hurt someone – including ourselves.

> Looking back on it now, I guess I was using sex as a means of hurting myself. I had such a low opinion of myself, I found all kinds of horrible, older men who were only too happy to collude with me in confirming how bad I was.

Husband number one 'raped' me after I had told him I wanted a divorce.

When I was in my early 20s, a very beautiful (married) girl unexpectedly made a play for me. I was living with a serious boyfriend, so I still don't understand why I was attracted to her. We had a couple of very erotic experiences, but I kept thinking it meant more to her than it did to me. One day she invited me to her place and we started making love in the living room. But I had an uneasy feeling, and suddenly noticed that the room seemed different, with an extra wall. Then I realised that her husband was watching us from behind a two-way mirror. It was really creepy – I got out of there as fast as I could.

Erotic risk-taking

Some people find it erotic to have sex in places where there is a risk of discovery – in public places, at work and so on.

When I worked in restaurants, there would be sex in walk-in freezers (I don't recommend that) or bathrooms, or after hours anywhere.

My lover and I really wanted to join the 'mile high club' but we found it rather difficult. There's always such a line of people and, since 9/11, the cabin staff seem very vigilant about where people are at all times. But last year we were travelling business class and the toilet entrance was situated away from the main corridor. We sneaked in and had a quickie, although I can't say it was very erotic – there's not much room and it's pretty uncomfortable bending over the loo with a fair bit of turbulence!

I've had sex a few times in the office, over a desk on a sofa – because either it's just now and we have to do it here, or as a pre-planned bit of excitement.

Outdoor sex is a common fantasy, although, in reality, it carries a number of risks – including getting arrested.

I once had sex in a nature reserve. It was jungle-like and we ended up on the ground, which was very exciting until we realised we were on top of a giant ants' nest.

During outdoor sex, frostbite of the breasts, leeches on the labia, neck cramp from trying to keep one eye peeled for wandering psychopaths, does not get a girl as aroused as her partner might think.

Kathy Lette

The combined erotic imaginations of two (or more!) people can lead to great creativity. Unfortunately, I have heard of many problems occurring when reality rudely interrupted the enacted fantasy.

This girl had not told me she was living with someone. We were in the middle of a full-on role-play – with her in a maid's outfit – when her guy came home suddenly. She made me hide under the bed and I was stuck there for hours until he fell asleep. It was like one of those crazy French farces.

We'd had a few drinks and ended up playing one of those dice games where we each wrote down sexy things we fancied doing, and numbered them from one to six. The first one we rolled was my girlfriend's choice – sex in a neighbour's swimming pool. Not only was this trespassing (the family was away on vacation), but the pool was over-looked by several other houses. The only saving grace was that it was fairly late at night, so there was a good chance people would be asleep. We crept into the garden, and slipped over to the pool. First she wanted me to give her oral sex sitting on the edge of the pool, like she'd seen in some French movie. Then we got in the water and, well, it might have been all those beers plus the fear of being caught, but I couldn't get hard for the life of me. I guess she's more turned on by danger than I am.

We had sex in a changing room in the lingerie section of a department store. I'm sure the girl in charge knew what was going on, but it seemed like she's seen it all before. Afterwards I did fork out for three bras and a couple of thongs – well, it seemed only fair.

I know it's a cliché, but I did have sex a few times in the broom cupboard at work, and once in the room where they keep the copy machines. I have my own office, but there are huge picture-glass windows, so privacy was an issue. But I must say, doing it standing up in a broom cupboard can be pretty heart-stopping, especially when you can hear your boss dressing down a fellow employee only a few feet away!

More than one

Some people are open and willing to try different combina-tions of sexual partnerships that may be unusual, or unacceptable to some people.

Nothing risqué, nothing gained.

Alexander Woollcott

I had a mother and daughter once. They were Scandinavian. I was in bed with the daughter at her home, and she said, '*Sshh* – someone's coming!' This woman came in and she said, 'It's my mother!' I thought, 'Oh no!' But the woman took her clothes off and got straight into bed and joined in. I thought it was great. The girl was laughing. They were making jokes in Danish; they'd obviously done it before.

One night in Birmingham, my friend Graham and I were staying with another guy and his wife. In the middle of the night, Graham woke me up. The guy wanted all three of us to fuck his wife, which we did. It was great. There was a bit of competition about who lasted the longest. Her husband wanted to watch. Then they got her into a position where she was sucking my cock and trying to pee on Graham's face, but she couldn't do it.

I met these two army chaps when I was trekking in the Himalayas. I liked them both, and none of us had had sex for a while. They both seemed into me, and I was trying to decide who to focus on when it suddenly occurred to me – why not have both? Let one of my fantasies come true? We were all in my hotel room and one of them excused himself to go to the loo. I took the opportunity to come on to the other one, kissing and touching him, and letting him know I was available to him. When the other man came back, the first one conveniently excused himself to go to the loo and so I started playing with the other one. They seemed confused at first, but eventually they got the idea, especially when I went down on one and put the other one's hand inside my pants. That was the most exciting real-life fantasy I've ever had, and the image that has made me reach orgasm on many, many occasions since.

When choosing between two evils. I always like to take the one I've never tried before.

Mae West

Out of the ordinary

When I ask people about their erotic life, some describe experiences that sound like the plots of porn movies (does life imitate 'art'?).

I was in an English holiday resort, when I woke up and realised that someone was sucking my cock. I was in my 20s. I'd been sound asleep. It was the cleaning lady. She had one of those nylon coats on that she'd opened up. I let her finish. Once I realised it was a woman, I didn't give a shit.

When a man and woman of unorthodox tastes make love, the man could be said to be introducing his foible into her quirk.

Kenneth Tynan

There is a broad tapestry of human sexual behaviour, and some people are extreme players!

I get my boyfriend to pretend to rape me. He hides in the bushes or in my closet and jumps out and 'forces' himself on me. I don't know exactly why I like that.

There was a girl I was with – she used to phone her friend and tell her what we were doing. She gave her a running commentary on the phone. But that whole hippie thing was going on – half the time you were stoned.

I'm into sensory deprivation. My partner is, too. We have equipment at home that helps us achieve this and we take it in turns to zip each other into this special bag.

I met this man who was into tickling. When he first asked me to tickle him, I thought he was joking, but when I discovered how much it turned him on – and how good sex could be once he was aroused by tickling – I was happy to oblige. I never asked him how he came to be turned on by that, but I always wondered.

The psychiatrist asked me if I thought sex was dirty and I said, 'It is if you're doing it right.
Woody Allen

Sadomasochistic behaviour is fairly common, and seems, on the face of it, to have emerged from European culture. But I've come across accounts of African tribes with traditions of girls whipping adolescent wooers with vine branches, so there may be something more universal about this kind of human sex play. After all, the pain and pleasure centres in the brain are very close together.

I like to be spanked. I don't know why, but it's one of the most erotic things I can think of. It used to be just a fantasy, but a few years ago I found out that many people are into the same thing. Now I have a sex partner who is a real expert. Sometimes he lays me over his knee and gives me a delicious hand spanking, touching my clitoris at the same time. I come very quickly that way. Sometimes he tells me to bring him my hairbrush and uses that – he'll sometimes insert the other end in my hole. He also has a whole collection of other instruments of sweet torture – paddles, canes and suede or leather floggers – even a cat 'o' nine tails. Some hurt more than others, but the way he does it is so exciting I don't mind.

Penetration was nice – I was usually the top. For some reason I gave off a vibe that I was a serious 'top'. Some gay men are attracted to bowed legs. I paddled guys and had three-ways a number of times. This one masochistic guy just loved being dominated. He wanted to be slammed around and face-fucked hard. Once I was with him and my boyfriend in a three-way, and we were roughing him up bad. He got so scared and slugged at us violently and broke my boyfriend's nose.

Many people find BDSM (bondage, domination and sado-masochism) extremely erotic, and it is yet another one of the normative range of human sexual interests. But there are important safety considerations, and anyone who is playing in this way needs to be sure it is safe, sane and consensual. For example, even spanking and light bondage can cause permanent damage if they are not done correctly. Getting some education from a reliable source is essential.

Sex means spank and beautiful means bottom.

Kenneth Tynan

My girlfriend is a real torturer. She likes to play with temperature, and is pretty creative. She likes to light a candle and drip the wax on me, then uses ice in different places – on my nipples and even up my arse. The element of surprise really works for me.

Fetishism is also extremely common. People can become fetishistic about almost anything, but those I hear most about are an erotic interest in feet, shoes, leather and vinyl....

I'm extremely turned on by certain kinds of female feet and footwear. The arch has to be high, the toes uniform, and they have to be nicely manicured with bright red polish. I like a high stiletto sandal or a high-heeled black lace-up boot – and thigh boots are the ultimate. Not many women are keen on letting me worship their feet, so I usually pay prostitutes for that service. Or I go to sex clubs and there are women there who might let me come on their shoes.

There is no unhappier creature on earth than a fetishist who yearns for a woman's shoe and has to embrace the whole woman.

Karl Kraus

Some men prefer leather, but I have a thing about latex. My girl dresses up in it from head to toe, and that really gets me off. I like the latex knickers with the dildo attached – and so does she – and also the latex bra with nipple holes. It's a harmless fetish, isn't it?

Again, the criteria for 'different' sex are 'safe, sane, and consensual'. The above scenario seems to satisfy all three.

I have what one textbook I read called 'an erotic interest in urine'. Basically, it turns me on to have a woman pee on me. A lot of ladies won't do it, though.

> *The only unnatural sex act is that which you cannot perform.*
>
> Dr Alfred Kinsey

Toxic sex

Sadly, some people get into toxic sexual relationships from which they find it difficult to withdraw. Their reasons for forming these unhealthy bonds usually lie in earlier, problematic familial relationships. Psychotherapy or counselling is usually required to help a person change their pattern of making such unhealthy choices.

He used to beat me up and then – when I was lying in a crumpled heap on the floor, crying hysterically – he would want to have sex with me. I would respond, too, because a little human kindness at that point meant everything. It was erotic, but really sick.

The ultimate toxic relationship is incest, and this is more common than people think.

When I was a teenager, I started having sex with my own father. Most people think of this as abuse, but the way I feel about it – I adore him and am really happy to express my love for him that way and have that closeness with him. Now I'm in my 30s I don't see him very often, but when I do, we usually have sex. It's only become a problem lately because I think my new stepmother caught on. Last time I visited, she kicked me out of the house.

This testimony will be shocking to most people, because the actions of father and daughter desecrate a major taboo. I'm not saying it's okay, but as a psychologist and sexologist my task is to avoid being judgemental of the individuals involved. I included that testimony simply as an illustration of just how diverse human sexual behaviour can be.

> *There's nothing inherently dirty about sex, but if you try real hard and use your imagination you can over-come that.*
>
> Lewis Grizzard

I have also heard many accounts of people who engage in sexual activity with their pets and other animals.

I masturbate my dog because I want him to have pleasure, too.

As is well illustrated by the testimonies in this chapter, there is an incredibly wide variety of human sexual behaviours that start being discovered and tried out in early adulthood – if not before! No matter how 'strange' they may seem, all of them are just part of a broad range of human sexual styles. I personally offer no judgement, but clearly some are not typical, and many are judged by most people to be inappropriate, unhealthy or wrong. In my view, any style of sexuality is okay, as long as fulfils the criteria I've already mentioned: truly safe, sane and consensual. The latter requires some special consideration, because it's not just about reaching the age of consent and saying 'yes' rather than 'no'; people who have suffered sexual abuse, those who are in a relationship where there is a power imbalance, and those who are not sound of mind for any reason are very often incapable of giving full and true consent.

Being sane means being clear of mind with unimpaired judgement – including being free from the influence of drugs or alcohol. Being safe includes not deliberately doing anything that might cause long-term physical or mental harm to anyone, including oneself, and not being at serious risk of transmitting or acquiring an STI. Those who were sexually active in the permissive, pre-AIDS years often long for that relatively risk-free, sexually open environment they could enjoy with impunity. The possibilities are still endless; however, these days, sex in our 20s is often largely about learning how to have pleasure that's also harmless.

I don't like casual sex. I like it as formal as possible. Blood tests, CVs, the works.

Kathy Lette

5

In Our 30s
Now Let's Do it Properly

Men reach their sexual peak at 18. Women reach theirs at 35.
Do you get the feeling that God is playing a practical joke?

Rita Rudner

Just when we thought we'd got it together – learned how to have sex with a partner, and have some idea who we are sexually – we start facing new challenges. All kinds of nemeses dampen our fire: children knocking at the door, elderly parents requiring care, peri-menopause (yes, it really can begin in our mid-30s!) and a sense that we're not kids any more. By now we should be giving some thought to taking proper care of our sexual health. Many people in their 30s have been in a primary relationship for quite a few years, and this can mean being faced with the challenge of trying to keep our sex lives fresh and exciting. Some people in their 30s start having to deal with certain sexual disorders, such as lowered desire. No wonder there's a question on many people's lips: 'Is *everyone* having more sex than I am?'

People desperately want to be 'normal', although, as I've pointed out, there's really no such thing. We should try not to compare ourselves to others. What's 'normal' for a mother of two young children and an infant is probably having very little sex – and she may not be enjoying it much when she does.

It was hard to keep my desires in check. I wanted sex when I wanted it, but there were the kids, their activities, our jobs, constant juggling. I wanted it to be simple, but this was not realistic.

Less busy people in their 30s who feel their sex lives need a bit of a boost may start searching for ways to enhance it, perhaps by trying out new erotic techniques, sex toys or looking online for erotic stimulation.

Okay, making whoopee doesn't necessarily require a computer and the ability to type with your nose, but don't knock it till you've tried it!

For some, the 30s is – or was – a wonderfully exciting time for sex.

In my 30s, I felt quite desirable and sensuous. Sometimes I would make love to two different men in one day. It was the 1970s, so there was the Pill and IUDs – and before AIDS. So you had permission to do anything or everything, whenever you wanted to. In those days I was pretty much run by my sexual feelings. I didn't get married until I was 48.

This testimony illustrates very well why we cannot necessarily generalise the nature of people's sex lives in each decade, because world history and our social environment have such a huge influence. For example, the arrival of the AIDS crisis profoundly changed our sexuality, making people far more cautious and less experimental.

I was in my 30s when the HIV/AIDS scare started. I was terrified, and realised that the party was over. All that carefree 'don't care who you do it with' stuff I'd enjoyed for many years was suddenly over.

I was married then, in a monogamous relationship, but at that time there was so much conflicting information. Some people were saying HIV could be dormant from years ago, so you could never know who had it. Essentially it made me scared of sex. I even made my fully faithful husband wear a condom.

Knowing what we want

By the time most people reach their 30s, they are fairly sure that they understand who they are sexually, although few recognise that our sexuality is never set in stone and that things can change. But many feel – perhaps after a certain amount of trial and error – that they are more or less familiar with the nuances of their sexual desires.

> I think I've only just recently started to acquire a good understanding about what turns me on and what I need – that is, without guilt! I now feel comfortable about my sexuality and my desires and I think I probably fall right into the 'normal' bracket – if there is such a thing – whereas a few years ago I probably would have tried to suppress even so much as the desire to masturbate, believing it to be deviant behaviour.

People in their 30s who have long-term partners are usually becoming more tolerant of each other's differences – including their sexual styles.

> After 14 years of being happily married I suddenly discovered that my husband liked to cross-dress. He had been borrowing my clothing when I wasn't home, dressing up and masturbating. When I first found out about it, I was devastated. I wanted a divorce. I didn't understand it at all,

felt terribly betrayed and thought he was actually gay or trans-gendered or something. Fortunately we had some counselling, which saved our marriage. It turned out he is just a heterosexual man who is turned on by female clothing – he hadn't told me because he felt ashamed of himself. Apparently lots of men have the same fetish. I had to stop him borrowing my clothes, because he was stretching them out, but we're still together, and I even bought him men's size 11 high heels for his birthday!

I love using my wife's underwear to masturbate with. She knows about it and says I'm a dirty bugger. But she leaves her undies around the bathroom for me, knowing exactly what I'm going to do with them! She's a sexy woman.

Most people in their 30s are also often reasonably clear about what gender they desire in a partner.

I'm utterly comfortable. I was quite effeminate as a kid. I had heaps of close female friends and few male ones as an adolescent. I dug Bowie, Depeche Mode, Pet Shop Boys and New Order, with my Clash, Pixies, Police and Beastie Boys. I have many times been asked to confirm my straightness. I've also been kissed by well-meaning men, but always disliked it intensely – the hairy boyishness of it freaks me right out. I have lots of close gay and lesbian friends, and I relate well to that whole scene. I'm very at home with who I turned out to be in this regard – proud even.

Creating a family

Fifty years ago it was more common for women in our society to have children in their 20s, and the effect that had on their sexuality may now be experienced more in a woman's fourth decade, as so many leave childbearing until later on.

> In my 30s I had two small children under five. Sex was the last thing on my mind. I wanted a good night's sleep, rather than a good night's rogering! I also had elderly parents to care for and a full-time job. 'Sex? What's that?' was my feeling.

> In my 30s I was too focused on my career to settle down, so I had a series of relationships with men I liked to have sex with, and would always break it off if they got too serious. My girlfriends joked that I behaved more like men than men do. But once I turned 38, the joke was on me. I suddenly wanted a husband, children – the full domestic picture. I looked around to find available men, and there weren't too many of them. Now, at one month before my 40th birthday, I'm living with a man to see how it goes. We're considering adoption.

There is no doubt that, no matter when a woman decides to have children, her procreative period is going to affect her sexuality. It will also affect her partner's sexuality – and all this is to be expected.

> Having kids really affected our sexuality – it went down-hill. Then it was only a couple of times a month.

> In our 30s, my wife was the breadwinner. Shortly after she gave birth to our twins, I took over as the main caregiver, and she went back to work. It was exhausting. She would come home enervated from her exciting day in the TV world and I would be asleep on the nursery floor. She was stimulated to

have sex – in fact she used to say my being in charge of child-care was a real turn-on for her – but my desire got lower and lower, perhaps through sheer baby overload.

Literature is mostly about having sex and not much about having children. Life is the other way round.

David Lodge

The processes of pregnancy, birth and being in a post-natal state may cause natural and expectable sexual changes. At such times, hormonal changes and related events may affect desire, arousal or orgasm. These issues are usually resolved in time, and should only be seen as problems if they persist. It seems to me that normative conditions, such as temporary lowered sexual desire – which may occasionally occur naturally for various good reasons in a woman's life – are sometimes seen as problems when they're not. Temporary sexual difficulties – in either partner – may even arise at the planning stage.

My wife wanted to plan our family, and she decided the best way to do this was by figuring out her ovulation period to make sure we took full advantage of it. But I found that making love to order put a lot of pressure on me. Doing it on the clock just wasn't exciting, and it affected my erectile capacity. Our babies were spaced perfectly, but our sex life took a while to repair.

The state of the union

Physiological changes are not the only factors affecting sexual desire. Relationship problems can also play their part and, in fact, may be the main reason for one or both partners' sexual disinterest.

> When I'm mad at my partner I withdraw sexually. Actually, I just don't want to go near him, and if he tries to touch me, I snap at him. I'm not deliberately with-holding sex from him – I just genuinely do not feel like it. To enjoy sex I have to feel close, loving and appreciated.

Sexual interest might wane for reasons that are situational, psychological, relational or physiological – and many are combinations of factors. Sexuality between two people is a metaphor for their relationship. When the 'state of the union' is unbalanced, the symptoms may be displayed in a couple's sex life; when it's right, lovemaking can be a profound, passionate expression of deep caring and commitment.

> We touched each other. In that moment we were as close as two people could possibly be. It was strong, deep and more passionate than I could ever have imagined – and such an incredible relief to finally share our bodies with each other. We were both moved to tears.

Sex can even include a deep spiritual element, although that's not common in Western cultures. But among Hindu people, for example, the notion of sex as a spiritual experience is accepted, understood and even fostered.

When things go wrong in a relationship, the tension, anger, frustration and so on will be reflected in a couple's sexuality. If sex disappears altogether, it is frequently the result of an impasse that has been reached, and without resolution both partners may spend extended periods living with sadness, bitterness and longing. In couples therapy, I have often heard things like, 'If only the sex were better, everything else would fall into place', but the opposite is usually true; if the relationship was in better shape and underlying resentments were aired and resolved, the sex would improve. Relationships require regular tune-ups.

If you have been married more than ten years, being good in bed means you don't steal the covers.

Brenda Davidson

Keeping up with the Joneses

Many people compare their sex life – especially its frequency – to others, and what others *say* they get up to. However, this is a mistake because so many people are ashamed of their lack of sex and tell exaggerated stories to compensate. It's an awful secret many couples hold, because a dwindling desire and lack of sexual connection are painful and sad. They rarely even talk about it to each other.

I can't even remember when or why we stopped having sex, but it just seemed to disappear amidst all the school runs, the stress of work and the crises with various family members. I didn't stop being attracted to him; it's more like I just lost my own interest in sex generally, because there was always something or someone else needing my time. But deep down I felt guilty and sad, and had a terrible feeling of having lost something that was once precious. I was also acutely aware and worried that he might find someone else – but another part of me didn't even care.

I've already mentioned that work stress and caring for young children or elderly relatives can negatively affect a couple's sexuality. This can often be solved by simple time-management – by sharing the household chores or hiring a babysitter every now and again. Planning uninterrupted time together for sex goes against the grain for people who prefer to cling to the notion that sex should be more spontaneous – but it's amazing how helpful it can be to set aside special times for intimacy.

The only way we can guarantee 'alone time' is to put it in our Blackberries. I write, 'Appointment with Mr Johnston' to remind me! It actually turns me on whenever I see it there in black and white. We take it in turns to arrange childcare, book a restaurant or movie, and decide what exactly we'll do afterwards. Sometimes we meet in a bar and pretend we're chatting each other up for the first time ...

Caring roles

Sometimes the stress and exhaustion of caring for a young family wears away at a woman's sense of her femininity, as it relates to sex. She comes to view herself primarily as a caretaker and loses touch with an important side of herself – the seductress. Constantly being 'mum' often tips a woman's identity into a maternal role a little too heavily, and that may affect her interest in *being* sexual. This phenomenon is not confined to women, as more men are taking on childcare roles, and more gay men (as well as lesbian couples) are raising children.

> To me as an older gay man it was a shock – I had no idea young gay men would want babies and all – that was the farthest thing from my mind growing up. Now I see gay men with baby strollers – it would never have crossed our minds in my day, that gay men would be emulating the straight lifestyle. One of the things we liked best about being gay was the freedom – nothing to encumber us. But having kids, etc.! Maybe if I was very wealthy and in my 30s, I might consider it.

It is often how we feel about ourselves – exciting lover versus harried caretaker – that inspires our libido. Likewise, it is frequently who we feel ourselves to be in the context of our partners – someone who can please, tease and share pleasure versus someone who lacks sexual inspiration – that affects our desire to make love with him or her. Clever partners will find ways to help a responsibility-focused partner reconnect with his or her sexual side.

> I didn't want to put any pressure on her after everything she'd been through with the twins, but I couldn't imagine going through any more days or even months of feeling that it was always me who wanted it and that she was just never inspired to want it, too. In the end I went to a store I know she likes and picked out some sexy lingerie for her. I got a saleswoman to help, agonised about the choice (and

the size!), but I wanted to show her I still view her as the gorgeous, desirable woman I met.

Giving compliments and sensitively sexual touches may help as well, or even taking her to a romantic movie. In bed, try to provide soothing first – caresses and sensual massage – before moving on to something more directly arousing. And most tired mothers will attest to the fact that one of the best types of foreplay is taking out the rubbish!

> Sometimes I get mad at him for not helping me enough – even though I know he's had a full work day, too. I just feel so overwhelmed that if he offers to do the smallest chore – set the table or change one nappy – I instantly warm to him and am far more likely to want intimacy when we finally get to bed.

Stressed and over-stretched

Men's sexuality can also suffer from overwork, stress and feeling that – after a day of enormous responsibility at work – they do not feel like being responsible for fabulous love-making when they get home. Many of the challenges that face both men and women in the world of work – job loss, redundancy, being provoked by a difficult boss or colleague – can have a devastating effect on a person's sense of self-worth, and that can have a knock-on effect on his or her sexuality. The pressures of trying to be successful in our society take a significant toll on our psyche, physical health and energy.

But, as I've already pointed out, relationship factors very often account for a lowered libido, and one of the most common feelings that can reduce a person's interest in having sex is having underlying anger or resentment towards one's partner.

> I had my first full-term pregnancy in my 30s, and found that my husband was not so great with pregnancy. That was difficult. I was hurt that he wasn't more loving with my body during those times.

> For several years now – certainly since our first child was born – it has been very difficult to get my wife's attention. She's a wonderful mother, obviously, but it seems whenever I want to be intimate with her she's got other things on her mind. I don't really say anything, but it's not easy to be a lower priority than wax-sealing her gooseberry jam.

It is important to be able to talk about deep issues and resolve differences, or sexuality can dwindle and the relationship may be doomed. The trick is to have frequent, calm talks in an environment of safety, with no distractions. The most useful style of communication is to express one's pure feelings about what is happening, without blaming the other, and – most importantly – asking for what one specifically needs. And life throws all kinds of tricky situations at us, so a vital task for people embarking on long-term relationships is to learn to support each other. For example, bereavement can have a detrimental effect on a person's sexual interest.

> My only sister died of uterine cancer. She was younger than me – just 29 years old. I nursed her through her treat-

ments and her final weeks. My husband was wonderful – took charge of the kids and the household – but something switched off in me and I just shrank if he tried to make love. It took many months to get my fire back.

Any kind of stress – perhaps relating to work, finances or childcare – can also reduce a person's libido. And being unable to pay the bills, losing one's job, dealing with taxation demands, being made redundant and many other problems that commonly occur in tough financial climates, can even lead to depression, which is known to be at the root of low desire in many people.

When I was let go at the plant, I found it really difficult to find my feet again. We had to rely on my wife's wage for a while, and I felt useless as a husband – useless as a man. That feeling affected how I felt about sex, too. My penis just wasn't feeling good, either.

Psychological challenges

Some people's brains make it hard for them to focus on sex. Engaging in lovemaking actually requires that we pay attention to our senses – in particular, touch and feeling – and follow a desired sequence of events. If we happen to struggle with such tasks, sex becomes more challenging.

I've been diagnosed with ADHD (attention deficit hyperactivity disorder). My brain seems to work overtime and I get distracted really easily. When I go to my girlfriend's flat and we're having sex in her bedroom, there's often a point when someone in the flat above flushes the toilet and you can hear it. This is so distracting to me I frequently lose my erection and I have to start over.

Sometimes people have personality issues or other psychological challenges that make it difficult for them to enjoy sex with a partner.

It's hard for me to trust people enough to allow myself to have sex with them. I've been told I have paranoid personality disorder, and that many of my concerns are unfounded, but I just can't stop imagining that someone I might have sex with could take advantage of me – perhaps without my even knowing.

I have a phobia about germs, and I always have to make sure everything around me is super-clean. Having sex is a real ordeal for me, and mostly I avoid it. Well, what am I going to do? Short of wiping him down with Dettol, it's just too hard.

A person's general psychological state will strongly influence his or her sexuality. The person who provided the following testimony suffers from a obsessive-compulsive disorder, which also plays itself out in his sexual behaviours. If the basic disorder is treated, his sexually compulsive behaviour will calm down.

I am compelled to masturbate many times a day ... sometimes up to 30 times. It ends up being painful and my privates are usually red raw – but I just have to do it. I can't stop. Of course, it's affected my work and I have no chance for a relationship – I suppose it's a problem I should get some help for, but I'm too embarrassed to tell anyone.

There is a current vogue for labelling anyone who gets publicly caught in an affair as a 'sex addict'. The PR strategy is usually to have the person first make a public *'mea culpa'* statement and apologise, then disappear for 'treatment', only to emerge with a new, 'reformed' image. I think this is unfortunate for several reasons. In the first place, I do not believe a person's sex life is anyone else's business, no matter who they are; and, secondly, I'm a bit uncomfortable with the concept of 'sexual addiction', because I think the term 'addiction' should be reserved for something that is not essentially good for us. Sex *is* a natural and healthy aspect of our lives, so shouldn't 'addiction' terminology be reserved for substances like alcohol, tobacco and crack cocaine? However, it is certainly possible for a person to become compulsive about sexuality, and that can lead to significant problems that require treatment. People who suffer from sexual compulsivity are usually obsessive or compulsive about other things in their lives, too, and it is the underlying disorder that needs to be treated, not the fact that they are sexual beings.

In my opinion, if society is going to be judgemental and punitive about a person's sexuality, it would be better to reserve it for people who coerce others – although most psychologists understand that even the most persistent sexual predators have a condition that requires treatment.

> I get this terrible urge to touch women – strange women. I know it's wrong and I've been caught and charged after I rubbed against a woman on the Underground, not knowing her husband was nearby. He grabbed me and called the police. The thing is, even though I know my urge can ruin my life, I can't stop. I think about doing it night and day, and eventually I just have to go out and do it.

When I come home, I masturbate while thinking about the women I've just felt. After I've ejaculated I feel guilty and ashamed – and resolve not to do it ever again. That lasts about a day until I get the urge again.

I am compelled to expose myself in public. I usually choose younger women or girls to show my genitals to – somehow if they register shock, that is a turn-on for me. I know my actions are unsociable and wrong, but it's hard for me to stop. I'm having treatment, but the pills I'm taking reduce my sexual drive almost completely – I don't like that but it helps keep me out of trouble.

Why do it?

By the time most people reach their 30s, sex may be familiar enough for it to have become routine. But they 'go though the motions' for any number of reasons. Sex holds different meanings for different people at different times. Some even use it as a means to an end.

> *Sex is hardly ever about sex.*
> Shirley MacLaine

I rarely felt like it, but I did it whenever he wanted it because I wanted to stay married. He had some very attractive female co-workers.

I knew that if I had sex with him he'd agree to the holiday in Majorca. I said there'd be a lot more of that if I was relaxed somewhere in a sunny place. It worked – we both got what we wanted.

When my woman's horny, she can be a real bitch. I go down on her and give her a great orgasm and ... what a difference! It's amazing how nice she can be – for the next day or so!

I longed for sex to be like it was when we first met – surprising and fresh and passionate. Somehow we had just got into this boring routine – a couple of minutes of him playing with my nipples and touching my clit, then four minutes of thrusting and it was all over. I suppose I contributed to this status quo – I wouldn't insist on more foreplay because I just wanted to get it over and done with. When I really wanted to have an orgasm I preferred to masturbate – it was far more reliable.

I'm too busy for a relationship, but sex is the best way I know of to lose weight and look good. When I'm feeling a bit bloated, I find someone to shag who's more interested in sex than eating. It always works.

I'm not exactly a virgin anymore, and I like sex, so it's not that hard for me to say 'yes' if I think it's reasonably likely that I'll enjoy it and if he treats me well. If he courts me nicely and I get a nice meal and nice wine, I'll probably go through with it. I regard it as one way to get to know a man better.

If I feel I'm getting a migraine I just get into bed and masturbate. It usually does the trick.

I have had guilt fucks – 'How did I get here? Now I've got to do it' sort of thing. And I've had validation fucks – 'See, I must be a good/cool/sexy guy because she just had me.'

I am fed up with men who use sex like a sleeping pill.

Toni Braxton

Maintaining the status quo

Many women have told me they often have sex just to placate their partners.

> I always knew when I was going to have to have sex with him – he'd get morose, testy and complain about little things. It just wasn't worth putting up with that, so if I was busy I'd give him a quick blow job and hope that would do the trick.

Just as it was true of some women in their 20s, some 30-year-olds fake both orgasm and general enjoyment. Some do this because they feel pressured to fulfil their partner's fantasies of being such fabulous lovers they can please a woman without much effort. Others do it because they're not in the mood and want to get it over with, or because they simply don't know how to ask for what they want.

> I really never enjoy sex as much as my partner thinks I do. I guess I'm programmed to give him a good time rather than the other way round. My mother always said, 'You'd better be good to him because if you don't there're a million other women who'll take your place.' She lived in fear of being ditched by my father, who had umpteen affairs.

> By the time I'd read enough feminist literature to realise that it was a mistake to fake orgasms, I'd been doing it for

so long I couldn't really change that. What was I going to do – confess? He'd be devastated.

A girl I was seeing told me she'd faked orgasm from time to time and it made me very wary and question every moment. I was never sure whether she was really enjoying herself or not. It spoiled our thing, because it's important to me that my partner is satisfied. Otherwise, what's the point? You might as well just jerk off.

I may not be a great actress, but I've become the greatest at screen orgasms. Ten seconds of heavy breathing, roll your head from side to side, simulate a slight asthma attack and die a little.

Candice Bergen

As I pointed out in the previous chapter, some women 'fake it' because they don't know that many – probably most – women do not climax during intercourse. In most cases, women need more direct clitoral stimulation.

My boyfriend watches a lot of porn and has internet sex with other women. It's upsetting to me, but frankly I don't blame him. He thinks there's something wrong with me because I never come. I mean, I can when I touch myself, but he doesn't know that.

The pressure to have 'the right kind of sex life' can seem particularly acute in our 30s. It's a time when some women realise that they have actually never experienced orgasm.

It was really embarrassing to realise that I didn't have the same pattern of sex that some of my friends have. I never discussed sex with anyone, and had never masturbated or anything until I was in my late 20s. When I was 31, I overheard some women at work talking about 'The Big O', and I had no idea what that was. I felt ashamed of my sheltered life, which had involved taking care of my mum most of my teenaged years and well into my 20s. I had heard the word 'orgasm', but I didn't know it was a special experience – as distinct from the general nice feeling you can get down there in certain situations. Once I had the idea that I was 'abnormal', I didn't want to tell anyone about it, and just tried to ignore it for another few years. Finally I got involved with a man who figured out what was going on and asked me to seek counselling. I got a workbook that was actually quite informative, and began to get to know my own body. Once I did actually have an orgasm, I kicked myself for missing out all that time. I'm still working on feeling comfortable with having sex with Graham, but at least I know that a lot of women don't have orgasms and some even just choose not to.

Some people are simply late starters, but that doesn't mean that they're abnormal. Not having orgasms – even not having sex at all – can be personal choices. They only become problems if there is a desire for that to change. Sex therapists can be helpful to those who wish to work on some aspect of their sexuality – either as individuals or with a partner.

Men make love more intensely at 20, but make love better at 30.
Catherine II of Russia

Women over 30 are at their best, but men over 30 are too old to recognise it.

Jean-Paul Belmondo

Better sex

Our society considers the ideal relationship to be one in which a couple seamlessly achieves a perfect balance of work, family and sex. But for the average person, this is an extremely difficult balance to find, and many people in their 30s find that maintaining a lively sex life is way down the list – the last chore at the end of the day. On the brighter side, others find that in their 30s they are finally in a position to have really great sex – although some have to work harder at achieving it than others.

> I put an ad in the paper, to see if I could find a woman who would be willing to try a few things that would be new to me. I made it clear that being in a wheelchair meant I had a few physical limitations, but that I was finally ready to experience things I'd been missing – mainly because I was too afraid to suggest them. I was afraid I'd get a 'do-gooder' who wasn't really into it, but actually I found an amazing woman who totally shared some of my own fantasies. She was able and willing to get herself in a position so that I could give oral sex for the first time, and she was also athletic enough to be able to try all kinds of positions – both in and out of my wheelchair – that were illuminating.

By the time they reach 30, many people feel that they know a lot about their own sexuality, enjoy it immensely and continue to try new styles and experiment – either with one partner or with several different people.

For three years in my 30s I was in a loving, sexual relationship with two other women. We all lived under the same roof. From time to time problems and jealousies arose, but essentially it was an amazing time. It ended when one of my partners became pregnant with a man she was also seeing. My other partner and I were willing to help raise the child, but the mother-to-be decided to be exclusive with the biological father.

I had happy serial-monogamous sex for most of my early 30s, though I experimented with infidelity early on. I'm not sure why, but I assume I was trying to assert power after the bollocking my ex gave me. At one point, I had four simultaneous 'casual' relationships going for a couple of weeks. Moron. I did not get caught and loved the sex, but I felt horrible with the disingenuousness of it all, as they were all really lovely. I was a regular Charles Aznavour, and it was very tiring in all senses. I'm remarried now, and have a very passionate and understanding sexual relationship with incredible trust and tenderness. She was quite timid sexually speaking – I was her first partner. But things have progressed well over the years, and the learning and experimentation never stop.

In their 30s, some lucky people find that their capacity for eroticism increases beyond their earlier expectations.

My boyfriend at the time was into Tantric sex, and together we explored it with a teacher – an amazing way to get totally high on sex. There's this spiritual element that I really liked, but doing the exercises increased both the heart connection and the erotic connection between us to a degree I never would have thought possible.

I don't know exactly where I got this idea, but I suddenly said to him, 'I want to be your slave.' He didn't seem surprised at all. He just said, 'Get over my knee', and I did. He gave me a delicious spanking, alternating between striking pain in my buttocks and stroking my clitoris so expertly that I came. It was a revelation, and I wanted more.

Fantasy life

A fantasy life can continue through our 30s – and well beyond. People I spoke to seemed to be gaining a new level of comfort with their fantasies – even the edgy ones.

I am lying on the sofa. My wife is masturbating herself on my face, slowly teasing both of us. We take our time savouring everything; she gets incredibly wet and worked up and, just as her crescendo of unfulfilled energy is about to dissipate, she tries something different. Perhaps she bears down just so, and grazes herself on my lips and tongue, just so. Something gives deep inside and she is coming for the first time ever – grinding, squeezing, very loud squealing, gushing wetness and the look of surprise and happiness on her face when she finally releases me.

But an uncomfortably large discrepancy can arise between a person's fantasy sex life and what they are really experiencing.

Feeling stuck in a boring sexual stalemate with a long-term partner is just one of the reasons why people may decide to seek sexual connections outside their primary relationship.

We married when I was 24, and I was faithful to my husband for ten years. But, finally, I gave in to my fantasy of having hot sex with this neighbour I really fancied. However, the sex wasn't that exciting, and he turned out to be a thoughtless womaniser. I don't know why I imagined he would fit my fantasy of someone who would really care about me and respect the risk I was taking just to be with him. Frankly, my affair was way more trouble and pain than it was worth. After it ended, I appreciated my husband a lot more.

I'm a horny man and I have needs. Women make themselves available to me and I do it with them if we get the opportunity. My wife and I have been married a long time. We basically have a good marriage and we get on pretty well, but she's busy with the kids and all her various activities – book club and what not. I still look after her sexually, although she doesn't seem that interested. I wouldn't want to hurt her, and when I have sex with other women (most of the time), I cover my tracks. I just don't see that it's an issue – unless I make a mistake and she finds out. That could be a problem.

My boyfriend was really turned on by the idea of me being with other men. I liked that in fantasy, but in reality it was an uncomfortable idea – even frightening. One night when we were out at a bar and had a few drinks, he got this guy's hand and shoved it up my dress. I was shocked but also excited. The guy started fingering me and we all got really aroused. We got in a taxi where they were both touching me, and by the time we got to the flat, I was ready to do almost anything. My boyfriend watched while I gave the guy oral sex, then both of them shagged me. Afterwards I was worried that I might have shown my boyfriend that I liked it a little too much – but he seemed really proud of me. I ended up being glad that I had allowed myself to be pushed into a new situation, although it did occur to me the whole thing could have gone badly wrong.

But not everyone is willing to take such sexual risks. What do more conservative couples do when they become apathetic about their sex lives and want to spice it up? Experimenting with sex toys is a common strategy employed by people in their 30s who are eager to enhance their sexual experiences, either alone or with a partner. Some seek new partners – either *in vivo* or on the internet – while some find the use of erotica, in the form of books, movies, DVDs, TV, telephone or the internet, enhances their erotic excitement.

Cybersex

It is quite clear to most people that sexual content is ubiquitous on the internet; in fact, it's pretty hard to avoid it. And those who type and masturbate at the same time are certainly redefining the art of multitasking.

I like to watch porn. I know it's mainly for men, but it gives me ideas – and the men I have sex with are all watching it, so I figure I need to make sure we're in synch. It's the real meaning of 'boning up'!

I have occasionally used sites as a masturbation aid. It's fine – though, like all wanking, it's nowhere near as good as the real thing. But it serves a need. At this level, it's no different from using a jizz mag or a porno DVD. Clearly, though, the net opens up much more dangerous and destructive opportunities. I wouldn't judge people who go that route but it's not for me, mainly because it's so much better when it's real.

Porn holds no attraction for me at all (the cold dirty internet killed any lingering interest there).

I believe that sexual media influences generally affect our sexuality far more than most people recognise – not always negatively, but they are a strong force that can often alter people's expectations and provide unrealistic notions of what sex is all about.

The messages I've received about sex from movies, magazines and so on have affected me hugely. I have been a keen student of sex since childhood. Cinema and books will get to you one way or another – love or hate them – or their message, whether its *Romeo and Juliet*, Beyonce or *United States of Tara* [an American TV show]. We filter, absorb and process the myth or mantra a thousand times a day. I still feel as though I'm my own sexual species, just as I feel I'm an island in most regards when it comes to the media.

The fierce debate about pornography/erotica continues, and it would seem that 'politically correct porn' is an oxymoron. The fact is, many people are drawn to it and, unfortunately, many receive the bulk of their sex education from it.

My wife was featured posing in a sex magazine. I couldn't wait to get hold of her glossy spread and wack off to it. I know I've got the real thing at home ... but seeing her all air-brushed like that was extra-hot.

The difference between pornography and erotica is lighting.

Gloria Leonard

I like watching other women in porn movies. I mean, I know they're faking and everything, but they have some amazing tricks up their sleeves – well, if they wore sleeves!

At first I find it stimulating ... but then it gets very 'samey', and it's really aimed at men who want to watch other men getting blow jobs as far as I can see.

I like the kind of porn that has a story – stuff that's designed for women. It's not so easy to find, but I'm not turned on by those endless 'cum shots' you see in most porn ... I want a bit of romance, and for the woman to be in charge and get a guy to go down on her.

As a heterosexual woman I was really surprised that I was really turned on by watching gay male porn. But then, there's two or more gorgeous men with huge cocks – what's not to like?

I hate porn, but my boyfriend likes to watch it while we're having sex. It really puts me off, and I think, 'Aren't I enough for him?' The other day I asked him to give me cunnilingus, and he said, 'Yes', but immediately put on some porn. I complained that it would stop me coming, so he said okay and set to work on my pussy. Well, halfway though I suddenly looked up and realised he had put the porn movie on with the sound muted. I was about to make a real fuss, but then I thought, 'Oh, fair enough' and lay back with my eyes closed to enjoy my own private fantasy – about George Clooney.

I do enjoy porn, especially if it's well done. Watching *Emmanuelle* is a much better experience than watching Valley porn. I love well-written sex, especially in the area of S&M, and there's lots of it.

Porn makes me feel physically sick. I just can't believe that guys think those women are really enjoying themselves, making those stupid faces and fake moans. If they understand that wrestling is all acting, why can't they see porn is, too? And the women with those gigantic plastic tits – I just think how painful it must have been to acquire those. I've got naturally large breasts and one guy actually asked me to lick my own nipples like he'd seen porn queens do. Yuck. It's got to the point where I feel I've got to shave my vulva, or they don't think I'm normal. And some of them look like they've had their labia surgically removed – that'll be the next thing, men will think the rest of us women are abnormal if we actually have genital lips!

Spicing things up

Our 30s can be a time when we're sufficiently comfortable about our sexual selves and our partners to allow full rein to our sexual creativity.

My partner and I like the drama of sex. Sometimes I'm a nurse performing a genital inspection, or a school teacher, or a precocious teenager (that one's the naughtiest!). We dress up and even use props – and sometimes we go to a hotel or other locations for a bit of variety.

We sometimes just go to the sex shop and wander round looking for inspiration. Once we found this lube that kind of burned – it was an excruciating sensation that took some getting used to. My partner's into rude clothing – knickers with no crotch, etc. Oh, all right, I admit I'm into them, too! And I guess I'm old fashioned, because I really like stockings and suspenders. Shame so few women wear them these days.

Some of the things I've seen in the sex shop, I'd never buy, but I fantasise about using them. There was this mechanical fuck machine – a kind of penis-chair you sit on and 'ride'. Wow!

My lover and I invested in this mesh sex hammock. One lies in it and the other can easily manipulate his or her body for perfect oral or anal access. We have to take it down when our parents come over, though.

My boyfriend had often had anal sex with his previous girlfriends and really liked it, but I was a virgin in that respect. When he brought it up, at first I said 'No', but then we discussed it. I said, 'It's going to hurt!' He said, 'I'll get you ready and it will be fine.' He used a lot of KY, and gradually stretched me using a dildo. He made sure I was really aroused all the time, by touching and kissing me where I loved it. Eventually he put on a condom and a lot more lube and did me in the arse. I have to say, it wasn't entirely pain-free, but it was really hot and quite a revelation.

> *Don't worry, it only seems kinky the first time.*
> Author unknown

An open mind

Sometimes partners' sexual interests do not immediately coincide. But instead of saying, 'You want me to do *what*? That's disgusting!', it's worth being a little open to trying new things (provided, of course, that they are consensual and not permanently harmful). If we don't push ourselves a little in the erotic arena, we will probably end up doing boring, safe things forever and ever – and never discover our erotic possibilities. Doing something different and edgy may require a bit of negotiation; in fact, it's best to discuss it beforehand to ensure both partners understand the boundaries and fully consent. There must be trust between those who choose to adventure into advanced sexual behaviours, but being daring and trying something new often lead to heightened eroticism, greater mutual pleasure and an even more satisfying sex life.

The bottom line is that you can try to spice up your sex life in as many ways as you can possibly imagine – and that can be an awful lot of fun. But, at the end of the day, if you are in a relationship, your experiments in sexual enhancement will probably be far less rewarding than an honest, emotionally intelligent exploration of your love connection – and self-exploration of the two individuals who comprise it. In our 30s we should be mature enough to achieve this. Fostering your own and your partner's individuality – allowing you to grow as two insightful, caring and open adults who are prepared for the adventures ahead (and cognisant of the dangers) – will preserve your sex life far better than a pair of furry handcuffs and a nylon nurse's outfit.

In Our 40s
Re-evaluating Our Sexual Needs

Women are most fascinating between the ages of 35 and 40, after they've won a few races and know how to pace themselves. Since few ever pass 40, maximum fascination can continue indefinitely.

Christian Dior

For many people, reaching 40 may herald the beginning of a sense of mortality. Approaching midlife is certainly sobering for many of us – even though we tend to fudge the exact age we think actually constitutes middle age. After all, if we're going to live to 101, at 40 we're nowhere near halfway! In earlier times, turning 40 meant that women in particular were 'past it' sexually speaking, but now we hear phrases like '60 is the new 40'. There are enough attractive 40-something female role models around to inspire women who are anxious about losing the ability to be considered sexually vibrant at this point; nevertheless, many worry about it.

In our 40s, it's not quite as easy to maintain health and fitness as it was in earlier decades. The relationship between our physical state and our sexual health is well established; some people begin to experience a poorer quality of sex. Of course, at this period in our lives, different people are at different stages of family and career. Some people have chosen to leave childbearing to their late 30s, or even beyond – so they may be just beginning to deal with the sleepless nights and lack of time, inclination and privacy for sex that others have experienced in the past. By contrast, some people in their 40s may have kids who have flown the nest, and may feel free to be more sexually adventurous. Others may have become bored with their sexual status quo. Some may be beginning to lose confidence as they notice signs of ageing. Given our youth-oriented society, many people in their 40s begin to sense a lack of interest from people they might have once attracted.

> Men are simply not looking at me the way they used to. Oh, they still flirt with me, and we'll have a great conversation, but at the end of the evening they say a discreet 'Goodbye', and disappear into the night with a 20-year-old on their arm. Then I have to feel foolish for thinking they were interested in me, and the self-loathing sets in.

A new confidence

However, many 40-something women seem to have become more comfortable in their skins, and to have taken on a more assertive role in their lives generally. They socialise comfortably with men – including being able to count them as platonic friends – and do not mind initiating dating or sex.

> I went to an all-girls school and had no brothers, so I never learned to be close to men who weren't my boyfriends until now. In the past, men were just so exotic to me, I didn't know how to relate to them unless we were dating. But now I feel blessed with three or four great relationships with men who are genuinely 'just friends'. I also have one 'fuck buddy', with whom I have completely no-strings-attached sex. Having said that, I am not in a serious relationship with anyone at this point. If I was, I imagine he might object to my current lifestyle. I imagine a lot of men would be threatened by it.

Other single women in their 40s follow the same rules that they did when they were 20.

Once I reached 40 (I was divorced at 38), my friends all said it was the time when women could ask men out, but I never subscribe to that. You can sort of let men know what you want, but I would never come right out with it. I don't think that works. I think it's the way we're made up – men want to do the chasing and women have to find some clever way of attracting them.

He who asks is a fool for five minutes, but he who does not remains a fool forever.

Chinese proverb

It has long been a cliché that some kind of panic button is flipped inside single, heterosexual men in their 40s, causing them to start driving 'sexy' convertibles and going out with women half their age.

I like the whisky old and the women young.

Errol Flynn

Acquiring a younger 'trophy' wife or girlfriend – or a 'toy boy' – is still fairly common practice among men and women in their 40s (and older), but in my clinical experience I have found such unions do not always fulfil the promise of recaptured youth and a lot of ego-stroking. There are often imbalances of power, status and culture between partners of dissimilar age, although many couples do manage to transcend those. But no matter what age each partner may be, if the purpose of a relationship is more to do with being reflected by a younger, wealthier, more powerful or more attractive person than it is about love and respect, then that 'use' of another may eventually lead to resentment and other negative emotions. These in turn could produce sexual problems.

Although the term 'over the hill' was once commonly used to describe women in their 40s, there has been a positive shift in the way they are now viewed – particularly in terms of their vibrancy. For example, a relatively new dating website, cougar.com, has been established in the USA for older women desiring – or being desired by – younger men. A recent movie script aimed at adolescent boys contained the line 'She's a MILF!' (Mother I'd Like to Fuck).

After my divorce, at 44, I went to an *ashram* in India to get a little 'me' time, and hopefully some personal growth. The only men who hit on me there were young men in their 20s, who were there for different reasons. They were looking for a little 'you and me' time and a great deal of penile growth.

Women with a past interest men because they hope history will repeat itself.

Mae West

Mae West, the epitome of the sexually aggressive 'older' screen siren, and several other assertive and outspoken *femmes fatales*, inspired a whole generation of early 20th-century movie-goers, and continue to do so. They were clearly women who liked sex (at least that was their public image), and were not afraid to appear every bit as predatory as men.

I like to wake up feeling a new man.

Jean Harlow

But not all men are comfortable with outspoken, sexually confident women. Even modern heterosexual feminists may continue to struggle with the integration of their strength, ability, intelligence and their wish to appeal to men.

In my sex fantasy, nobody ever loves me for my mind.

Nora Ephron

The impact of ageing

For the first time, women in their 40s may notice wrinkles and the effects of gravity on their bodies. Many find this distressing (after all, women tend to feel they are in a beauty competition every day of their entire lives), and begin to feel they need to hide or camouflage their bodies. To achieve this, some embark on major reconstruction.

I had my first facelift when I was 41, and I've had more work done every few years since then. I think it's a mistake to do it all at once – it's far too noticeable. This way I can just keep gravity at bay – forever, if necessary. My husband doesn't understand why I do it. He says he would love my body even if I allowed it to age – but you just can't trust men. He says that now, but ten years from now he might run off with his secretary, and then where would I be?

Lack of body confidence can strongly affect anyone's sexuality. Self-consciousness and embarrassment distract us from focusing on pleasure, and obstruct the type of partner connection that promotes eroticism. This can occur in both men and women and, of course, culturally prescribed values in our society – such as the emphasis on slimness – can certainly play their part.

Women say they feel more comfortable undressing in front of men than they do undressing in front of other women. They say that women are too judgemental, where, of course, men are just grateful.

Robert De Niro

Gay men in their 40s have few screen role models, and many have complained to me that they are no longer universally regarded as being sexually vibrant. Some adapt their roles to a 'sugar daddy' status in the hope of attracting young men who value security more than youthful sex. Others, especially those in committed unions, seem more relaxed about the fact that they no longer have the muscle tone or smooth faces of younger men.

Bob is always trying to get me to go to the gym more. It's not like he's a perfect specimen himself, but he excuses himself because he's older and makes more money than I do. I guess he thinks I've got to keep up my status as arm candy. That's all fine and well, but I've got a full-time job, too.

Having a satisfying sex life is by no means dependent on age and appearance, but many people think it is. Being considered sexually desirable by those we want to attract is not something that many people want to relinquish without a fight.

> *The man's desire is for the woman. The woman's desire is for the desire of the man.*
>
> Samuel Taylor Coleridge

Women and gay men seem to have a harder time with this issue than heterosexual men, who often find they can attract women through their apparent ability to be a provider – and that a little power and wealth goes a long way.

> I know I'm not the most attractive man in the universe, and I don't even look after myself particularly well (I like beer too much). If a woman sees me bending over, she's going to be turned off by my flabby backside, but if she sees me in my Ferrari it's a whole different story. OK, I'm a pig, but don't judge me – judge the women who run after me!

If we allow ourselves to be influenced by societal views that sex is only for the young, we will be handicapped in our enjoyment of lifelong sexual happiness. Nevertheless, it is perfectly true that single people in their 40s and beyond begin to be aware that their age is becoming more of an issue, in terms of potential partners.

> In my early 40s, I was very sexually active – one person at time. These relationships were always rather intense. Sex

was one of my favourite parts of any relationship – I had to be very sexually interested in order to be involved. I had realised from the time I was very young that if I really desired a man, I always got him – but that was until I turned 49 and Julio came along. He was beautiful and ten years younger – he'd been a model. I'd never been with a man like that before – I threw myself at him. I lured him to my apartment and into my bed, but then it went the other way. He knew what I wanted, but he didn't want me. I was so shaken – that had never happened to me before. And once you've been burned, you don't want to try again.

Sex in the house

Many people in their 40s are parents of teenagers. As they try to help their children with the many issues of adolescent sexuality, they are often made even more acutely aware of their own sexual struggles – dwindling libido, affairs and a secret yearning for the kind of unstoppable sexual passion (and nubile bodies) their youngsters have. All kinds of unresolved issues can play out between parents and their sexually burgeoning children, and, in many families, sexuality may begin to be the 'elephant in the room'.

Mother seemed envious of me. I didn't fully pick it up at the time, but I think she looked at her own sheltered adolescence, the fact that she married the first man who came along – with whom she lived unhappily ever after – and projected all her fears and wishes and longing on to me. She was super-protective and I was not allowed to date until I was nearly 20. If a boy called up, she would be very cold, or even rude to him.

My 20-year-old daughter came home from university with a broken heart. She was inconsolable for nearly a year. I tried to soothe her, help her through it, but it coincided with my own deep grief when my secret, long-term love affair ended. In a way, I really understood what she was going though; the problem was, I couldn't share my own pain with anyone – especially her. I felt very conflicted.

I found it hard to be welcoming towards my daughter's boyfriends. I understood that she was becoming a young woman and wanted to seek the company of men her age, but they always seemed to arrive with a sexual agenda that was perfectly transparent to me as a man myself – after all, I'd been that age; I knew the score. But she was just in some dizzy, romantic fantasy.

For better, for worse

Being single in our 40s carries both advantages and disadvantages, and it's not easy to negotiate the dating world when we perceive ourselves to be in competition with younger people. But maintaining long-term partnerships through our 40s is not easy, either. Marriages can flounder at any age – and the challenge of sexual fidelity can arise at any time during our sexual life span – but our 40s commonly inspire the moment, possibly because an affair can seem to be a remedy for relationship boredom and the sadness of lost youth.

In my 40s, I suddenly realised that I simply couldn't get all my needs met with just one man. So I started looking around for other men who offered things my husband failed to provide – great sex, for example. This worked pretty well, and made me happier. I felt guilty, but I told myself these other men actually made it possible for me to stay married.

> *Thanks, I enjoyed every inch of it.*
>
> Mae West

We had two children and so, by my 40s, I was a dad and facing an increasingly demanding workload. By my mid-40s, our sex life had become mechanistic and routine, and the issue of my other kinkier tastes was becoming more pressing. I started to seek sexual connections outside the marriage, but always looking for that extra element.

I am not suggesting that every 40-year-old is incapable of fidelity.

> *I gave up screwing around a long time ago. I came to the conclusion that sex is a sublimation of the work instinct.*
>
> David Lodge

Being the creatures we are, at around 40 many committed people begin to be more challenged than they previously were by the prospect of 'till death do us part'. This may have something to do with the approach of midlife, and the 'crisis' that frequently seems to accompany it. When a person of 40-something years begins to subtract her age from her life expectancy, she rarely likes the result.

It was little things at first, but they all added up. I was in a trendy clothing store and a sales assistant asked if I was 'shopping for my daughter'. Delivery men stopped flirting with me. Doors that were previously open no longer seemed to be so. Then one evening I was talking to an attractive man around my own age at a party and all of a sudden I noticed his eyes were wandering around the room, not at all focused on me. He made some pitiful excuse about taking a leak and walked straight over to chat up a much younger woman. All my life I'd been considered a great beauty, and it was painful to lose that.

A sense of loss that comes with ageing can cause people to re-evaluate even long-held principles relating to their current existence, their self-concepts and their relationships, in a manner that can lead to a profound shift. Values may begin to disintegrate, even though their replacements may be entirely at odds with what is socially acceptable. Some people become downright cynical about the idea of monogamy, while others begin to reconsider the whole notion of love and how they relate to others.

> *A man can have two, maybe three, love affairs while he's married. But three is the absolute maximum. After that you're cheating.*
>
> Yves Montand

In many societies, including our own, hypocrisy abounds. Although it's not openly condoned, studies have suggested that a very high proportion of 'committed' people have extra-relational sex. It's difficult to know exactly how common it is, because people are understandably wary of revealing their affairs to researchers.

I have affairs because, although I'm bored with my husband, I don't want to leave him. I don't want our children to suffer, either, so I try to get my needs satisfied and keep the family together. It's not easy, though, and I've nearly been caught a few times.

In my 40s, my sexuality seemed to wane a bit. I had affairs, though, and that kept me in touch with the more sexual side. But I didn't do that after our daughter was born. Having a child meant that sex definitely took a back seat to getting some sleep.

What's more, the prospect of forbidden sex is extremely exciting at any age.

When I was in my early 40s, I moved to the city. I was practically living with my boyfriend. We had some issues because he drank too much and the sex wasn't great. But we were staying at his parents' house for the weekend. There I met his brother, who had been paralysed in an accident. His brother ended up coming on to me and I responded. He was beautiful, a big athlete sitting there in a wheelchair. We didn't get undressed, but he was kissing me and I sat on his lap. He had an erection, although he said he couldn't feel anything there. He was touching me. He said, 'I can imagine doing it.' I was completely turned on, but I was terrified my boyfriend or their parents would catch us. I wanted to continue later, when we could be alone, but this guy went and told his brother –

my boyfriend! First my boyfriend was devastated, and then – and this is so weird – he asked me to marry him. I said, 'No.'

There are many reasons why a person might choose to have an affair.

I had very little time for sex. My husband had a string of affairs … I don't actually blame him!

I began to seek sex elsewhere because I was mad at my husband. I couldn't get what I wanted by asking – he just never listened to me. It was a relief to be with people who seemed to appreciate me.

There's nothing wrong with our relationship. We have good sex, and my wife is a wonderful person – and a great mother. No, when I met Sophie I was not looking for anything more. The truth is … it just happened. I felt horribly guilty. It would have been much easier if I'd hated my wife.

Of course, the discovery of an unsanctioned affair can be devastating to a marriage, and may lead to divorce. Most of us have been brought up to accept the fairytale of 'happily ever after', so the shock, disbelief, sadness and sense of betrayal can be so great that it puts an end to the relationship. But, in fact, many couples manage to get beyond a partner's philandering and use it as an opportunity to re-examine and reaffirm the relationship.

I nearly left him, in fact I had it all arranged – including a mediator who was going to deal with the divorce. But something inside me told me to try to be a bit more mature and consider what was really important. It wasn't as if our sex life was the most important thing in our marriage – in fact, it was way down on the list. And I had a lot to lose. The betrayal side was painful, and I have never managed to trust him again as far as women are concerned – every time he 'works late' I still imagine the worst – but at the end of the day I think I made the right choice to stay. We do care about each other, and have a pretty good marriage – and it would have been devastating for the children. Maybe when they've left home, I'll strike out on my own, but for now I'm staying put.

I say I don't sleep with married men, but what I mean is that I don't sleep with happily married men.

Britt Ekland

The truth is that monogamy is not easy. We value it in our society, but there are other cultures, for example some Inuit tribes, where sexuality outside marriage is sanctioned – although usually according to strictly prescribed rules and conditions. Even in our society there are people who choose to have open marriages, or other types of relationships that depart from the traditional coupling style.

We became 'swingers' a few years ago. We're both in our 40s, and we don't have kids. Both of us have a pretty high sex drive, and are open to different possibilities, so we decided to experiment with other married people. We belong to a private group that organises swingers' parties – usually in a discreet suburban home. There are rules about practising safe sex and 'no' means 'no' – that kind of thing – but apart from that, pretty much anything goes. We pair off with people we're attracted to in different rooms and tell each other about it afterwards. It's a lot of fun, although I wouldn't recommend it for everyone. Problems? Every now and again one of us wants to see someone we've been with again – without our spouses – but that's against our rules.

Paying the price

In trying to meet the challenges of monogamy, many people to whom I have spoken have decided that paying professional sex workers for erotic experiences is preferable to having affairs. They consider the anonymity to be less threatening to the marriage than getting involved with someone who might potentially disrupt the primary relationship with emotions and demands.

> *The big difference between sex for money and sex for*
> *free is that sex for money usually costs a lot less.*
> Brendan Francis

Paying for sex with a prostitute (or a gold-digging lover) is not for everyone, and many people are critical of the sex industry for all kinds of very good reasons. But the fact remains that sex workers will always be available if a person wants to hire them.

My boyfriend is a lot younger than me (I'm in my 40s), and although he say he loves me, I'm always worried that he might fancy younger women. I try to make our sex life as exciting as possible because I want him to stick around. On his birthday I took him to a gentlemen's club. There were lots of girls stripping on stage – all different types in terms of size, colour, ethnicity and so on, and I asked him to point out the one he liked best. He did – she was a bit like a younger version of me! I paid for a private room and the three of us retired inside. First she took off all her clothes (except her high heels) and gave him a lap dance. I took my top off, and the two of us played with each other while he watched – I could tell that was really turning him on! Then we both worked on him until he came … he said it was his favourite present ever …

There's no greater fan of the opposite sex, and I have the bills to prove it.

Alan Jay Lerner

For one night only

Some people are simply not interested in a relationship, preferring to seek sexual experiences that are not 'meaningful' and apparently devoid of emotional attachment. These are not necessarily just one-night stands – some people meet for regular sex, on the understanding that it's purely about physical pleasure.

We were friends and we both knew exactly what it was about: sexual gratification, pure and simple. Our situations were different – his wife was unable to make love due to ill-health and lack of interest, and I was in a long-distance relationship with a man with whom I was very dissatisfied (and eventually left). My two friends who knew about our 'arrangement' both warned me that I would be the one to start having feelings I couldn't hide – but that didn't happen. Actually, it was he who turned around after two years and offered to leave his wife for me. But that was not what I wanted. I didn't want us to get to the point where I'd have to start washing his underwear. I loved the passion, excitement and irresponsibility of things exactly the way they were.

The perfect lover is one who turns into a pizza at four am.

Charles Pierce

Getting it up

Although sexual dysfunction can occur at any time, the 40s is commonly the time when some start to struggle with sexual problems such as erectile issues, orgasmic problems or dyspareunia (painful sex).

I had no idea smoking affected my erections. They should put that on the pack.

Since my mid-30s I've had a long struggle with vulvar vestibulitis [pain and/or inflammation at the entrance to the vagina]. The first doctor I saw thought it was a psychological problem, because things apparently 'looked normal', but the pain I was having was affecting my sex life and my relationship, and making me very anxious. I finally found support online, and a practitioner who knew what to do.

I've never had an orgasm. This didn't bother me until I reached my 40s, started being more open with other women, and realised that they experienced something I didn't. I got a book, *Becoming Orgasmic,* and have started having some sex counselling. I have yet to climax, but I'm discovering a lot about my body and sexuality – I had no idea how naïve I was.

In the past I'd had the odd problem getting hard, but I usually put it down to having too many beers, or to stress, etc. But it gradually dawned on me, when I was around 45, that my erections were not quite as immediate as they once were. I could be with the most desirable woman in the world and that still didn't make a difference. I worried that I was soon going to be completely impotent, like my father was at the same age. I went to see my doctor and he reassured me that it was normal to be slowing down a bit at my age, and that it wouldn't affect my ability to be a good lover. That was quite a relief. Now I wonder if my father could have had the same reassurance, maybe he wouldn't have just given up and shut down the way he did.

Yes, one of the biggest sexual myths is that men automatically lose their ability to have erections as they age. They don't, but they may start to take a little longer to get hard, just as ageing women also take a little longer to produce the necessary amount of lubrication for intercourse. A fuller discussion of the physiological changes that may occur as people age will be found in Chapter 6, but suffice it to say that from this point in life on, maintaining one's sexual health may require a little extra work.

When my husband was younger (now he's 49) he had these *boing!* erections, pointing straight up to heaven. Over the years, these have lowered, and now they sort of point at the wall. He doesn't have them so readily, either, and when I first noticed this, I thought it was me. I thought he was bored or not so attracted to me anymore. But we talked about it and I eventually learned not to take it personally. Now I help get him started by paying more direct attention to his penis.

The angle of the dangle is proportional to the heat of the meat provided that the urge to surge remains constant.

Author unknown

That's not true. And all kinds of things can influence a man's erectile capacity, including smoking, drinking and taking various types of drugs – prescription and otherwise. Women's sexuality can also be affected by medication and other substances – as well as natural hormonal changes that affect the way our bodies work. They can have arousal, lubricating or orgasmic difficulties, often without realising why.

We got married when we were both 18. Fifteen years later, my husband became clinically depressed and his doctor gave him some pills to improve his mood. Unfortunately, this medication took away his sex drive altogether, so we went from having very little sex to having no sex at all. I didn't realise that it was the pills until about 18 months later, when I caught a TV documentary about it. It happens to a lot of people. My husband asked for a change in medication to something without sexual side-effects, but in the meantime I had started having sex with a co-worker. It was a mess, and nearly ruined our marriage. That's the sort of thing your doctor should tell you.

I had no idea my cold remedy was causing my vaginal dryness, although I suppose it stands to reason. If it's drying up the mucus in your nose, I suppose it doesn't confine itself to one area.

The problem I was having getting hard appeared rather suddenly – one minute my girlfriends thought I was a bit of a stud, then the next minute both Larraine and Bettina had the same complaint. My doctor did some tests and discovered that I had some vascular issues. It was a relief to know there was a reason for it – and that it could be treated.

Like men, women can have trouble becoming physiologically aroused – specifically, becoming sufficiently lubricated for comfortable vaginal penetration. This issue will particularly affect those who enter early menopause, but it can creep up on any woman as she begins to age because producing less vaginal lubrication is not as immediately apparent as being unable to get an erection. Some women are taken by surprise when intercourse suddenly becomes painful. But putting up with the pain is a mistake, as repetition can lead to a more serious problem known as 'vaginismis' (a condition where vaginal muscle spasm prevents penile entry).

I entered menopause at 43, and it was a shock to realise that it was happening so early. I thought I had at least another ten years or so. I took hormone therapy, because it was before there was all that concern about safety, and I barely noticed any sexual problems – or any side-effects at all, once I started on the HT. But when I stopped taking it four years ago, I found that my desire plummeted for a while. It wasn't just that I lost interest in having sex so much – it was more that I felt drier and intercourse was painful. I put up with it because I didn't want to disappoint my husband, but after a while it was really hard for my vagina to open for intercourse at all. I went to a sex therapist, and had treatment for vaginismus.

It can't have escaped anyone that there are all kinds of sexual 'enhancement' drugs on the market for both men and women, but it's worth considering that when nature slows down our responses, we can counteract that in a highly pleasurable and natural way by putting a few brakes on our lovemaking – instead of rushing – and taking all the time we need to become fully aroused.

Anything worth doing well is worth doing slowly.
Gypsy Rose Lee

Of course, a little additional over-the-counter lubrication provides extra insurance against dryness and irritation – especially if you're planning a sexual marathon with an impatient man. But teaching your partner exactly what you like is always worth the effort. No one's a mind-reader!

What women really want is three hours of goddamned foreplay.
Dan Greenburg

As well as the issues described above, there are a few other things that can lead to sexual problems when we are in our 40s. For example, repetitive sex in long-term relationships can become extremely boring.

It's always the same pattern. Clockwork. He does half a minute of perfunctory twiddling upstairs, then it's down to the basement for four minutes of grinding – and Bob's your uncle. I keep wanting to say something but, quite honestly, I'm pretty busy, too.

> *I can never understand why most people have sex so quickly. You'd think they didn't enjoy it, the way they plunge in, thrash up and down, and then turn their backs on each other and go to sleep.*
>
> Graham Masterton

Creating excitement

For some people, being creative in bed simply means rearranging the pillowcases. However, just as they might have done in their 30s, 40-somethings who feel that their sex lives need a boost may experiment with different styles of coupling, or other new methods of enhancing eroticism such as sex toys or acting out fantasies. Others may try to revive a flagging drive by using erotic literature or audio/visual material – which, in some cases, can certainly help.

I was never really one for porn, but one day I was channel-surfing, and instead of flicking quickly past the sex channels, I decided to check them out. It was a revelation.

Most of it was aimed at men, but I found it quite a turn-on just seeing people having sex – albeit simulated in many cases, I suppose. Anyway, I got to understand what all the fuss was about. I learned a few things, too, and tried them out on my husband. For example, I'd never been keen on getting on top and didn't quite know how to move my hips the right way but, after receiving this visual example, I decided to give it a go. My husband was so surprised, he thought I'd either gone mad or was having an affair! I showed him the sexy channel and we've been using it for 'research' ever since!

Madame Bovary *is the sexiest book imaginable. The woman's virtually a nymphomaniac but you won't find a vulgar word in the entire thing.*

Noël Coward

Erotica is not always the answer to the problem of a dwindling erotic connection. Poor-quality sex (or lack of it) can be a very painful issue in any relationship, and it is wise to address it – at least by talking about it. Sexuality is extremely important to many people and, although they may not say so, dissatisfaction can make one or both partners extremely miserable. In fact, it can even become a relationship 'deal-breaker'.

I had a difficult time in my 40s. My husband was not very sexual.

For whatever complicated reason that was never sorted out in therapy, I have never been truly, sensually turned on by my husband. He feels the same about me. In order to keep some semblance of a complete marriage, we have tried hard to keep up the sexual part of our marriage. When the marriage was at issue over deception on his part, I was able to rouse some deep need in myself and actually make it happen more often – and in a more pleasurable way.

How exactly do you keep your marriage sexually alive after a very long time together? Instead of putting up with lack of passion, some people allow themselves – and their partners – to continue to develop as sexual human beings. One excellent strategy for achieving this – and busting that boring status quo – is for partners to work on their individual capacity for experiencing both sides of the pleasure equation. Some people are more comfortable in receiving or taking pleasure than they are in giving it, while others are the opposite. If a 'receiver' can lessen the focus on his own progression to orgasm and instead practise new pleasuring skills with his partner's guidance, the couple's combined erotic experience can be greatly enhanced. Likewise, if a person who tends to dismiss his or her pleasure in favour of being accommodating – or hoping to achieve the status of 'a perfect lover' – switches roles and allows a partner to provide pleasure, there will be multiple benefits.

Sex is a two-way treat.
Franklin P. Jones

It's never been easy for me to just lie back and enjoy myself, and that has interfered with my ability to have orgasms. My partner is very generous, and loves to spend ages down there giving me oral pleasure, but if it goes on too long I find myself worrying that he's hurting his back or getting irritated. I often get to the point when I start turning off, and so I just pull his head up and ask for inter- course. But I can't come when he's inside me, so I end up frustrated and trying to give myself an orgasm in the shower. It makes me so mad, and I can see that he gets disappointed, too.

It totally goes against the grain for me to totter round in high heels and a teddy. If my feminist friends saw me, they'd be shocked. But quite honestly it makes me *sooo* hot to allow myself to be his plaything!

> *Strong women leave big hickeys.*
>
> Madonna

Couples who manage to maintain their individuality may be better equipped to foster a more exciting, long-term sexual connection. Being too enmeshed – and feeling that a partner's actions are always predictable – is not conducive to main- taining a flourishing sex life.

People grow up with differing attitudes to the notion of pleasure in general – not just sex, but relaxation, savouring taste and texture, and so on. Some learn early on that pleasure is a gift – that it can be allowed in their lives to be cherished and sought after. But other people learn more limiting messages as they are growing up – that suffering is better for the soul, and that allowing oneself to enjoy pleasure will court accompanying feelings of guilt.

Sex is as important as eating or drinking, and we ought to allow the one appetite to be satisfied with as little restraint or false modesty as the other.

Marquis de Sade

Learning the art of catching those negative thoughts and replacing them with more positive 'self-talk' is one way to deal with long-standing sexual guilt.

Sometimes when he's touching me – as opposed to when I'm doing something to him – this nagging voice inside says, 'You shouldn't be expecting him to spend so much time on this.' I think I've learned that the voice is my mother's – she was very much one who believed in 'Take care of the man at all costs.' Now I wear a rubber band on my wrist. My therapist taught me to snap it, to jolt me away from those thoughts when I notice them. Instead, I try to say to myself like a mantra, 'I deserve to enjoy sex as much as he does – and he *likes* giving me pleasure!'

I find it hard to change that part of me that says I have to give a 'perfect performance' in bed. I worry so much about getting a 'good review' afterwards that I don't really enjoy it at the time. Sometimes my anxiety affects my erection, and the whole thing becomes a self-fulfilling prophecy. I have to try very hard to tell myself I don't have to get an A+ and focus on being in the moment.

Relaxing into it

In our 40s – if not before – it is worth examining our individual attitudes. If taking a leisurely bath is not something you can do without keeping one guilty eye on the clock – and an ear out for signs from others that there are other things to attend to – it is likely that sexuality will also be a hurried, awkward and stolen respite. Many people could benefit from making sex a higher priority, although some think that that would require changing an attitude that's culturally prescribed.

> *Continental people have a sex life; the English have hot-water bottles.*
>
> George Mikes

Some people even find it difficult to take a holiday, or allow themselves to enjoy a massage. Experiencing sexual pleasure or sensuality requires being able to focus on it without too many distractions or feelings of guilt, embarrassment, worry or anxiety. This is traditionally a little more difficult for women than for men, since there still exists a legacy from former eras which suggests that allowing oneself pleasure is unseemly in a 'lady'.

> *Sex hasn't been the same since women started enjoying it.*
>
> Lewis Grizzard

Yet our 40s may be the perfect time to begin savouring sex and sensuality more. After all, what's the rush?

> *For flavour, instant sex will never supersede the stuff you have to peel and cook.*
>
> Quentin Crisp

Reducing tension and stress by exercising and learning to say 'no' to people who would overwhelm you with unnecessary demands and projects can help to foster a healthy sex life. In particular, yoga and meditation are tried-and-tested methods of being more at peace with yourself, so that fun and pleasure can be welcomed into your life. Laughing more, being able to see the funny side of life's situations – including sex – will help with general relaxation and can reduce anxiety.

I love being silly in bed. I draw imaginary pictures on his back and ask him to guess what it is. Sometimes I nip him to the point where he starts to get annoyed – then I switch course and go down on him.

If somebody makes me laugh I'm his slave for life.
Bette Midler

We still horseplay during sex a lot – it's about the only time I feel like a kid again. Sometimes it gets a bit too much, though – like when my partner pins me down and 'play forces' me. It's on the edge of saying 'yes' and saying 'no', and it slightly scares me sometimes. I do know he'd never actually hurt or rape me, though.

You have to accept that part of the sizzle of sex comes from the danger of sex. You can be overpowered.
Camille Paglia

Sex has long been considered dangerous – especially for those who have embarked on spiritual paths. But choosing not to have sex – or not being allowed to – can present a whole different set of adult sexual challenges.

> I became a nun when I was in my 20s, but that doesn't mean I don't notice men or have sexual thoughts about them. I know I betray myself when occasionally I giggle and blush. I have chosen a higher path, but that does not mean I don't struggle with my womanly passions.

I want to be liberated and still be able to have a nice ass and shake it.

Shirley MacLaine

Different needs

A lack of sexual feelings can be as much of a problem as unwanted ones. For example, discrepancies between two partners' level of desire or frequency of needs can be perceived as a problem at any stage of a couple's relationship. Although this can certainly cause sadness and resentment, the issue is often temporary. It's perfectly expectable that each person's desire should fluctuate from time to time, as he or she goes through different stages and different challenges in life. Occasionally it can be a serious problem – depending on the reasons and the length of time it continues – but some couples become overly worried about short-term desire discrepancies.

> He started saying I was a 'nympho' and that I needed to chill out. I reminded him that two years ago, when I was post-partum and he had gone back to the gym, it was *me* telling him that *he* was oversexed! Then we had a good laugh and decided to leave the name-calling to our kids.

Critical language is never useful, nor is forcing yourself to be sexual with a partner when you really don't feel in the mood. Within any relationship, it should be okay to say 'no'.

Sex and self-image

People in their 40s who take care of their bodies through a healthy diet and exercise and take steps to reduce their stress, will feel better about themselves. They will have a better body image and feel more attractive (if we feel attractive, others tend to think think we are too). The result? Your libido will be higher.

> I find that if I pay attention to the way I look – maybe dress up, get my nails done, wear some lacy underwear – I am more open to responding to subtle advances by others. I rarely sleep with people I've only just met, but the point is that I like to feel that the option is there. The days when the option is not there are the days I wear my reducing bra and old knickers.

Depression, anxiety and sleep problems (such as insomnia or sleep apnoea) can all affect sex and relationships. The arrival of such problems should be taken seriously, and treatment should be sought. Likewise, having to face serious physical illness or disability can present serious challenges to the maintenance of our sex lives at any age.

> One of the awful things about going through chemo was constantly getting thrush. It just never seemed to go away, I suppose that's because my immune system was down.

But the worst thing was feeling a burden to my husband and family. I somehow decided I wasn't good enough for anything – including sex. We had a couple of failed attempts at lovemaking, which reaffirmed this. But eventually I got well enough to take care of the family again and my confidence began to be restored – and then our sex life returned.

Our sexuality is certainly very much connected to our self-image and sense of self-worth, and it can deteriorate if those become devalued. Above all, hanging on to a view of ourselves as vibrant sexual beings – and ignoring the ageism that would suggest people over 40 (or those suffering from physical challenges) are not – will play a huge part in maintaining a healthy and enjoyable sex life.

Never be ashamed of passion. If you are strongly sexed, you are richly endowed.

Margaret Sanger

Getting flirty

Sometimes people in committed relationships are afraid to flirt, but I happen to think it can be a good thing. Social dancing is probably the most common and acceptable way for people to engage in a little 'safe' hanky-panky.

Dancing is a perpendicular expression of a horizontal desire.

George Bernard Shaw

Obviously, destructive flirting – for example, to deliberately hurt one's partner or in a business situation – is fraught with potential problems. But if there's no threat of a lawsuit, and if you're a good judge of how it is being received (in other words, not too seriously), flirting playfully can be uplifting and fun. Note: this advice is not for people who tend to over-step boundaries!

> *There are times not to flirt. When you're sick. When you're with children. When you're on the witness stand.*
>
> Joyce Jillson

Generally allowing yourself to be more playful can be life-affirming and increase your optimism and joyful outlook on life. Too often, couples get so bogged down in their duties, responsibilities and work, they forget to have fun together.

> It had been years since we took time off and holidayed together. But last year my partner said, 'I think we need a break – just the two of us.' With our finances not so great, I was reluctant, but even the budget trip we took made a real difference. You forget how much more you feel like having sex when you're warm and relaxed. Not having to get the 7.15 train in the morning helps as well.

A little imagination

Sometimes, we need to throw caution to the wind and try something new. I've already pointed out that following the same pattern in bed, will usually lead to sexual *ennui*. Not everyone is willing to take risks – either in the bedroom or out of it – but there can be benefits to occasionally doing something we fear. Even taking up a new hobby – or trying a little thrill-seeking – can get your adrenaline going and foster a zest for living that may transfer to one's sex life.

> *An improper mind is a perpetual feast.*
> Logan Pearsall Smith

Some people harbour hidden desires for certain sexual styles they're afraid to try. Some only fantasise about them, but others seem to be braver.

> I decided: what can I lose? He might tell me that I'm disgusting, but it's worth a try. Well, he did say I was disgusting – but in a good way!

At 40, a person might be lucky enough to have reached the point where he or she feels safe enough to tell a partner about particular fantasies (you never know, they just might be shared – and if not, who really cares?). Many people have found it rewarding to not only describe a fantasy, but to suggest an actual performance (provided, of course, that it is harmless and consensual).

> I told her I imagined her waiting for me on the bed, completely naked with just her long, black boots on. A few nights later I came home to exactly that image!

> I'm proud to say that I'm pretty kinky, and most of my sexual scenes nowadays start off as fantasies that I first

imagine, then plan, then act out with a like-minded wild woman.

I've noticed that some people in their 40s, who have been very sexually experimental earlier in their lives, sometimes want to try something more 'vanilla' – in other words, more conventional. Even people who are lifestylers in BDSM (bondage, domination and sado-masochism) can experience burnout and gravitate towards something simpler and more intimate in a traditional sense. Sexually speaking, you are allowed to change your mind!

> *Some mornings, it's just not worth chewing through the leather straps.*
>
> Emo Phillips

Communication

I've already pointed out that if underlying anger, guilt, resentment or other negative emotions are present in a relationship, they will affect our sex lives. Learning to fight and resolve conflicts – and even make up with great sex – is an important skill to acquire.

> *There are some things that happen in the dark between two people that make everything that happens in the light seem all right.*
>
> Erica Jong

Sex should not be the last chore of the evening. Planning time for it may not match fantasies of spontaneity, but it should ensure that intimacy actually occurs without interruption. Keeping a sexual score is counterproductive, and the essence of developing into skilled, intelligent lovers is achieving good sexual communication.

One way to heighten pleasure is to avoid distractions and try to focus fully on sensations. If other thoughts creep in, push them gently aside. Experiment with different types of touching (both giving and receiving) and stroking, and allow pleasure to permeate your whole body.

> Our sex therapist gave us this 'homework exercise', where we took it in turns to explore each other's bodies without touching each other's genitals. Starting with our hands, we moved to faces, then backs then fronts – leaving out breasts, anus and genitals. I could not have imagined it would be as exciting as it was. It was tantalising to have forbidden areas, but more than that we discovered all kinds of special areas that each of us loves to be stroked – butts, forearm and feet in her case, and feet, torso and butt in mine. It was a revelation.

> *Sex, unlike war, is far too grave a matter to be left to the privates.*
>
> Michael Haaren

Being able to guide your partner in a non-threatening way can be the key to not only to getting what you want, but also helping your partner to feel good about pleasing you.

> *Sex is conversation carried out by other means.*
>
> Peter Ustinov

I'm not used to being open about my sexual needs, but once I understood that he really wanted to please me – and was really grateful for any tips I could give him about that – I began to guide his hand to where it felt best, and even took the initiative to reposition us if it wasn't working.

In our 40s, we should be able to resist the patterns of sexual behaviour that are being set up for us by porn and internet sex. We can take it in turns to bring each other to climax exactly the way we want to.

> *More experienced and sensitive lovers enjoy their partner's climactic transports, which they are unable to do if they orgasm simultaneously.*
>
> Francis Stubbs

Some people are afraid of intimacy. That's not the same as being afraid of sex; they can be confident about that, yet fear what accompanies it – being vulnerable to rejection or at risk of suffering performance failure. For some people, showing another human being who they truly are is terrifying and painful.

> *When you sleep with someone, you take off a lot more than your clothes.*
>
> Anna Quindlen

If two people share the erotic responsibility – taking it in turns to initiate it, making sure there are no interruptions (mobiles off – check!) and setting up their environment for sex in whatever way is most pleasing to each other (whether that be lighting scented candles or getting out the blindfold, feathers, ice cubes or paddles!) – the stage is set for an extended period of delightful relaxation and mutual pleasure. In our 40s we are just starting to be ready for the serious business of sexual enhancement – a process that may continue into later decades.

Cellulite is highly correlated with sexual expertise.
David Schnarch

In order to move beyond the sameness and predictability that can annihilate passion, a couple's best bet is to work on improving their interpersonal connection, their lovemaking skills and their level of sexual sophistication. It's also a matter of attitude; unfortunately, some people in their 40s and beyond are stuck in a rut.

Oh, come on! It's been 25 years! Enough already!

By contrast, colluding in and supporting each other's sexual growth – both individually and collectively – is an optimistic, life-affirming and loving process. Oh, and did I mention it can lead to unbelievably hot eroticism? In fact, it can supersede the excitement of earlier years by a long shot.

The true feeling of sex is that of a deep intimacy, but above all of a deep complicity.
James Dickey

7

In Our 50s
Preparing for Sexual Longevity

If you want to improve sex, ask, 'What do you enjoy?
What do you feel? Because I care.'

William Masters

n our 50s, new challenges may require us to work harder to maintain our sexual health. Navigating menopause, dealing with hormonal changes and having potentially serious diseases such as cancer can all affect sexuality; however many people have fantastic sex during this decade – partly because they are smart enough to slow down and enjoy it more. Some are becoming empty-nesters and actually have more uninterrupted time to spend in the pursuit of pleasure.

It is commonly believed that we automatically lose our sexual desire and ability as we get older. This is absolutely *not* true! But certain changes do take place, and it's worth being aware of these so that, if necessary, they can be counter-balanced in appropriate ways. For example, many women find that in their 50s – and beyond – their lubricating process takes longer; in other words, the way their vaginas become slippery inside is different from the way they when they were in their 20s – and they may not produce as much fluid as they did in earlier years.

I remember when I was much younger, I'd suddenly be aware of two things that seemed to happen simultaneously – my mental lust for someone and a 'wet' feeling in my crotch. Sometimes the lust thing was so strong, it would make me dizzy, while I used to feel embarrassed about the wetness because I thought it would gush out and everyone would know.

Things are a bit different now. I have to ask my partner to slow down because I need time to get wet enough inside. When I'm too dry, sex can hurt.

These days I sort of know when I want to have sex with my partner, but it can take me by surprise. Once we start, though, I really get into it.

I always get ready eventually, but if he enters me too early it doesn't feel comfortable. We use personal lubricants sometimes, but my favourite way to have sex is for him to make me come with his tongue first. Then I'm wonderfully wet – and enjoy intercourse much more.

Some women experience no difference in the amount or quality of their vaginal lubrication, while others notice a thinning of their mucus.

I used to think it was the consistency of Béarnaise sauce; now it's more of a vinaigrette!

Researchers tell us that as women age, both the length and the width of the vagina decrease. In canvassing personal opinions about this, I found that few women in their 50s or beyond were aware of such changes, and several women said they didn't believe this had occurred. But it's subjective, isn't it? All of these women were sexually active.

I've been having sex with the same man for over 30 years. We've always 'fit together' nicely, and I'm sure I would have noticed if that had changed.

During my 50s, I had seven or eight sexual partners, each with different-sized penises that ranged from smallish to on the large side, and some were quite wide. I seemed to be able to accommodate each of them perfectly well.

When I was 58, I was travelling abroad and had an affair with a much younger man. He was pretty athletic in bed, and his penis was quite big, and wide on the end. I was a bit nervous about keeping up with him, but actually managed it quite well – except that my vagina didn't seem to stretch as well as it did when I was younger, and after prolonged intercourse there tended to be a bit of blood. He just thought I was having a period! As if!

Ask any married woman the difference between a husband and a toy boy, and she'll tell you the same thing. About three hours.

Kathy Lette

An extended period of thrusting isn't always what a woman wants – at any age – but it may be even less desirable for women who are not lubricating as prolifically as they once did, and who are not on hormone replacement therapy (which supports the lubricating process). Another sexual change thought to occur in ageing women is that as they approach orgasm, the feeling of inevitability is less obvious and doesn't last as long. I asked a few women about this, and most of them found it difficult to imagine.

I've never even thought about what happens just before I come. It's usually something like, 'Don't stop what you're doing or I'll have to kill you!'

Once I know I'm going to come, I'm usually just trying to stay in that delicious state for as long as possible. I don't think that's changed at all.

Now that you've described it, I get it. You're talking about that period of thrashing about trying to come before the kids come barging in. Yeah, it's definitely got shorter since they got old enough to know what we're doing!

That's one of the problems with sexual research – it's hard for people to describe their sexual responses, even if they're willing to try. Here's one 56-year-old woman's subjective description of her most recent sexual experience. It really illustrates some discrepancies that can occur between sexual partners of different ages – although these do not necessarily inhibit pleasure at all.

My boyfriend catches me in the shower and wants to get in with me. I let him in and he stands behind me, and starts soaping up my breasts – which I love. I can feel him getting hard against my bottom. He touches my stomach, which I don't love because, unlike him, I've got a bit of a spare tyre (he's 15 years younger), but I'm grateful for my gym work-outs that have left me in reasonable shape. I am distracted by thinking that I need to lower the bathroom lighting for occasions such as this. I pull my focus back to him, wind my arms round him and feel his firm backside. Then I slip one hand between my butt and him and start stroking his cock. He takes the hint and starts 'soaping' my vulva, and I get even more turned on. The soap helps to make me feel wet and ready, but I'm worried about letting him enter me because the soap and water combination might make me uncomfortably dry. He tries to bend me over to enter me from the rear, but I resist this and instead distract him by turning round, kneeling and sucking him. There's a taste of soap – I have to aim more water on his cock to get it off, then go at it with relish. He is enormously excited – and way ahead of me. I want him to slow down and wish we could dry off and go to the bedroom for a longer session, but he's too far gone for that. He comes in my mouth and I hide my disappointment. I could ask him to touch me until I come, but this time I decide to let him off. He's so happy. I lock him out of the bathroom, return to my shower – and make myself come. I'm definitely very aroused, and it doesn't take too long. I never want to make a big deal about being out of step with him, because I want to keep him happy.

Younger men

It is not uncommon for women in their 50s and beyond to turn to younger men for sexual pleasure.

I don't like the term 'cougar', but I suppose I fall into that category. I am definitely very attracted to younger men, and not at all interested in men my own age. I'm always surprised when a very young man seems interested in me, too – but I do have a few things to offer. My experience seems to be a plus, and I talk to them about their careers and give useful advice. I'm also pretty good in the sack, and they appreciate that. I teach them things younger women never showed them. They don't stay around too long, though – a year or two at the most – and then they find girls their own age. I tend to fall in love with them (I wish I could be more like men and keep my emotions out of it) and I've had my heart broken a few times.

Many men are attracted to older women, although it is usually believed to be more common for younger women to want older men. For a young man, there can be considerable benefits to be gained from being with an older women. Aside from her sexual expertise, many men appreciate being taken care of in emotional, financial and other ways.

> *Twenty goes into 50 a lot easier than 50 goes into 20.*
>
> Bette Midler

Now that I'm 56 – no longer a young chick – I'm always surprised that the men who seem to be interested in me are much younger. They may look good, but I think, 'Oh my God, I have nothing to talk to them about.' My ego is soothed, but I get depressed because I think there isn't going to be any kind of a relationship.

> *Older women are best because they think they might be doing it for the last time.*
>
> Ian Fleming

The problem with ageing

As men age, they too undergo certain changes – although these do not have to interfere with their ability to continue having satisfying sex throughout their lives. When men are young, their erections happen quite instantaneously; for example, whenever visual cues trigger them.

She gave me a smile I could feel in my hip pocket.
Raymond Chandler

But as I explained earlier, ageing men typically take a bit longer to get an erection. It doesn't happen so much on cue, and it may not always be quite as firm as it used to be.

My body used to know that I wanted a guy even before I did. My erections were frequent and completely spontaneous – sometimes embarrassingly so. These days I tend to think 'he's hot' quite a few minutes before I get that tight feeling in my jeans. In other words, I'll know in my mind that I want to have sex with him – but my erection takes a bit longer to get going.

I started noticing that Bob didn't seem quite as pleased to see me naked as he used to (you know that old Mae West line: 'Is that a gun in your pocket or are you just pleased to see me?'), and it really worried me. I thought I was no longer turning him on. I even wondered if he was having an affair with someone who did. Luckily I heard a doctor on the radio saying that it's normal for men, as they get older, to take a bit longer to get hard and that their partners shouldn't take it personally.

Men of a certain age usually require more direct stimulation of their penises in order to get hard enough for intercourse; so, if they haven't done so already, this is a good time for their partners to perfect their manual and oral skills. Unfortunately, that doesn't always happen.

> Over the years I usually had orgasms with my husband's penetration. He gave me oral sex early on in our lives – the first time I had an orgasm that way I nearly hit the roof! It was a huge surprise. I guess it was my preferred style of sex. But after he began to have problems with erections, he chose not to give me pleasure with his tongue anymore. I was on oestrogen after my hysterectomy and it made me feel very sexy, so I was unhappy that my husband just didn't seem interested.

Men in their 50s and beyond will not usually have the type of 'point-to-the-ceiling' erections that are characteristic of younger men. Some do not even achieve a completely stiff erection until just before they orgasm. But people find all kinds of creative ways to get things going.

> I've had to get a lot better at making him hard with my mouth. Earlier in our lives he'd be hard or semi-hard when I started, but now I'm usually starting from scratch. That used to put me off, but now I'm pretty confident that if I persevere he's going to get erect enough for a great bonk. Not bad for a couple of grandparents, eh?

> Lately my partner has had some dysfunction with maintaining an erection ... Viagra has sorted that. And porn helps with libido problems.

One of the most worrying sexual issues that men can face as they age is their fear of losing 'potency', and that fear itself can create such anxiety that it makes it less likely an erection will occur.

> He was humiliated twice, three times – so he was not going to try again. I've never been that confident. I'd never had to encourage him before, so I guess I thought he didn't like me.

> We joked about the effects of Viagra when we saw the ads on TV. He said, 'Never!' He wouldn't want to be embarrassed if it didn't work.

> *An erection is a mysterious thing. There's always that fear, each time one goes, that you won't be seeing it again.*
>
> Kirk Douglas

If only men could understand that, as far as most women are concerned, 'potency' or sexual prowess is not really about having reliably hard penises, because they're not reliant on a penis for either pleasure or orgasm. But for a man, being hard is a sign of success, and not getting hard equals failing.

> Once I'm hard, the sex is as good as ever. Oh, but I can't go again as quickly as I used to.

The period of time between a man's orgasm and when he can get an erection again is known as the 'refractory period'. As a man ages, this usually becomes a longer interval. It is also true that men of any age will take longer to ejaculate with each subsequent orgasm (unlike women, who may find that additional orgasms happen faster after the first one).

Sex is more fun than cars, but cars refuel quicker than men.

Germaine Greer

Once upon a time I could come and then get hard again within a few minutes – although it usually took a bit longer to come the second and third time round. Now I'm not really ready again for quite a few hours – and sometimes for even a day or two.

I can make love to two women in one day, but to the same woman only once every two days. It strikes me that God's trying to tell me something.

Losing the ability to be orgasmic again and again can be tough for men who have previously been extremely sexually active, or whose partners expect repeat performances.

I used to pride myself on being able to do it several times in one night – but that was a good 20 years ago. Nowadays I can only manage once – or maybe twice on a really good night with a very exciting partner. But I've learned to value quality over quantity.

Why is food better than sex? Because you don't have to wait an hour for seconds.

Author unknown

Remaining orgasmic

By contrast, women of any age seem to remain capable of having multiple orgasms – in other words, one after the other.

I have always liked to have several orgasms in the one lovemaking session, and I've found my partners are usually tickled pink that I can do that. After it's all over, I sometimes masturbate once more for good luck. I suppose I'm just greedy! This has not changed over the years; in fact, I now know more about my body and am better at teaching my lovers how to please me. Any shyness I once had about that has completely disappeared over the years.

Some older men and women say that the intensity of their orgasms has diminished, while others claim that their orgasms are just as wonderful as they were in their teens.

I definitely had stronger orgasms when I was first married. Now the earth doesn't move quite so much – but it's still very good.

When I was in my 20s, I took my orgasms for granted. In the right situation they just happened. Now I find that I have to really focus on staying relaxed – and I usually fantasise to help me get 'over the edge' – even when I'm with a partner.

I suppose it might be because I no longer have issues with enjoying sex – my concerns about right or wrong, about pregnancy and about being interrupted by children are long gone – but I definitely enjoy it more and always have great orgasms. I'm much better at letting my partner know what I want, too – that didn't happen when I was younger.

Sex toys or other sexual-enhancement products can be helpful in increasing excitement that will lead to orgasm, and some people in their 50s are experimenting with them for the first time in their lives.

> I use vibrators (Rampant Rabbit) and tried a butt plug ... but my husband was not happy with the butt plug so I have discontinued.

> My partner and I sometimes just wander round a sex shop to see if there's anything that turns us on. Half the time we don't buy anything – just the ideas we get in there turn us on so much we race home to bed.

Experimenting with different styles of sexual enhancement is the right idea, but the same things don't always work for both partners.

> Nowadays we watch quite a bit of porn online ... but I find it is really all aimed at men ... rather unsatisfactory from my point of view

Some women in their 50s have reported having less desire and less clitoral sensitivity than they did when they were younger.

> I got to the point where I just didn't feel like it. I forced myself to try, though, because my husband wanted to keep our sex lives going, and when he says he still fancies me, I believe him. I'd hate him to have sex with someone else, so I did my best to seem interested.

I frequently hear older people – both men and women – say that it takes them a bit longer to reach orgasm.

At 19, I remember doing anything I could to avoid ejaculating too fast – for example, thinking about unpleasant things like exams – because I tended to have a real problem holding off long enough for my partners' liking. But now I have no such problem; in fact, I'd say I'm a much better lover now because it takes me a lot longer to come.

I noticed that once I started on hormone therapy, including a little testosterone, my orgasms – which had become a bit lacklustre – returned to the way they were before.

Some women find that hormone replacement therapy (HRT) can restore orgasmic capacity, improve desire and vaginal elasticity, and increase lubrication. For many, this will mean that intercourse is less likely to be painful. However, choosing to take hormone replacement therapy – oestrogen, testosterone, or any other hormone or combination – is a personal (and controversial) decision that should be made in consultation with your doctor, after a careful weighing-up of the risks and benefits. There are a number of herbal, homoeopathic and other 'natural' agents that may help to counteract the negative symptoms of ageing and menopause, but these too must be carefully evaluated.

For quite a while I avoided asking my doctor about HRT because I'd read some worrying things about links with cancer and heart problems. But I finally felt so terrible, and had so little interest in sex, I decided to give it a go. It may be risky, but at least I have my sex life back.

I'm not keen on taking hormones, and I've found that natural oestrogen supplements have helped to counteract my internal dryness. I use a personal lubricant to help make intercourse comfortable, and although I'd never been interested in porn, I've recently found that certain rather naughty DVDs can really get me going.

Stopping HRT – combined with not getting enough sexual intercourse – caused me physical pain on the few occasions when I did make love. I finally sought help, and learned to be more comfortable by using a topical cream and stretching the entry to my vagina.

My doctor gave me some hormones – oestrogen and some testosterone – and I must say I felt like myself again after just a few days. My sister was very critical of my choice and said I should 'age gracefully' – whatever that means. I told her my sex life was really important to me, and I wasn't going to give it up without a fight.

I became newly single when I was 51. I found it very difficult to begin dating again, but when I finally found someone, I was very nervous about having sex. I thought he would find my vagina too dry and that I would be in pain. The first time we made love I had armed myself with a gallon of KY, but the funny thing was, I really didn't need it. I was so turned on, there was no problem down there at all.

Resolution

As both men and women age, they usually experience a faster return to an unaroused state after orgasm. This is known as 'resolution', although that term – as well as the phenomenon it describes – means nothing to most people. But, for women, the clitoris retreats back under its hood faster than it might have done in the past, and men will lose their erections even more rapidly once orgasm has occurred. Other age-related changes include having fewer orgasmic contractions (for both men and women), and men's ejaculations may not occur with quite so much force as before.

> When we were younger, I remember that when I was giving my husband a hand job, he'd frequently get me in the eye. But now, 34 years later, he sort of dribbles on his stomach.

To some degree, sex works on a 'use it or lose it' basis. So we need to keep going if we want to ... well ... keep going! For women, keeping up an active sex life really does help to maintain a healthy vagina. Of course, it must be said that women's sexuality is not all about vaginal penetration, and her pleasure and orgasms are certainly not dependent upon having something inside her. But vaginas can lose elasticity and generally atrophy; so, if we wish to retain the possibility of having intercourse throughout our lives, something of a penetrative nature must be done to keep things in good working order.

> I haven't had a partner for three years, but I continue to masturbate. Usually I just use my fingers, but once a week or so I use a vibrator inside that helps me get that yummy 'full' feeling I get from intercourse with a man.

Sick and tired

A fifty-year-old who starts having sexual problems needs to become a detective. Knowing that arousal, desire or pain issues don't automatically appear with ageing, but are usually due to hormonal changes, illness or medication side-effects, one can set to work to discern the exact cause and find ways to fix it or take compensatory measures.

Women are like ovens. We need five to 15 minutes to heat up.

Sandra Bullock

Older women may need even more than 15 minutes to 'warm up', but that does not have to be a negative thing. Many people have great sex during this decade; they can enjoy a slow build because they have more leisure time. They can make love without having to listen out for the kids or rush off to work.

Once our youngest left home, there was finally some 'us' time. It was hard to get used to no one knocking at the door, no school 'emergencies' and no chauffeur duties. We looked at each other one day and said, 'Why are we sitting here watching TV?' We started having slow, lazy sex – and we didn't even have to close the door! It felt decadent and delicious, and it's been that way ever since.

At any age, serious diseases such as cancer can affect a person's sexuality. It is not only the disease itself; treatments such as chemotherapy and prescribed drugs can also lead to sexual problems.

While I was going through chemotherapy, I didn't feel much like sex as a pursuit of pleasure. But I definitely needed it as a source of comfort and reassurance. I feel really lucky that I have a partner who understood that.

After I had cancer, I was not allowed to have any more oestrogen supplements, although my doctor said I could use a little topical oestrogen cream in my vagina to help with the dryness. This did help, and my partner and I worked hard to keep our sex life alive – even during chemo. I can't say I always felt sexy at all, but his holding and stroking me – and just letting me know he fancied me and actually wanted to have sex with the bald, scarred me – was enormously comforting. We became closer than we'd ever been.

Different medical conditions can affect different people in different ways.

After I had my TURP (transurethral resection of the prostate) I simply couldn't get an erection, and I thought my sex life was over. But, over time, I started getting partial erections and was able to orgasm, even though I no longer ejaculated. Now, on occasion, I can even have intercourse, even though my penis is never fully erect.

After I got prostate cancer, I was inactive for about three months during treatment. The small uncertainty after my prostate operation may have made me more careful about being ready for sex; it's slightly less spontaneous. But I can still see someone and just want it right then.

The treatments for many diseases can reduce sexual desire and functioning, and it's important to ask about the sexual side-effects of prescribed medication and other therapies.

I had no idea that my beta-blockers were killing my sex life – I just thought I'd gone off it because I was getting older. But when I met Barbara, I really wanted to be able to make love with her. My doctor came up with some alternatives to treat my condition, which did not affect my functioning, and I felt like I had a whole new lease of life. But I still couldn't get away from the fact that I'd started taking those pills without realising just how much they'd affect me as a man.

I was married to Jimmy for 32 years. He died of heart disease six years ago, and I started taking antidepressants to try to cope. Then when I met Arthur I noticed that, although I was attracted to him, things weren't quite right downstairs.

Certain antidepressants and a host of other medications – prescription and otherwise – can inhibit sex drive or create other kinds of sexual side-effects. It's worth checking with one's doctor, who may be able to prescribe different medication that does not affect sexuality.

Negotiating the change

Maintaining sexual health in our 50s and beyond definitely requires some vigilance, thought, decision-making – and sexual practice! Women in particular have some important decisions to make about how to manage the natural symptoms of menopause and hormonal changes, including how these might affect their sexuality and relationship. As I mentioned earlier, many women find that going through menopause has a significant negative effect on their sex lives, while others barely notice it.

Menopause did not affect my sexuality at all ... in fact, I wasn't really aware of the menopause. I had a full-time job and elderly parents and relatives, so it was difficult to fit in sex. At 49, I noticed menopausal symptoms. I started immediately on hormone therapy and continued on it for 11 years. Menopause didn't hit hard until I followed the medical advice to stop hormone replacement. Then everything deteriorated very fast. My libido really went. I had a nasty, drying-up sensation. At that point in my life I thought the idea of using a lubricant was bizarre, because I had never previously had problems – far from it.

Menopause, of course, is a natural passage of change for women, and should not be considered a disease or something that must be 'fixed'. Many women do suffer from uncomfortable symptoms and some sexual changes – either lowered desire or the effects of oestrogen depletion, such as vaginal dryness leading to painful intercourse.

I can't tell if menopause has affected my sexuality. I've not lost lubrication – I notice it's there during masturbation. But I've not had intercourse in three years. I'm still interested in sex, but have not found the opportunity to follow through. Certainly there is some trepidation about body image, after children, etc.

It was a surprise to me that I felt sore when he tried to put it in. I felt as though something had torn and, as he continued thrusting, it started to really hurt. I was in two minds about how to handle it – on the one hand, this was the first time I'd had intercourse for nearly a year and I didn't want to blow it. On the other hand, it was so painful, I just was not enjoying. Finally he stopped. 'You're a bit dry, honey. Got some lube?' Unfortunately, I didn't, because I wasn't expecting this. 'I've got something better,' I managed to say before going down on him. Damn. I guess I am officially a 'menopausal woman'.

Whether menopausal symptoms are evident or not, vaginal atrophy can occur as a woman ages and, in my opinion, it is wise to take this into consideration. In particular, if a woman wishes to continue to be sexual with a partner in a way that involves vaginal penetration, she would do well to take some steps to prevent vaginal atrophy and keep her vagina healthy enough to allow for intercourse. Even women without partners can do this – keeping their vaginas stretched by using a well-lubricated dildo can do the trick. This also applies to women of any age who have had a hysterectomy, or have gone through any other medical procedure that reduces the body's capacity for producing female sex hormones.

Giving it up

Some people in their 50s stop having sex with other people, either by choice or otherwise, and there can be a number of reasons for this.

When my youngest was 16 or 17, we were still sharing a bed but I was getting increasingly bored with the mechanics of sex. There was such a disengagement, I wanted a divorce. Although I wanted to leave I didn't know how I could. I was in this country all by myself – I had lost my original citizenship, so I stuck it out. Finally I said, 'I'm done. I'm bored. I want a separate bedroom.' And it's been the same ever since.

Damn! What sex life? It makes me *really* happy that I had such a great and active one while I was younger.

I wouldn't change a thing about my past sex life, but it's gone. I want to figure out how to have a sex life again.

All through my 30s and 40s I was busy with the children, and barely had time for sex – and I know that was difficult for my poor husband, whose libido stayed constant for those decades. But now things have reversed – my children have grown and I'm ready and wanting sex, but my husband's interest has diminished. It really doesn't seem fair.

Some people stop having sex because they lose their sexual confidence, as a result of body-image problems.

I'm less secure about my body now. I've aged ... had babies, and fewer people see it. When I was young, I had no qualms about getting naked, and strutting my stuff. Now, I'm not so sure – although I'm still not what I'd call self-conscious.

As I get older, I would say that I'm more bodily self-conscious in general. But I have no problems with arousal if I have an interested partner, and no problems with orgasm. The desire part is more complicated.

I don't think of my chin hairs being chin hairs anymore, but stray eyebrows.

Dr Sharon O'Connor

Feelings of physical inadequacy are more likely to emerge if a woman in her 50s considers herself in competition with younger women.

> Men and women seem so different about sex – men can have a quickie without feeling bad. I suppose a few women can – if you believe that character in *Sex and the City* – but I'm not one of them. I wish I were. I'm suspicious now, and I understand that about me. I don't want to fall into that thing where he'll get bored and wants out. It's a conundrum. Part of me wants to get back into a relationship, while the other says I don't want to go through another depression of feeling rejected because he wants a 20-year-old.

Deciding not to have a sex life is a personal choice, and there are plenty of people – including married folks – who have chosen not to bother with it.

> I couldn't care less about having sex. I think my sexual drive went way down since I turned 50. This maybe came with menopause at around 49. I'm confused about whether it's more to do with my hormones, my relationship with my husband, or just the way I feel about myself. I feel a lot better about myself than I did before, though, but I still don't feel like a sexual person. But I'm much happier with myself. I feel strong and healthy despite my high blood pressure.

A decision not to be sexual must be respected; however, it seems sad that there are many people – of all ages – who would like to have sex but, due to various circumstances, have given up all hope that they will be able to have a satisfying sex life at any time in the future.

Nobody knows how sad I feel inside that I have never really had satisfying relations. I feel that I've failed as a physical human being, because I don't even know what it's like. In my 40s, I still had hope that someone would come along, but now I'm 57 and I think that's out of the question. I know my weight doesn't help. If I weren't obese, maybe I could attract someone.

Part of me feels sad because I used to really enjoy it – those feelings that you just couldn't wait. I remember when I was in my 40s – leaving work in the middle of the day and going downtown to have sex, then going back to the office. If I was going to have sex with anyone, it would be my young gym trainer. But even though I realise that the actual physical part would be fun, I couldn't face the anguish I would feel when he dumped me for someone his own age. I want a whole relationship, not just to have sex, whereas before I could get past that. But, as I've got older, I want the whole package. I don't want to wake up feeling stupid.

The issue for me now, in my 50s, is not so much sex but the way I feel about myself and my body, which affects my sexuality. I just don't feel so powerful as a woman because I don't have that edge of confidence in my ability to attract any man I want – how I miss that! But many of my female friends say they don't care about it anymore. I wonder if they're telling the truth!

I live with a great deal of sadness. I would often try to initiate and he wouldn't respond. He's having fantasies about other women all the time. For me sex has to be really special, really set aside. The home thing is just not conducive. I've always wanted to do something like take a trip, but he'd rather work. I feel like I gave up. Sad.

By contrast, I spoke with a number of people who found their 50s to be the most sexually liberating time of their lives.

Just before my menopause symptoms kicked in, I suddenly had a spurt of sexual energy that I could barely control. It was like I was in my early 20s again. Although I made some bad mistakes with men at that time, it was definitely fun!

Now in my 50s, I've started to rediscover my partner and our sex life – even bought sex aids. Things improved dramatically.

Quite honestly, reaching 50 turned my sexual world upside down. I was bored with my husband and we hadn't had sex at all for several years, but didn't want to end our marriage, which was good in many ways. I suppose I was panicking a bit about ageing at the exact time that I met a young man who really got my hormones going. He made me feel like a teenager. I felt guilty about our age difference, and there were all kinds of problems between us, but the sex was so fantastic I didn't care. I realised that even being menopausal doesn't have to stop you having the best, the wildest experiences ever.

Turning 50 has really freed me from all that body consciousness I had when I was younger. When I was in my 30s and 40s, I used to make sure my man never saw me naked from behind. Now I say to myself, 'He's not with me because of my looks, so I can relax and leave the light on.'

Starting over

At this age, some people find that it is much harder to re-establish an active sex life after the loss of a partner or divorce. From an emotional point of view, it is not easy to reconnect with a new partner, but there is also the fact that finding a way to meet new people or to attract them in a comfortable fashion seems to get harder as we grow older.

Feeling inadequate as a lover maybe made me less likely to get out there after 25 years with one partner.

I have not had sex in the last few years. I'm in the process of a divorce, and have not got out there and had sex yet. Honestly, it's a scary thought.

I wouldn't know where to start. I'm not very computer literate and wouldn't know the first thing about getting on some social network or whatever people do to meet people or get laid now. What, am I going to get myself a 'Face page' at my age?

However, just because a person's sex life is halted for some reason, that does not mean he or she is doomed to a sexless life forever. Some take an unconventional – even unsanctioned – path to sexual fulfilment.

It seems awful to admit this, because I do love my husband, but roughly about the time he started going grey, I stopped being attracted to him. I found myself looking at younger men, and eventually started having liaisons with them – nothing serious, but enough to put the twinkle back in my eyes.

Our sex life was getting a bit stale, so my husband very kindly suggested that I have a bit of excitement elsewhere. He even went online and found a gorgeous young man who worked as a hooker for both men and women. The first time I met with him, I was terribly nervous. I couldn't decide what to wear! But when he arrived, he put me at ease and I had a wonderful experience. I didn't have an orgasm, though; in fact, I suppose my desire to please men generally stopped me just lying back and letting him pleasure me. I found myself trying to please him instead! I met with that young man many times, but eventually I started to have some feelings for him. That made me crazy. He told me I shouldn't confuse sex and love, but I think a lot of women have trouble separating the two.

My husband has had several affairs, but I know they were based entirely on sex. I am happy with that ... I knew he would always come back to me. Well, he has so far!

One of the most common obstacles to sexual relationships for single people in their 50s is simply finding someone appropriate.

I hear about people in my situation who have happy sex lives, but I think a lot of people my age (56) aren't having sex. I have little desire. I don't hang out with a lot of single women – more men, both gay and straight. In the world of gay men in their 60s, if you're not young and buff you're not desirable. My best friend is 65 and he's complaining all the time. The single women I do know are divorced. One is married to a man who lives in another country. No one talks about it, but I just know people go months at a time with no sex.

At 52, I experienced menopause and my desire started dropping. I'm prepared to go along without having sex. I try not to think about it too much. I think more about wishing I had a companion. I really enjoy men. If I can have interesting conversations – funny ones – with someone, that's what I'd want.

I have a history of going for unavailable men, so now, in my 50s, my world's full of them. The first one I really loved was married. I was living in another city and was so mad for this man, I had to get away. He was still crazy for me, too, but he would have lost a lot and in the end he took money over me. He was also alcoholic. I am so glad it did not work out, but he remarried and yet he still calls me. Then there's another man – married, too – who wants to have an affair with me. He's very smart and clever, but I said, 'I'm not doing that.' I was never attracted to the ones who were available to me.

A sense of humour is what I'm attracted to. He writes the best emails – I sort of fell in love with him via email. Then he came into town and I said, 'Nothing's going to happen.' He wanted to get his kids situated first. I blasted him: 'You're playing with me! We both know what this is about.'

I'm attracted to men who are remote. I'm always wanting more. I guess I want to feel like nothing bad could happen to me either physically or mentally – someone who's so clear about right and wrong he would always step in to defend me. I would feel safe when I'm with him – like my father.

Single people of any age – but especially in midlife – face stereotyping. They often report that it seems hard for their married friends to leave well alone when it comes to match-making.

I hate to be 'fixed up', because what other people feel is appropriate for me never is. My theory about rich men is that they're generally a mess – arrogant for the most part, and spoiled, and used to getting their own way and throwing their weight around – all attributes I don't want to be attached to. On other hand, I don't want to be with some loser I'm supporting. I don't like cheap men either, but I want to be able to pull my own weight – and for him to do so, too. Therefore, being fixed up is hard. I feel I'd like to have a good sex life, and to achieve that it would have to be something you can't describe – animal-like. For me, it could be in any age group. It doesn't have to be young and hunky by any stretch.

I want a man who's kind and understanding. Is that too much to ask of a millionaire?

Zsa Zsa Gabor

It's never very easy to meet the right partner, especially in large cities.

I tried a dating website once. I got about 600 responses and I never answered one. One was this very heavy-set bus driver who had a little boy. He stated that 'anyone who wanted to date him had to date his kid as well'. It was sweet, but not for me. Then there were all these guys with handlebar moustaches and tattoos. I thought, 'This isn't me, either!' Then sometimes I think I want theatre people, but lots of times they're narcissists and you end up feeding whatever it is they need, and you think, 'That's not going to be easy either.'

I was sexually dormant for ten years after my friend died of AIDS. I was 52. I went out to gay bars occasionally, but I didn't have sex for long time. If I'd hired a hustler or wanted to go to bed with someone my own age, maybe I could have got laid, but I liked younger men. I'm just not interested in people my own age. But people in their early 30s usually want someone their age. I wasn't interested enough in sex to want to pay for it.

I feel good that there's somebody I might want – I don't need a trophy guy. Having had sex with a younger man – he was an athlete in bed – I didn't like that, either. I suppose he was trying to impress me, but afterwards he said, 'I just want to be friends.' I think it was because he didn't like how I was in bed. That was ten years ago. Now I'd be so nervous to try again.

Some people feel that they enjoy their single lives, or are too set in their ways to bother with partnerships. They are willing to forgo having regular sex in favour of enjoying occasional lovemaking on a more casual basis when opportunity arises.

Getting older – it's easier than in the 20s – you understand how things work. You can get on by yourself. I don't feel like I need to have a boyfriend. Beforehand, it just happened rather more easily. Now I'm in my 50s and don't have a boyfriend. That's okay, but I don't want to be this age without a boyfriend and look terrible. I don't want to be an awful-looking old maid. That's why I work out every day – so I look good and keep the stress levels down. I feel that can hold it together. I really like my own company.

I've been alone so long I don't know how I would be with someone now. I fantasise that we'd have our own flats and we'd stay together sometimes. I like having my own thoughts and not having to talk. When I was first with someone, it was like a drug – I was always thinking about him, and I couldn't concentrate on other things. I was in 'la la land' and it took me over. That's a little bit scary – the thought of going back to that crazy 'can't wait to have sex again' kind of thing. It's losing control, and I don't want to lose control. I would go back to it if I thought this person was in it for the long haul and I was not going to be dumped – someone I was able to trust. I have the feeling I might find it in an older fellow who's not that attractive himself anymore, but is funny.

Special challenges

Some gay men, lesbians and bisexual people may have unique challenges as they age. For example, some believe that the competition to be young, vital and attractive is more acute in the gay world than it is for heterosexual people.

I'm not happy with the way my vulva has aged. My labia hang lower than they used to, and everything just looks, well, older. It affects the way I am with partners now.

It's harder to find sexual partners now. My last lover was 15 years younger. He was a real wild man – all emotion, all spirit and a lot of spunk. We were together for six years, until he died of AIDS. He was also a terrible drug addict, and smoked crack all the time. I lived with him once he got sick.

My cousin is 55. She's a lesbian and she was raised a strict Catholic. When she was about 20, she came out and attracted a lot of attention because she's very butch. She's a police officer. She came to visit me and brought her girl-friend – they were both very mannish. But recently she became 'born again'. Now she doesn't think of herself as gay, even though she lives with a woman. She thinks she's given up lesbianism for God. She actually believes all that bullshit about 'homos' going to hell, so she's trying to live a straight life before she dies. She's in denial about her sexuality – she thinks she can just walk away from being a lesbian.

There can also be exceptional challenges for middle-aged people living with physical or mental disabilities.

I'm bipolar, and sex has been a problem for me all my life. It's not so much sex, it's just that when I have an episode I can't make the right decisions about whether it's a good idea to go to bed with someone or not. Even at my age, I have to have someone taking care of me in case I do something stupid. That means at times I have to leave decisions about sexual appropriateness to someone else – not fun for a 54-year-old adult.

When I enquired about personal definitions of sexuality, people in their 50s certainly seem more resolved in their acceptance of their own and others' sexual path and exploration.

My definition would involve two people who are attracted to each other, comfortable with themselves and their sexuality, and interested in playing and finding what they each like sexually. It would involve an exploration of each other's bodies and sensory joy.

My personal definition of great sexuality would be being totally intimate and trusting with each other – and totally in synch with each other's needs. If you have that, whatever you specifically do feels great.

In Our 60s
Rediscovering Pleasure

What is sex like in one's 60s? It's exactly like it is at 30; you get just as hurt when it goes wrong.

Joan Rivers

I n our culture, there's a general notion that sex ends before 'old age'. So, our 60s – and even earlier – are considered to be a sexless time. There is absolutely no reason why this has to be true but, nonetheless, many people believe it. Not only that, but younger people are often highly judgemental about sexuality between older people, and the latter are usually secretive about their continuing erotic lives for fear of shocking them. But do we really need to worry about that?

Setting a good example for your children takes all the fun out of middle age.

William Feather

Adult children would seem to prefer that their parents play roles of 'dear old Mum and Pop', and confine themselves to bingo as opposed to ripping off each other's clothes for an evening of erotic fun. But, whether younger people can accept it or not – and there are many prejudices about sexuality later in life – sex is extremely important to many older adults. Having a happy and comfortable sex life at this age usually improves our overall quality of life, so it's worth trying to stay healthy enough to maintain it. What's more, our sexuality can actually improve as we age. Affection, sensuality and even hot, lusty eroticism are all possible and common in people of 60 and beyond.

However, we may have to do a little maintenance work. Some people accept the natural physiological changes that occur in one's 60s, but others are not happy about them and worry that they are doomed to a sexless old age.

> It's been 20 years since I had sex. I got a pacemaker three years ago, when I was 64; for many years I've felt estranged from my husband and our relationship has became a marriage of convenience. But the thought of never having sex again my whole life makes me very sad.

Perhaps we buy into the idea that sex should and does end prior to middle age, because of the lingering puritanical notion that sex is only for procreation – and once you become incapable of that you have to retire your pelvis.

> I know my parents stopped having sex when they were in their mid-40s, and moved into separate bedrooms. I'm not sure why – they were both healthy and in good shape. But, when I reached the same age, I had to fight the feeling that it was all over for me, too. Fortunately, my wife made it clear that she was never going to give up – and now (in our 60s) we're still getting fresh.

> *Puritanism – the haunting fear that someone, some-where, might be having a good time.*
>
> H.L. Mencken

Although people try to be stoic, many are secretly terrified about their approaching old age. Fortunately, some are also obstinate:

Fuck ageing gracefully! I'm going to go kicking and screaming.

But many men and women are still sexy and vital in their 60s (and beyond), and are capable of a rich sex life. They are often sexually confident – and their experience counts for a lot. They know their own bodies, they know how to give another person pleasure – and they're not afraid to try new things.

I've finally realised that sex is precious, and something to aim for. Early on it was always available – and often just an annoyance (someone wanting it when I didn't). But now I spend more time preparing for it, savouring it and giggling about it after.

What exactly do we need to know in order to make love successfully and satisfyingly at this age? We certainly have to pay attention to maintaining our sexual health – and our overall health, as well. The views of many younger people – that middle-aged people are, or should be, non-sexual – are quite wrong. Sometimes our 60s can bring some big surprises.

To be honest, I would say this is the best sexual time of my life (apart from three years at university when I was 18 to 21). My partner and I now experiment … we finally have time for sex, and actually plan 'sex evenings'. We use sex aids, lots of lube – and pornography helps! Plus there is Viagra …

Gone are many of the elements that made sexuality stressful earlier in life – for example, not having enough time to really enjoy it. Some people certainly have bodily concerns, but if they can let go of their need for perfection, let it all hang out and simply focus on all the wonderful sensations that their bodies can give them, they might have the best sex they've ever experienced.

Honestly, it's such a relief now to be beyond all that preciousness – 'Is my tummy hanging out?' 'Is my backside too large?' At one point my lover said to me, 'Look, neither of us is 25 anymore – let's just enjoy ourselves!' It was so freeing. Somehow he gave me permission to enjoy sex the way it should have been for all those years when I was judging myself – and my partner – quite unnecessarily.

I have a much older body now. I work out and eat well, etc., but there is no dispute that I am not the fit, muscled, slim guy that I was in my 20s. And that body doesn't perform so well – not only sexually. There's nothing very sexy about not hearing whatever sweet nothings are being whispered to you. But I have always been confident about myself (too confident, maybe); I still happily walk around naked in front of a partner; maybe I should stop. I am happy with my body (less two inches on the waist, of course) for a man of 62. My mind, on the other hand, is as deep and exciting and inventive as it ever was – which helps.

I feel great about my body *now*. When I was teenager, I wished I had bigger tits … but I don't want bigger tits now, and would not ever contemplate having any cosmetic surgery, although perhaps I would consider some if I had a mastectomy or suchlike. But I am happier than ever about my body. I wish it was less wrinkled and that I had less 'cellulite' but, hey, *why*? Who is going to be looking at it at my age (my mid-60s)?

I'm constantly tortured about my body – I have always thought it was not good enough, especially my huge rear – but the funny thing is that it turns out he actually likes that.

Failing to adopt an accepting attitude towards our own ageing bodies can certainly put us under a lot of unnecessary pressure. Sure, many people are aroused by looks, but sexuality is really about touch and feeling – and that never goes away.

I feel I'm competing with all those beautiful younger women – even the ones who don't look after their bodies are still gorgeous simply because they're young. I look back at my own youth and think, 'Why didn't I appreciate my own body more then?' I always thought there was something imperfect about it, whether it was a bit of cellulite, a pimple or two, or a slightly bloated tummy – how I'd love to have just those problems now!

Getting better all the time

In our 60s, surely we are finally wise enough to have fully mature, sophisticated sex and allow ourselves to embrace whatever it is that turns us – and our partners – on.

I have definitely become less inhibited in my sexuality lately. Trying new things just doesn't seem to be so threatening or scary as it once was. My husband has been leading me into quite a few new adventures – in all these years together, I never knew he was so kinky!

At this point, we are hopefully far better at communicating our needs to a partner. In middle age, as a result of hormonal shifts, both men and women tend to become rather more androgynous, with women becoming more assertive and men becoming more comfortable with intimacy and closeness. The natural independence that women gain at this time helps them to make their desires known more clearly, and to assert themselves sexually.

I'd never really been comfortable with taking charge sexually before. But when Steve developed arthritis in his back, it was best for me to get on top for intercourse. At first I found the thrusting a bit tiring, but eventually I built up my muscle tone and learned to give him a pretty good ride! I'm proud of myself, actually. Even at my age I feel like a bit of a 'babe' – and the workout definitely beats going to the gym!

Many men naturally acquire more nurturing skills at this age, and some are able to utilise these in their lovemaking. So many women feel they become much better lovers.

When I was younger I used to jump out of bed as soon as I'd ejaculated – into the shower and off to work. Now I understand what my wife was complaining about all those years ago. These days I actually enjoy snuggling afterwards, and now that I'm retired, I finally have time for it.

I've finally learned that there are more erogenous zones in her body than just her genitals and breasts. It's been fun discovering just exactly where they all are – and she says I've yet to locate a few more …

Changing positions

It is fairly common for people to start having a few age-related physiological challenges in their 60s and beyond – bad knees, hip or back problems, and so on – which can dictate their sexual style or choice of position.

> These days we like to lie in a spooning position, and he holds me and plays with my clitoris. It's wonderfully comfortable. When I'm ready, he pulls my leg over his and enters me from behind. We both love it that way – he continues playing with my clitoris while he's slowly thrusting and we can both come that way. I wish we'd found out how great that is much earlier in our lives. I guess we just did the missionary thing because that's all we knew about then.

Having physical challenges can encourage people to be extra-creative and resourceful – and actually improve their sex lives, as long as they grasp the opportunity and don't just give up. Out of necessity, many people who have been physically challenged since they were young discovered this years ago; the rest of us are way behind in that regard.

> After my accident (at 28), I went for about a year thinking I'd never have sex again. But I learned from others in the same situation that sex can be incredible, even with a spinal-cord injury. My wife and I have discovered that my wheelchair can be an amazing sex aid! We've found all kinds of ways to use it for balancing, to achieve different positions both for penetration and oral sex. I'm lucky that she's so athletic, but

even if she wasn't, I know we'd find a way. It's important to me to be able to pleasure her, too – and I know she also loves our sex life now.

In the course of my work as a psychologist and sex therapist, I have often been filled with admiration for people who have persevered arduously to reclaim their sex lives after serious injury and illness, and also by those who have been severely physically challenged since birth – many of whom require the help of carers to position them for sex. There's usually a way – if there is a will. It's all about mindset and determination, and I've seen plenty of evidence that people with disabilities can actually have not just a functioning sex life, but fantastically erotic experiences, no matter what their particular physical challenge might be.

Even for healthy ageing people, there can be a few obstacles to enjoying sexuality in our 60s and beyond. Problems such as painful joints and certain other typical age-related medical conditions can certainly affect one's sexual style, but there really is nothing that cannot be overcome somehow. If we put our minds to it, the quality of sex can improve dramatically and continue on that path throughout the rest of our lives. And it's worth keeping in mind their athleticism in bed may be highly overrated. Simply following the body's lead in a comfortable, relaxed fashion can be particularly rewarding.

These days I mainly enjoy lazy sex. The athletic stuff was fun when I was younger, but there's just no need for all that now (was there ever?). Just lying comfortably and touching, holding, stroking – that's what does it for me.

Becoming aroused

As I've already mentioned, from about our 40s onwards, many people notice that it can take a bit longer to become aroused. For men, getting an erection is not as immediate as it used to be; for women, becoming lubricated is a slower process. But, as I've also pointed out before, failing to exhibit signs of physical arousal rapidly does not mean desire is absent.

Partners of people who've reached middle age need to remind themselves not to take it personally if they do not trigger an immediate response when they undress or make sexual advances. Instead of backing off, they can help by providing some direct genital stimulation to hasten the process.

> I actually like having to work for it. I'll touch her and she'll be really dry, but gradually, after a few minutes of teasing and stroking her, everything starts to become nice and warm and moist. It's a reward, and I know she really wants me physically then – her body has caught up to her mind.

Men in their 60s will certainly have the occasional erectile failure – just like every man does from time to time, at any earlier age. The problem is, at this age a man is likely to over-react and imagine that it means more than it actually does.

> I had the occasional problem getting it up when I was younger, but then I put it down to too much beer, or maybe even too much jerking off. Now I worry that it means I'm well and truly over the hill, and can soon kiss my sex life goodbye.

How a person conceptualises his or her sexuality becomes a most important deciding factor in the quality of sex in middle age. If a man believes that his sexual prowess lies solely in his erectile ability, he is bound to have a sense of severe disappointment and loss of confidence if he, say, develops a medical condition that affects his erections. But the truth is that men can be excellent lovers without using their penises, and both they and their partners can achieve great satisfaction.

> His penis may be flaccid, but he's still got a tongue. I told him that one day, and I'm delighted to say he took the hint.

> I'm old enough and wise enough to ask for what I want. If my partner doesn't respond appropriately or seems unsure, I have no problem showing him.

> Quite honestly, I'd rather have oral sex than intercourse. There's always the worry about lubricating enough to avoid sex being painful – with oral sex, I can just lie back and think of … whomever!

Similarly, if a woman defines herself by her appearance – firm breasts and so on – their natural drooping may plunge her into despair.

> I used to love being on top, but now I don't dare let my partner face my saggy tummy and breasts. Rear entry is good. If I really stretch my ass, the cellulite smoothes out!

> I prefer to lie on my back during sex. It counteracts the effect of gravity, and I imagine I look years younger!

Lying on her back is fine and well, but what about all the many other exciting positions she could be trying, if she wasn't so worried about her looks! However, female sexuality can include a kind of auto-eroticism (being turned on by oneself), so maintaining a healthy attitude and confidence in our attractiveness can help our libido. If we feel attractive and confident, others will be attracted to us. Maintaining a fitness regime, adhering to a healthy diet, keeping alcohol consumption to a minimum and generally staying as healthy and stress-free as possible will help. Fortunately, women in their 60s tend to have more time for body maintenance than they might have done in their childbearing years.

What libido?

Certain women actually experience a higher level of sexual desire after menopause; nonetheless, some people in their 60s do not.

> I wish my libido was higher, and that I didn't have to rely on sex aids (such as a vibrator) and porn ... but, hey, why complain about what you cannot change?

> I'd like to know how can I increase my libido as an older woman. I raised this with my doctor, and he suggested 'more lubrication' or the website 'Go ask Alice', which he said he refers patients to!

As people age, they are still capable of strong orgasms that can be just as intense as they were at a younger age. Woman can still be multi-orgasmic, while men may experience orgasm slightly differently – less genitally focused and perhaps more global, like a full-body sensation, but just as good.

I almost feel guilty about how much more pleasure I get now that it's not all about making babies ... I said 'almost'!

No pressure

Sex is really good for us! It helps reduce our stress levels, can play a role in preventing depression, improves our muscular tone and provides us with a general sense of well-being.

If I make love and have a great orgasm, it makes a huge difference to the way I feel about myself and my life. It feels life-affirming – even youthening. The next day I'm walking about all fluffed up, and betting myself that the kids at work would never believe what we got up to!

For it is a maxim I have learned to trust with all of my heart that everyone without exception enjoys a sexual life far more active and more rewarding than can be guessed at even by his close friends.

Brendan Gill

But some of us do have to re-evaluate our attitudes towards sex. For example, if we accept that a lovemaking session doesn't have to end in orgasm, we can be freer to enjoy pure pleasure for its own sake. Conversely, if we view sex in a goal-oriented fashion – i.e. if we don't have a 'big O' or ejaculate it's a disaster – we're setting ourselves up for potential failure. We should learn – at every age – to release ourselves from the pressure of turning sex into a performance at which we must excel. Interestingly, women are prone to acquiring a little performance anxiety as they age.

He assumed I would know what I was doing and be super-confident in bed. I hadn't told him that I'd only been with one man before him – my husband of 40 years! But this man had different expectations, and I obviously didn't meet them, because I didn't hear from him again. I feel I need to go back to sex school and start again!

I'm experienced at sex, so I can usually manage to please a man. I teach them things, too. The only trouble is they run off and use their new skills to impress younger women. Little shits! But that's life!

I found that the people in their 60s who were enjoying their sex lives the most tended to be those who had managed to move away from established, boring patterns and were open to trying new things.

My husband finally told me that he felt bad about the fact that we don't have intercourse anymore. 'We should be having sex, don't you think?' he said to me. 'But we do have sex ...' I protested. 'Giving me a hand job isn't exactly sex, now is it?' I had to convince him that it was. Although I am not up for intercourse anymore, we lie together and snuggle, and I whisper erotic stories in his ear while bringing him to orgasm ... and that's very satisfying for both of us. I love to make him feel good, and he says he thoroughly enjoys the experience as well. Who says we have to do it the same way that we did when we were starting a family?

When change occurs

Many people in their 60s find a way to bring back romance in their lives, since middle age is a time when one can fulfil not just sexual fantasies, but also the desire for a deeper connection. By contrast, the same things that cause sexual problems in a relationship earlier in life still apply – such as anger and resentment towards our partners.

> I felt very isolated from my husband when my mother died … I felt he had done very little to help me during her final illness and frailty.

Some people even erroneously think that women lose interest in sex before men do. This may be a hangover from previous eras, when women were not supposed to enjoy sex. Whatever the reason for this lingering belief, it is incorrect. Barring illness, desire-lowering medications and certain other physiological or psychological conditions, women can maintain sexual interest throughout their lives – as can men. But desire can fluctuate for either gender, and it is important to respect that in each other.

> When my wife lost her sister, her libido disappeared. I knew she needed support and comfort more than sex, and I tried to be patient. When her desire returned, she seemed even more into it than before. It was worth the wait.

Gay men I spoke to who were in their 60s were particularly aware of their libido and how it affected their lives.

> My libido is as strong – if not stronger – as it was when I was 21. And that's a problem for me as a gay man. There are fewer guys who want to have sex with me.

My desire started going down in my early 60s. This was also to do with the fact that sex stopped being safe. In the early 90s, all my gay friends were dying so I didn't really actively run after sex for 10 to 12 years.

Many gay men to whom I spoke – at this age and even younger – complained that they were having a tough time ageing.

The gay world is youth-oriented. After they turn 45, a lot of gay men feel invisible when they go out.

The whole bar scene has changed. It used to be how people met for sex, but now they hook up on the internet and at the gym. It's radically different. In the late 60s, there were just three or four gay bars, but now it's dispersed. Every neighbourhood has one, so bars don't have the same intense sexual feelings as they had in the 70s. Then you could easily get anonymous sex. In the 80s, too, bars were meeting places. You might see the person again or you might not. You never had to make any commitment in order to get into somebody's pants.

I'm definitely feeling very isolated. I have a friend the same age, who is also gay, but he married a woman and it's easier for him. I'm having a really hard time.

I'm not sure it's any worse for us gay men than it is for heteros without partners. We all feel more isolated as we get older. But feeling that you're losing your looks – that doesn't seem to bother straight men as much. It's not so much a daily beauty contest for them. Straight women, though, they feel it just like we do.

Now we're in our 60s, the thing I'd most like to change about the way my partner is sexually is that I wish he didn't need to depend on Viagra.

The problem with erections

Although men in their 60s may not achieve the hard erections that they did earlier in life, they can usually still reach sufficient stiffness for intercourse. In any case, as the penny finally drops that women appreciate many non-penetrative styles of lovemaking – often in preference to intercourse – men can make up for any erectile difficulty by being better at pleasuring a woman in the ways that really count, including manually and orally. At 60 there is often a slower build-up to orgasm and – guess what? – that's exactly what their partners, at least the female ones, always wanted!

It's more about connection and attachment, whereas at 30 it was more about sex. I feel more comfortable with my regular partner and can always get to orgasm. At 30, it was all dependent on having the right friction.

Illness actually has far more effect on a person's sexuality than ageing itself does. If men are healthy physically active and keep up sexual activity (remember, 'use it or lose it!), they can often carry on getting erections their entire lives without having to rely on any little blue pill. Erectile problems are most often caused by illness, alcohol abuse, medication, diabetes and hypertension – and there can be psychological reasons, such as depression or relationship issues at the root, too. Although drugs like Viagra, Levitra and Cialis have helped many people, there have also been some problems – for example, certain side-effects, and the fact that it can sometimes put partners out of step with each other.

My husband stopped being able to have erections many years ago, and I was unable to persuade him to see his doctor. With very little discussion, our sex life abruptly ended. I was sad about it, but eventually adjusted to a sexless existence. But when he turned 60, all of a sudden he came home one day with some pills that made him functional again. Then he was chasing after me, eager to try out his new 'toy'. Well, I was horrified. I mean, it had been at least ten years. I had lost the inclination, but I did try it – and it hurt like hell. I had to tell him he'd missed his window of opportunity.

The above scenario is quite common, but a sex therapist can help couples adjust to changes in each other's sexual interest and ability. It's worth seeking help if there are any significant alterations in one's sexual responses, including those that appear to be due to illness or surgery.

My drive is reduced, and performance can be an issue following the prostate surgery I had ten years ago. But sex is still an important part of my life.

I had some erectile issues following surgery or, more specifically, radiation post-operatively. This was easily solved by the use of Viagra-type drugs as necessary. Libido has rarely, if ever, been a problem. Reaching orgasm has not been affected, although it takes longer and the recovery time is slower now. Premature ejaculation still sometimes happens. Such problems have been intermittent, infrequent and I have never sought help, other than a post-operative prescription of Viagra.

Remaining sexual

Women may actually become more orgasmic in their 60s, as hormonal shifts increase their libido and orgasmic capacity. However, for a variety of reasons, many are challenged by a change in their sexual responses.

Now I masturbate only about once a month. My orgasms are not as long-lasting, not as intense. I tried testosterone, but it didn't do much. Maybe I need to increase it. I only take a sixth of what my doctor gave me – I'm just not motivated to change things. Mind you, if there was somebody I wanted to have sex with, I'd be popping six of those things.

At 67, I can still give myself orgasms, but I have problems with my lower back and I have poor bladder control – stress incontinence. I also feel like I have dead nerves down there – maybe cut nerve endings. I talked to a urologist and my doctor says to do Kegel exercises. But it feels dead, like I have no control. I like to think I'll have sex with someone again. But sex isn't as important as a relationship.

I feel I need to have a relationship with the person I'm having sex with. Sex with a new partner is a little more daunting. I don't feel as free to initiate with a new partner. I feel battle-scarred. And my desire isn't there until I get started, but once I get going I can have great orgasms.

I will show you a love potion without drugs or herb
or any witch's spell; if you wish to be loved, love.

Hecato of Rhodes

Women who go for long periods without having intercourse often worry about losing their ability to be sexual again.

If you don't have sex soon, you'll end up with a
Barbie stump. That little bit of moulded plastic
between the legs of a Barbie doll. That'll be you.
You'll heal over.

Kathy Lette

Well, fortunately, that's not going to happen, but vaginal atrophy is a real concern and it is recommended that if women plan to have intercourse again at some time in the future they work on maintaining their sexual health by adding a clean penile-shaped vibrator or dildo – with added lubrication – to their repertoire of self-pleasuring.

Doing without

I have detected considerable sadness and longing among a number of people who have been living without sexual experiences with others for some time.

It's as though this whole part of me has died. I really miss it. Not sure I'll ever find it again, but I think about it – and hope for it – a lot.

I haven't had sex for a long time. But then, I had so much sex earlier in my life I think I might have used up my quota.

I would love to have reached this point with an ongoing and satisfying sexual relationship at the centre of my life. I have no idea how I could have done that – particularly given the ongoing importance of the S&M element in my needs.

I know a few guys who I would guess have managed to maintain a long-term physical relationship. I know a few who have stayed very married despite having little or no physical contact with their partners. I know guys who have remained in a marriage with a long-term, outside secondary affair. I know guys who have, in later middle life, given it all up for a new love. I truly wouldn't look at anyone I can think of (that I know personally) and envy them, or indeed pity them. I believe I have been incredibly lucky for 40-odd years, and if the equation has ended up short of perfect now, I'm not sure that I would want to make the changes in the past that could possibly correct the current situation.

My extra-marital relationship has ended, and there's no resumption of sex at home with my wife. My ongoing sexual interest is served by a couple of long-standing professional mistresses with whom I have personal relationships.

People find all kinds of creative ways to find sexual fulfilment in their 60s, and sometimes those are outside what is generally accepted as appropriate and right. But middle-aged people are lucky in that they are willing to be bloody-minded about being happy in their remaining years – and why not?

Coping with loss

Hopefully, by the time we reach our 60s we have achieved the ability to enjoy a superior level of intimacy, and are more emotionally mature and self-confident. Sexual communication may also be easier. Men may become more sensual at midlife, something that their partners usually truly appreciate. But, unfortunately, one of the main issues for people in their 60s is the loss of a partner – or the lack of available partners – for one reason or another.

Maybe at this age women in our society shouldn't expect too much from men. They aren't going to see you as a person – or, if they do, it's very transitory. And the dating scene is tough. It seems to be all about sex at our age – just about having sex, and not so much about companionship.

My sister was married to a shit, and she was about to leave him when he walked out on her one night. She's been on eharmony.com lately. I see her struggles and I say that even at our age these men are just predatory. She's educated, too.

I've been alone too long. I doubt that I'll ever be with someone full time again. I don't want to be figuring out what to cook for dinner everyday – that would be too boring.

I've been madly in love for years with someone of mixed race. I've always been very close to my family and I'm not sure they'd accept him. If he was madly in love with me, too, I suppose I might be able to overcome that problem, but he's not.

I'm not great with finances, and not being married sort of keeps me a little girl – even at my age. I suppose it's ridiculous, but if I run out of money I can call my father. Still, not having a partner, I feel sort of out at sea sometimes.

I have men in my life that are very smart – some that are wonderfully playful, one with a great sense of humour and one with a fabulous body – I just haven't been able to find it all in one straight guy. If I did, it would be love forever.

My mother said it was simple to keep a man; you must be a maid in the living room, a cook in the kitchen and a whore in the bedroom. I said I'd hire the other two and take care of the bedroom bit.

Jerry Hall

Sometimes we have to be extra brave in order to seek a partner, especially after heartbreak or bereavement. It's not easy.

I married when I was a virgin nearly 50 years ago. I've been attracted to other men, but they've been married. I think I could have had sex with this particular man I was really attracted to, if I'd acted on it. But we didn't. The reason was that he was married and his nephew went to school with my son, so I felt I couldn't get away with it. So

I've only ever had sex with one man my entire life. I'm sad about that.

She who hesitates is celibate.

Kathy Lette

In our 60s, we often lose ageing parents, other family members or friends, and bereavement can have a significant effect on our sexuality.

The loss of my brother two years ago affected me deeply in many areas. It made me a sadder person, and maybe has made me less cavalier about life and about sex.

As the next decade – our 70s – looms, many people have fears about approaching old age. They may not voice it, but facing one's own mortality is a particularly tough order in our youth-orientated society.

I'm worried about entering my 70s. I think I have to stay strong. I have friends complaining about aching here and there in their bodies, and I'm afraid of it. Then I think, 'Well, if I'm still stylish and I still have my sense of humour, I'll still be OK.' But at 70 – I don't know. My mum is 70, and she's still having a good time. I've noticed Viagra in my father's medicine cabinet. He had prostate cancer that caused some problems.

I have this fantasy about finding a beautiful young man who will be with me until the end. Be the last person I'd see when I die. Of course sex would be nice, and I believe that keeps a woman young – but it's the thought of sleeping in his protective, strong arms every night and feeling safe and at peace and adored. But yeah, it's just a fantasy. Who'd want this saggy old body?

Quality not quantity

For 60-something people who are in a relationship, one of the main things on their minds regarding sexuality tends to be frequency. Some lament the fact that they may not do it as often as they used to in previous decades. If only they could understand that it's quality, not quantity, that's the name of the game now!

I rarely talk to my friends about their sex lives, but I get the impression that most folk my age – i.e. mid-60s – do it rather rarely. But I could be wrong; we don't discuss it. I do know that one of my husband's friends recently said to him, 'I haven't had sex in two years.' He is 'happily married'.

My sex life now makes me feel full of life – much better than earlier. When I had more regular sex in the past (a couple of times a day), I never stayed with those guys. It felt so disruptive – I couldn't sustain it. I had a relationship with one guy that was very sexual – I couldn't stand being the object with him, or that much intense sex. I made a choice to be with someone who didn't have that intensity.

I'd love to *want* sex every minute. Now I feel lucky if it's once a week. I think it's really sad with my husband now. I was always told what a great lover I was. When I met my husband, he didn't say that. We finally went to a therapist to improve our sex life, and he said to this person that he was never really physically attracted to me. I felt like he wasn't with me for sex, and that was a good thing. I knew I couldn't trust a man who was lusting after me – he'd soon be after someone else.

Overcoming ageism

When I asked people how sex in their 60s might be different from sex in earlier years, there were a lot of favourable comparisons.

Sex at 60 is only different from sex at 30 because I have to use more lubricant.

Now is the best time of my life. But no point in 'looking back' and saying, 'I wish ...'.

In our culture, there's a great deal of ageism relating to sex. Love and sex in films are usually the domain of the young. Ageing women are portrayed in archetypal images – the crone or the nurturer, not so much the one getting her pussy licked on a regular basis. In fairy tales, older women are usually wicked. Snow White's queen was a paragon of sexual jealousy, who lost out to the beauty of youth. But then, even the wicked queen was probably getting more sex than Cinderella.

A few recent films – such as *It's Complicated* with Meryl Streep – are portraying older men and women as sexually active, but double standards still abound. For example, what do you call an attractive older man who goes out with women half his age? There is no equivalent male word for 'cougar'.

I've started being interested in younger men, and I've been surprised to discover that quite a few young men are actually interested in older women. And they're not even Italian!

But no matter what age we are, an active sex life does carry a risk of contracting STDs, so precautions must be taken; in fact, some studies show that in the older age group sexually transmitted disease is actually on the rise, possibly because they do not believe they need to practise safe sex.

The main factors that will help us maintain sexuality throughout our lives are staying healthy (with regular exercise, a healthy diet and maintaining a balanced weight), positive attitudes towards sexuality and our bodies, being creative in our approach to lovemaking and having access to a partner with whom we can experiment and develop useful strategies if problems arise. Maintaining the non-sexual fun in a relationship and a zest for life, being affectionate and comforting to each other, not obsessing about how often you are or are not 'doing it', being OK about saying 'no' to each other at times and considering counselling if things go wrong will all help. Even those without a partner can – and do – enjoy pleasure and/or thrilling orgasms via masturbation.

Try to put a positive spin on things – you're only two people short of a threesome.

Kathy Lette

Partner or not, our fantasy lives usually continue into our 60s and beyond.

Now I think more of specific men or individuals, rather than *just sex*. In other words, I imagine I'm with, say, George Clooney. But my husband wouldn't like me to be thinking of other men when we are having sex (I think).

The bottom line is that people about to turn 60 can be hopeful about their sexuality as they enter this decade – and every other one for the rest of their lives. As those I've spoken to have attested, plenty of people in their 60s are having great sex.

I can remember when the air was clean and sex was dirty.

George Burns

9

In Our 70s
Lovers' Peak

Just because there's snow on the roof doesn't mean the boiler has gone out.

Author unknown

M ore people are living longer and demanding a better quality of life in later years, so doesn't it make sense that, as a society, we should avoid being judgemental and disapproving of sexuality among elders – and recognise that sex is a source of pleasure and comfort, no matter how old a person might be?

Don't let the wrinkles fool you. You'd be surprised what we older folk get up to!

I only take Viagra when I'm with more than one woman.

Jack Nicholson

From the discussions I've had with people in their 70s and 80s – and even beyond – it is clear that, for many of them, sexuality ranks pretty high on their list of priorities. Some may want more of it; others are actively looking for a partner. Many long for information about sexuality at their particular age and how to navigate bodily issues that can make sexuality a bit more challenging in the later years.

The movies are all about romance between young people. There seems to be little recognition that older people could be having the same feelings – let alone acting on them. But my friends and I – mainly single at this point – are interested in similar things, only we keep quiet about it because we don't want to shock our kids.

Many people in their 70s and beyond have complained to me that they would like to be taken more seriously as sexual beings.

The young people get all the attention, don't they? When I have sexual feelings I feel as though I shouldn't be having them, as though I'm an aberration – that I should stop all this nonsense and focus on knitting. Well, at 78, my eyesight's too poor for knitting now, but it doesn't hinder me when I have … relations.

There's one gentlemen here in our senior residence who's quite a wolf. He chases all the ladies and doesn't want to take 'no' for an answer. Some of the ladies flirt back, but I wouldn't want to be thought cheap.

Many people in their 70s are sexually active; by that I mean that they enjoy at least some aspect of sexuality, such as self-pleasuring, sensual touch (genital or otherwise), intercourse with others, oral sex and many other kinds of sexual contact. But not everyone values sex at this or any other age and, of course, it is perfectly possible to have a happy life – and a good relationship – without it.

Sex is off my radar. I'd rather finish the crossword puzzle.

The specifics of sex may vary as we age, but it is still possible to enjoy it as an important aspect of our connection with others and a healthy, lifelong source of pleasure and comfort.

> One of my lady friends said, 'You're a dirty old man' (we were in bed at the time and she was giggling when she said it). I said, 'I may be a dirty old man, but you're nearly 70 – what does that make you?' She thought for a moment, and then she said, 'I'm a SOW!' 'What's that?' I asked. 'Sexy old woman,' she replied. 'I just made that up.'

Masturbation is a common and useful form of sexual expression for people in their 70s and older.

> *Don't knock masturbation. It's sex with someone I love.*
>
> Woody Allen

For example, if one partner wants to be sexual but the other does not, there's no reason why the less-interested party shouldn't hold the other while they bring themselves to climax; in fact, this is something that could happen at any age. For women without partners who think that they might want to have intercourse at some point in the future and need to keep their vaginas from atrophying, using a penile-shaped vibrator with a clitoris stimulator may be a good solution.

> I hope my kids never find my stack of sex toys. I feel like putting them in a box labelled 'CENSORED! In the event of my death *Open at your peril*!'

My yoga teacher is my inspiration. He's Swedish, six foot four inches, and to say he's a sight for sore eyes is an understatement. It gets pretty warm in the room, and after 15 minutes or so his shirt is damp and he's sweating so much every muscle in his body is defined and popping out. I put my mat near the front so I can see him – even smell him – better. Most days I go home and think about him while I use my vibrator. That class is worth every penny …

At 78, I definitely don't advertise my sexuality as far as my family is concerned. I am quite sure that if my children knew how hot and heavy Burt and I get they'd be quite shocked.

Some would consider the woman who provided the above quote to be one of the lucky ones. Many people at this age report experiencing great difficulty in finding sexual partners. There may indeed be fewer available same-age partners for women, since they tend to live a little longer than men. Nevertheless, I hear complaints about lack of partners from people of every age.

I miss how easy it was to meet sexual partners when I was younger. Throughout the 80s, I was still promiscuous – out there looking for sex. I spent far too many hours in gay bars looking for sex. In my era, just a look from someone in a bar across the way, maybe smiling or not, and then – that was it! People even used to hook up on the street. You'd walk past each other, turn around to look back, and before you knew it you'd both be in bed. Now, at my age, that's not going to happen.

The only reason I would take up jogging is so that I could hear heavy breathing again.

Erma Bombeck

Changing our perceptions

Elder sex is certainly a taboo in our culture, but I have visited many societies – in various parts of the South Pacific, for example – where open displays of highly sexual teasing, dancing, flirting and ribald songs and jokes are performed by elders in public rituals. The first time I witnessed this – in a formal Maneaba greeting ceremony, held in my honour in Kiribati – I was astounded. For someone from Western culture, it was so unusual. Younger people were expected to stay in the background – considered to be 'unready' for public displays of sexuality! Men and women took it in turns to invite strangers to dance in a gyrating, suggestive manner (it was impolite to refuse), and as I enjoyed this novelty with one of the oldest men on the island, I couldn't help imagining how this would be viewed in a Western setting: with shock, disbelief and disgust. Pity.

I suppose our Western attitudes towards elder sex emanate from Puritan values that decreed sexuality is only for procreation and, once that is no longer viable – especially for women – it's an aberration.

Lord give me chastity – but not yet.

St Augustine

In more liberal sections of Western society, some greater level of openness about sexuality among elders may be creeping in, but we still have a long way to go in recognising that not only does pleasurable sex improve our quality of life, but it is also the right of every human being, no matter what age, to be respected in their consensual sexual choices and behaviour.

> *However carefully you phrase the history of your sex life, you're bound to emerge as a boaster, a braggart, a liar or a laughing stock.*
>
> William Rushton

But our society is certainly youth-obsessed, especially when it comes to love, romance and sex. There is, for example, an overall sense in the media that unless people look good (young and healthy), the sexual images conjured up – for instance, of older relatives – are decidedly yucky.

> *Using Viagra is like putting a new flagpole on a condemned building.*
>
> Harvey Korman

In fact, comedians get a fair bit of mileage out of propagating the notion that viable sex is only for the young.

> *At my age, I want two girls at once. I fall asleep and they have each other to talk to.*
>
> Rodney Dangerfield

One of the biggest taboos is the idea of sex between people of vastly different age groups.

I still appreciate beautiful young women, and I don't care if I come into the category of 'dirty old man', but I still have those thoughts. Of course, I don't approach them – that would be asking for trouble. But looking's free, isn't it?

I still look at young men, and I can joke with my husband about it. The other night we were watching TV and an ad came on for an exercise machine that was being promoted by a gorgeous young man with a well-defined torso. I said to my husband, 'I'd like to get one of those ...' Then I paused, and said, 'And the exercise machine could be useful, too!' He spluttered into his tea, but I think it turns him on to know I'm still interested.

Yet, despite the common prejudices, many older people I spoke to are still loving, caring – and vibrant – sexual beings.

My wife and I have had 53 years of lovemaking. Oh, we fight and quarrel sometimes, like every other couple, but we're far from 'past it'.

I keep waiting for my libido to go away, but it just doesn't! In some ways I wish it would ...

Honestly, I feel like an 18-year-old in a 71-year-old body. I look at a nice young man I see on the street, and for a moment I actually think about what it would be like to have sex with him. Then I catch sight of myself in a shop window and realise that he's way out of my league. It's not fair. But even just wanting it makes me feel alive!

Adapting to change

Older people certainly do have personal concerns about various natural, age-related changes in their bodies – including those they think might make them less attractive, as well as those that directly affect their ability to become aroused and reach orgasm, or have pain-free sex. But if we have previously enjoyed sexuality in our lives, and have kept our bodies (including our genitals) reasonably healthy, we should be able to continue. However, that does involve a little adaptation. It may also require acceptance, and being open to adjusting positions.

> We've changed the way we do things. Once upon a time we used to have sex standing up, on the floor, on the kitchen table; now it's a soft surface and the easiest way possible. Frankly, I wouldn't say it's any less enjoyable – just less likely to cause rug burn!

> *A good sex life isn't something you're born with, any more than you're born with the ability to cook, to crochet or take shorthand.*
>
> Graham Masterton

Sexual flexibility is also important – at any age. I'm not talking about being able to lift your legs ceilingwards and part them at a 180-degree angle, but, rather, recognising that if something works on one occasion, that doesn't necessarily mean it's going to work every time. The mood may be different, and it needs to be correctly read. Some people are too rigid in their ways – they establish a pattern that they're

382

unwilling to change, and that can lead to boring, repetitive, or disappointing sex.

> *He said, 'I can't remember when we last had sex' and I said, 'Well I can, and that's why we ain't doing it.'*
>
> Rosanne Barr

Performance issues

If people in their 70s can avoid focusing too much on performance, they may have much better sex. Discovering that pleasure is an end in itself – and does not have to lead to orgasm – can vastly enrich sexual experiences for both men and women. This is actually true of any age, but now it's crucial. What's more, despite the fact that men grow up thinking that size and hardness are all that matters, *not* relying on erections is the key to long-term sexual success.

> *Generally speaking, it is in love as it is in war, where the longest weapon carries it.*
>
> John Leland

My erections will always be important to me, but they're not essential like they once were. When I get them now it's great, but I've learned to do without them. My wife has been very helpful with that. At first, when I got a good one, I'd say, 'Cancel everything! Let's use this while it's good.' But eventually she said, 'You know, your timing isn't necessarily my timing and anyway I can enjoy lovemaking without it.' That kind of hit at my masculinity, but she was right. She loves to be touched just as much as she enjoys anything else ...

Men can certainly please partners in many ways aside from intercourse, but they have to get over the notion that without an impressive hard-on they've lost their masculinity. Women of the same age can help by being reassuring and showing men how they like to be pleasured in non-coital ways. Nevertheless, there are some men who really struggle with erectile loss.

> I don't have a partner, so my issue is masturbation. It's difficult to masturbate without an erection – I can manage it with a partial one but since my prostatectomy I don't always get even that. It makes me feel depressed.

> *I would read* Playboy *more often but my glasses keep steaming over.*
>
> George Burns

The plain fact is that, for most men in their 70s, erections are simply not going to be exactly the same as when they were 20. But, being knowledgeable about what pleases a partner – and perhaps even using fantasy, erotica or anything that might increase excitement – a person can still have fantastic sex and be an excellent lover.

> Once upon a time my partner thought his main job was to pose in front of me with a six-pack and a massive erection. Now that he can't rely on either, he's had to learn other

things – especially how to please me without using his penis. Quite honestly, that's made him a much better lover – at least as far as I'm concerned.

Drugs to improve erectile capacity have become big business and are helpful to many people, but they don't work for everyone. Thankfully, anyone can enjoy intimacy in many forms aside from intercourse.

People forget how great kissing is. I wish more men liked it as much as I do. At this age, I really would welcome a return to all that romantic spooning I did when I was in my late teens.

Kissing, and I mean like, yummy, smacking kissing, is the most delicious, most beautiful and passionate thing that two people can do, bar none. Better than sex, hands down.

Drew Barrymore

Savouring the moment

Earlier in life, sexual encounters tend to be goal-orientated – all about a race to climax. In our 70s (if we haven't discovered this before), we should definitely start slowing down and enjoy each moment for its own sake.

Our courtship was fast and furious – I was fast and she was furious.

Max Kauffman

Having to make accommodations for some of the menopause-related changes in a woman's sexual response (such as dryness) can actually help the process of making sex more thoughtful and caring – and therefore more pleasurable. And sex can even become more creative as people strive to find erotically inventive ways to overcome physical issues such as aches and pains, discomfort in the joints and not being able to sustain positions that were once easy.

> Sex isn't so frustrating as it used to be. When I was younger I was never sure if I was going to have an orgasm. Now I know exactly how to have one if I want it. But sometimes I don't want one and that's okay, too.

> I don't mind letting her know what I want – when I first noticed that it was taking me longer to get hard, I didn't want to say anything. As a matter of fact, I sometimes said I'd just had too much to drink because I was afraid I wasn't going to get an erection at all. Now I can let her know exactly how I want to be stroked – and she does the same for me. The timing is trickier, but the end result is a lot better.

Recognising that both partners have a right to pleasure – and being able to let each other know exactly how – is something that doesn't always occur between younger partners. But not everyone at 70 wants to have an orgasm – or always can – and it's worth recognising that sex without climax is not a failure.

Post-menopausal bliss

As I mentioned earlier, menopause used to signify the end of a woman's sex life, but we now know that this is not true at all. As a matter of fact, many post-menopausal women report higher interest in sex. Women in their 70s are long past menopause. They no longer have to worry about pregnancy and usually have more time to focus on lovemaking. Most importantly, they may have a greater awareness of who they are sexually. Many really know what they want – and are not ashamed to communicate that to a partner. Men, in return, are pleased to be with a woman who knows herself, has good lovemaking skills and is willing to communicate her desires clearly. There can certainly be challenges at 70 and beyond, but whatever needs to be worked out can be achieved if people can only talk about it.

I don't care that his erections are not that reliable, but since he was diagnosed with sleep apnoea and got his C-PAP machine, I have missed cuddling with him at night. It's also not that sexy. But I made a deal with him that, every morning when he takes off his mask, we would spend time together either making love or just holding each other. I need that closeness, and so does he.

It's been 20 years since I went through menopause. I learned to adjust – took hormones at first, then stopped and had to deal with all the hot flushes and so on. But now that's all behind me and I'm used to putting the lube beside the bed.

Everyone said my sex life would be over once I had my hysterectomy, but they were wrong. It actually had little effect on my sex life.

Do looks matter?

How we feel about our bodies affects how comfortable we are allowing ourselves to be naked with others and sharing them during lovemaking – something that is, in fact, true of any age.

Keeping up my exercise regime is essential to me. There have been times when I've let it drop and I've noticed a matching drop in my libido – probably because I didn't feel too good about myself. I know I'm never going to be model-thin again, but if my arms aren't too flabby, my tummy is reasonably toned and I can get into my best dresses, I feel all right about myself.

I couldn't care less how I look now. I just let it all hang out. My husband has given up, too, but there's a simple solution: turn out the lights.

I have a whole wardrobe of lacy nightgowns – and I made matching covers for my colostomy bag. It all helps me to feel alluring and forget my issues – and it's less distracting for my partner, too, when unsightly things are camouflaged.

The funny thing is, I don't really notice my wife's ageing signs – wrinkles and so on. Oh, I know she's got them, but when you're with someone for years and years, you kind of see them as they always were. She's still very appealing to me.

I still fancy my husband, but over the past ten years he has put on an enormous amount of weight. I worry about that for his heath first and foremost, but it's also not something I find attractive. It also makes lovemaking a bit more difficult.

My partner and I try to stay fit and athletic at least. In the gay community, that's a priority, but we also feel it helps us feel sexier and more alive, even though we're in our 70s.

I don't feel great about my looks, but my husband seems to think I'm still sexy. He tells me I'm beautiful and romances me just like he did when we were younger. My friends think I'm really lucky – I guess I am.

I'm in my 70s, but I tell people I'm younger. I don't date men my age, or anyone with a paunch. I think it's our duty to stay reasonably slim and toned – after all, it's not that difficult, is it? Walking, jogging – or dancing and eating healthy food? What's the point of living if you're just going to become a couch potato and never have sex again? That's how I feel anyway.

You're never too old to become younger.
Mae West

Many people in their 70s do not consider looks a priority. Single people of this age who are searching for partners often consider a wide range of attributes, with physical appearance often being a fair way down the list.

I want companionship with someone my age who's bright and funny – someone who's lived through the same sorts of things I have: the same eras, who knows the same pop songs, remembers the Rolling Stones first time round. I don't care about cellulite; the other stuff is much more important.

I lost my wife and started to date a couple of years later. One woman I went out with was 20 years younger than me – 55. She was good-looking with big boobs (I've always been a boob man!), but she still wasn't my generation and we didn't have that much in common. At first I thought it wasn't going to work, but I found that as I opened myself to being interested in her point of view and started doing things she enjoyed – things I'd never done before, like ballroom dancing – I found her world was refreshing. I eventually married a woman closer to my own age, but that first period was a revelation.

I want a woman who knows what she wants, and is confident in herself and her sexuality – no matter what she looks like.

I'm less judgemental about the way a man looks now; after all, I'm no spring chicken. I want someone who's fun to be with, who can be comforting and – this is vital – who likes to cuddle and kiss and knows how to be sweet.

Sexual confidence

The way we feel about ourselves as sexual beings greatly affects our sexual responses. If we regard ourselves as attractive lovers who can provide significant pleasure for our partners, we will have optimal desire and sexual responses. But if we lose our confidence and instead come to see ourselves as unattractive, poorly functioning or impaired, that will have a significant effect on our sexual experience and the way we relate erotically to others.

> My wife thought I was a competent lover, and she taught me how to do things the way she liked it. But, after we divorced, I met a woman who made me feel like I was the best lover in the world. Then I noticed an improvement in my prowess, and I was willing to try all kinds of things I'd avoided in the past.

Trying a new partner is not a reliable way to improve our sexual functioning, but summoning a higher level of sexual confidence – perhaps through practice, better communication with a partner and a willingness to try new things – will certainly help.

> After my husband died I didn't want anyone else for a long time. But gradually I let friends introduce me to a few people. It was quite nice to meet men and feel desirable again, but the thought of having sexual relations with them terrified me. I felt like a schoolgirl – I'd only had sex with two men in my entire life, and I had no idea what these other men might expect. I didn't even know if I was physically capable of anything after so many years of separate beds.

Enough is enough

Not everyone maintains an interest in being sexual throughout their 70s. It is a matter of personal choice, and if someone is disinterested it certainly does not indicate that there's something wrong with them – or that they cannot be happy without having some kind of sexual experience. It goes without saying that the same thing applies to people of all ages.

I'm just not interested. There's really no particular reason – my body's not in bad shape for my age, and I get offers every now and again, but it's not something I really want to try again. To tell the truth, I've never really been that interested in doing it. I've always had too many other things to think about.

We've been married for 44 years, but we have not had sex for 20 or so. Still, we love each other, value our life together and have a great family life. I know I don't miss sex; in fact, I'm relieved that's all behind me. I think my husband masturbates sometimes – I discreetly leave him be. But I think he'd let me know if he still wanted sex with me.

I had so much sex in the 70s and 80s, if I don't have it again I don't give a shit.

Information underload

Some people in their 70s say that they might feel more open to having sex if they could get proper information and advice about the sexual issues that are bothering them. Research has found that there are a number of sexual questions that senior people would love to bring up with their doctors, but are afraid to ask – questions such as whether it's healthy to have intercourse at their age; how to protect themselves from contracting sexually transmitted infections; and the treatments that might be available for erectile difficulties, vaginal dryness or a lowering of desire. Not only do many men and women in their 70s long for facts on these issues, but they'd very much like to have accurate information imparted in a respectful, nonjudgemental manner. Unfortunately, this is not always forthcoming.

> I feel awkward about bringing up certain subjects with my GP. I'm afraid of being shrugged off as someone who shouldn't even be worried about such things at my age.

> My doctor knew my late husband. Somehow it just didn't feel right to bring up the issue of sexual safety. It would seem disrespectful to Jerry, even though he passed away ten years ago.

The truth is that many doctors are uncomfortable discussing sexuality. They have not always been taught the best ways to be helpful with sexual problems arising from various medical conditions or their treatments. But just because a person is older, terminally ill or disabled does not mean that he or she is disinterested in sex or wants to stop making love. If anything, such people may need it more than others. However, there is a view that sex should be the last thing on the minds of elderly people – particularly those with serious medical problems. This is neither true nor fair, and the dearth of support and information can make the process of trying to have a sex life that much more difficult.

> My doctor said to me, 'Let's just worry about getting you well.' I felt frustrated that my questions weren't answered. Losing my ability to be sexual would seriously make me want to give up living altogether.

Of course, it's not always easy to bring up the subject of sexuality with your doctor, particularly because many people get the sense that their GPs are rushed off their feet. Sex therapy *is* available for many people; however, the idea of consulting with a sex therapist is not something with which everyone is comfortable.

> We sought sex therapy because we heard it might be possible for us to have sex, despite our physical challenges. You would think that two people with spinal-cord injuries would never be able to be intimate, but our therapist found wonderful carers who helped to place us together. Despite misgivings, we even managed to have intercourse. We had to get over the lack of privacy but, for us, it was one of the most beautiful and special moments of our lives.

Many 70-somethings have a particular need for information, not only because they may have been out of the loop for a while – or have only had one partner for most of their sex lives – but because a mythology based on hearsay and scare stories has built up around the subject. In many cases, people genuinely don't know what's safe – and what's not – and times have definitely changed on the sexual front.

> I hear a lot about problems … you can get from sex. You read about all kinds of nasty diseases. I'd like to know if you can get anything from kissing and touching, which is what I mainly do.

There's no substitute for moonlight and kissing.
Barbara Cartland

Sex and health

It is a myth that practising safe sex is more important for young people than for seniors. Unfortunately, STIs are on the rise for people in the older age bracket, so using protection is vital. Heterosexual seniors who may be entering the dating arena for the first time in many years may not be accustomed to using condoms. Not only that, but condom use can be more difficult if you are already struggling with tentative or partial erections. One solution is to have 'outercourse' (non-penetrative sexual activities), until you are either able to have intercourse using a condom, or are confident about the safety and reliability of your partner (perhaps by arranging for you both to be tested).

Studies indicate that many people in their 70s are simply not concerned about STIs, and rarely ask a potential partner if he or she is HIV positive. Many are out of touch and think diseases such as herpes, HIV and hepatitis C are not transmissible at this age. But the risks of transmission of HIV may be even greater for people in the older age bracket. Their immune systems are less robust, and the vaginal wall is thinner and more prone to tearing, which means that infection may enter more easily.

I know about the risks, but at my age I'd probably play Russian roulette if I thought it would get me into bed with a beautiful woman!

However, sex is generally healthy for us, although many people do not believe that. Some even think it may stop medical treatments from working.

I was on antibiotics and my girlfriend told me that I shouldn't be drinking or having sex. She said she heard that both sex and alcohol affect your blood and stop the medication working.

Sex does not affect antibiotic treatment, although, as I mentioned in earlier chapters, alcohol, certain drugs (prescription, over-the-counter and recreational) and smoking can affect sexuality in a number of ways.

Coping with illness

Sometimes sex draws to a halt when illness or age-related problems strike. For example, having a chronic illness can lead to sexual problems, either through physiological changes or as a result of what happens in a person's psyche when faced with serious health challenges. But there are many people living with illness or disability who still wish to continue – or enhance – their sexuality.

Having MS has certainly taken its toll on our sex life; however, we made it a game to see how many ways we could have sex in my wheelchair ...

Since I no longer have genital sensations, I have become more attuned to sensual feelings in other parts of my body. For example, I love having my hair washed and my scalp massaged. My wife gets in the shower naked with me, washes me and massages me in all the places I like. I touch her and make her come. It's jolly exciting – just as good as having sex any other way. Sometimes I get an erection and she sits on my lap and pleasures herself. A lot of people think that people with disabilities can't have sex, but they're dead wrong. Many of us regularly have erotic experiences just like anyone else.

Loss of sexuality can seriously affect a person's quality of life, and people challenged by illness or disability often need a knowledgeable person to listen empathically to their concerns and offer some suggestions. Even a few simple ideas, such as how to minimise pain or adopt positions that make sex more comfortable – especially for those suffering from chronic fatigue, back pain and arthritis – can really help people coping with health challenges to get the comfort and pleasure they need. Having sexual intimacy when a person is coping with major health problems is life-affirming, and highly beneficial.

Once we started using strategically placed heat pads – and occasionally ice – our lovemaking improved.

People with spinal-cord injury, cerebral palsy, multiple sclerosis or hearing or visual impairment and many others who are living with disabilities, pain, illness or chronic conditions – and their partners – need special help working out how to have a satisfying sex life. This includes how to find the positions that work best, how to use sex toys to best advantage, how to make sex safe, ways to give and receive the most pleasure, how to find the best time for their lovemaking and what to do if they get tired, experience pain or get spasms during sex. Some need basic instruction in sexual response and anatomy.

Lying on my back is no longer an option, but I'm not sure if it would be safe for us to do it some other way. We've heard about 'rear entry', but we've never done it. I'd be afraid to try without knowing if it would be safe or not ...

People who experience chronic pain as a result of problems such as cancer, heart or neurological conditions, or diabetes, will usually have sex less often than they used to. But even people who are terminally ill or extremely debilitated often say that pleasurable touch and intimate connections are very important to them.

Even when I was in hospital, he would break the rules and slide into bed with me for a moment or two. Just feeling his body beside me, hearing his heartbeat – it was so helpful. In those few minutes I felt hopeful and less afraid.

Up to half of all men who need treatment for prostate cancer express strong concerns about the fact that they are facing possible erectile problems (or loss). The treatments for prostate cancer – radiation, surgery and hormone therapy – can lead to erectile dysfunction, at least temporarily. Even the psychological concerns – including sense of body betrayal and disintegration, and fear and anxiety about sexual performance – can affect sexual functioning. The arrival of drugs like Viagra, Cialis and Levitra has certainly been appreciated by many.

The first time I was prescribed Viagra, after my surgery, I was afraid to use it. I had heard that only a certain percentage of people are helped and I thought to myself, 'What if I'm one of the people who never gets an erection again?' I couldn't face the thought. But I finally bit the bullet and, thank God, it worked. Not ejaculating isn't such a big deal – I just wanted to be able to get it up from time to time.

Some of the common sexual problems that can occur in the case of serious illness include low sexual desire, erectile problems, female lubrication problems, difficulty achieving orgasm and painful sex. Men with heart problems, diabetes, high cholesterol, cancers of the prostate and pelvis, end-stage kidney disease, multiple sclerosis and hypertension can experience erectile failure resulting from their conditions. In particular, many people with cardiovascular disease worry that sex may trigger another heart attack.

> Bypass surgery was a tough experience, but it was comforting to have Jim there with me – he'd been through it himself five years earlier, so he knew the ropes. He knew I'd be afraid of getting back to our sex life again – for fear of having a heart attack.

Problems achieving vaginal lubrication are often experienced by women who have received treatment for ovarian cancer, or by those who suffer from multiple sclerosis or spinal-cord injury. Some enter an illness-induced menopause and suffer the associated symptoms of vaginal dryness and hot flushes, and their vaginas may lose elasticity. Certain women can use oestrogen supplements to counteract those symptoms, but others are advised not to do so for fear of stimulating future cancerous conditions. Emotionally, many women facing serious health issues lose their sexual confidence or are afraid of vaginal pain – and women who have undergone mastectomy may find it difficult to overcome their sense of being 'less of a sexual woman' as a result.

When I had my mastectomy he was as scared as I was. And my daughter started acting out – it was very stressful. But I said to him, 'Just cuddle me.' Cancer isn't contagious, and you don't have to fix this. Just be with me.

Even after hysterectomy, some women can still have orgasms, but other problems such as lowered self-appreciation, body-image issues, pain during sex, tiredness and nausea can all interfere with every aspect of their sexual responses. But for women who have had genital or pelvic surgery, it is often the relationship with their partners that makes it more or less likely that they will achieve orgasm, rather than the extent of the surgery itself. Having a sense of still being attractive is another important factor – and partners can help with this.

I told her she'd always been beautiful to me and, no matter what, she always would be. I meant every word.

Women with gynaecological cancer will commonly experience pain in their genitals and, in fact, many kinds of chronic pain can lead to sexual problems. Pain can make certain kinds of movement difficult, including sexual thrusting, twisting or bending to perform manual or oral sex. Being in pain can make a person constantly tired, and can lead to depression – which in turn reduces interest in sex.

I have to work out the timing for sex around my pain medication for my arthritis so we can do it when I am reasonably pain-free. We use heat pads to help ease my joints. But it's possible.

Sex is identical to comedy in that it involves timing.
Phyllis Diller

Dyspareunia (painful sex) can develop when there is dryness in the vagina. Some men feel pain in their penises, testicles, prostate – or find that ejaculation becomes painful. Sometimes a man's penis becomes curved due to a problem known as Peyronie's disease, and that can be painful – as can acute prostatitis. It is mainly desire and arousal that are affected by chronic illness and pain, although some people have multiple sexual problems. Medication, surgery and other treatments can further complicate the picture. Sexual problems are common after any chronic illness, and people cope with them in various ways. Learning to pleasure each other in non-penetrative ways may be the answer at first. People in happy marriages tend to cope better, and the health challenges can even help bring people closer together. However, those marriages that are already in trouble may not sustain the course when challenged by severe illness or disability.

When I was diagnosed with MS my husband was helpful at first, but eventually he started spending more and more time at the office. My family was mad at him – they assumed he was having an affair with a co-worker. But the truth is, it was me who was playing around. I had met a man who really wanted to be with me despite my MS, and we were the ones having the torrid affair. No one would have guessed that. My husband eventually left me, and I'm no longer with my other lover, but I doubt our marriage would have lasted anyway.

Some men have problems reaching orgasm, especially if they have experienced damage to their central nervous system due to spinal-cord injury, stroke, multiple sclerosis or brain tumour. But some men who have had radical treatments, such as having their penis amputated, can still reach orgasm. Certain conditions can render orgasm less intense – for example, in the case of men who no longer ejaculate, or who do not have completely firm erections. And quite a number of prescribed medications make it difficult for men to reach orgasm, including certain types of antidepressants. Sadly, some people who would like to improve their sexual responses simply give up.

After my prostatectomy my erections were kind of floppy. I was given instructions to try to climax even though I wasn't hard. At first I thought, 'What's the point?' but eventually two things happened. First, I found I was actually able to climax when I masturbated. Secondly, over time, my erections became a bit firmer.

The way individuals react psychologically to becoming ill varies. Some people become angry and withdrawn, and take it out on their partners and families. Serious illness or disability in the family can be enormously stressful to all. But getting health professionals to teach couples how best to manage physical handicaps – or what the specific impact of a particular disease might be on sexual functioning or treatment – can make the difference between maintaining sexual connections or not.

I lost my leg in an accident and it took me a while to feel comfortable having intercourse. My balance and the muscle tone on my good leg were affected – as well as the feeling that the remains of my lost leg were unsightly. But I got some help figuring it out – using a supporting rubber wedge and some positive thinking!

I couldn't feel much in my genitals, but I was advised to try using a vibrator to help get sensation back. It did help, along with working extra hard on conjuring up fantasies that really work for me. I guess that if and when I find a partner that may help, too.

Being able to communicate with each other about what each partner needs is essential. So is being able to mention technical difficulties and ask to change things if necessary – and also to have general, frank discussions about what is important and what is pleasurable for both. It is best to be flexible about trying new positions, and to find creative ways to reach orgasm – manual or oral caressing is often the most comfortable. Finding new ways to enhance excitement is important, and being helped to feel attractive – despite the physical challenges – becomes quite crucial.

Caring and sharing

Illness and physical disability can cause or increase relationship conflict. People with serious illness who lose the ability to take care of themselves and become dependent on a partner can feel humiliated, ashamed or anxious. And partners might find it hard to flip-flop between performing caretaking chores and being sexy. Becoming a partner's caretaker can cause serious problems in the relationship, so it is important to be able to discuss issues as they arise.

I was an athlete. I prided myself on my strength, independence and virility. All of a sudden I was a man who couldn't even wipe his own butt. My partner was fantastically helpful – a saint, in fact – but, in truth, I found myself feeling emasculated and resenting her for it.

It's always a good idea for the partner with an illness or disability to stay as independent as possible, so that caretaking is limited for the healthy partner. Other problems in life – extended family conflict, time-management issues, childcare, financial problems, household chores and work issues – can all be compounded by illness or disability. Couples may need to work extra hard to achieve open communication and improve their conflict-resolution skills.

Being able to share our feelings about Bob's health issues made an enormous difference. We started having regular discussions about everything we were dealing with. Both of us needed to express how worried and frightened we were. We held each other and everything would seem all right.

A little comfort

Some of the best attributes of an older lover are experience, patience and a greater level of sensuality. This is certainly what most women of this age want – far more than a rock-hard erection. Fortunately, many people in their 70s are simply not as hung up about sex as younger people are. They tend to be more comfortable with sensual variety, and some are better than younger lovers at sexual communication.

I get offers from other men, but I prefer sex with my husband ... I can tell him where to touch, what to do, etc., without embarrassment.

Since men and women both become more androgynous as they age – the result of changing hormones – men acquire more interest in cuddling and hugging: the things that women have prioritised for years.

> *Among men, sex sometimes results in intimacy, among women, intimacy sometimes results in sex.*
> Barbara Cartland

Many people in their 70s and beyond have expressed the need for physical soothing and sensual touch, as well as verbal reassurance. Of course, genital stroking is usually nice at any age, but the entire skin surface can become a global erogenous zone, and provide enormous pleasure if we are touched and stroked the right way.

I never knew my skin itself could give me so much pleasure. Oh, I've enjoyed Swedish massages for many years, but having a lover caress me all over is almost better than real sex – and often all I really want.

Many adults have forgotten the delights of non-coital sexuality because they have become accustomed to 'going straight for the money'. But women in particular tend to love slow romantic connections, sensuous embraces and seductive words.

His voice was as intimate as the rustle of sheets.

Dorothy Parker

As people age, they may gain a better understanding of what really constitutes love, especially the empathic, accepting aspects of it – in other words, older people may find true intimacy easier to achieve.

At 79 I'm still trying to develop as a human being. I like to attend lectures, I read a lot, and have managed to keep abreast of basic computer skills – I would like to find a woman who's on a similar path.

The idea of being with a partner who loves sex as much as I do, and who values closeness, sharing and intimacy – that's a real turn-on.

Whether we are in good health or not, in our 70s sex is not so much about plumbing, and not just driven by lust and hormones. We would do well to focus on enriching sexual and sensual experiences. It's quality, not quantity, that counts.

Sex just doesn't happen as much as it used to, so I think we both look forward to it more.

There are some things that are better than bad sex: peanut butter and jelly. But in general, I can't think of anything better than good sex.

Billy Joel

Advance planning

Getting it on may not be as spontaneous as it once was, but even when we're in our 30s, it's wise to plan it, in order to make sure it happens and to get the best out of it.

> *If you're going to have spontaneous sex on the kitchen sink, you have to do the dishes first.*
>
> Dr Marty Klein

Sadly, privacy is often a pressing issue, too, especially for those living in assisted living places for elderly people. It's always wise to ask a nursing home about their policy regarding sex prior to signing up.

> There was a room specially reserved for people in the home who wanted to be private with each other. The problem was, it was right off the main sitting area, so everyone could see who went in and out. Some people actually parked themselves on the couch opposite the door, so they could stick their noses in other people's business and then gossip about it.

Some people in their 70s have smartly come to the conclusion that sexuality should probably be talked about ahead of time – especially if one partner has certain problems that may need to be accommodated.

> I'm a grown-up. I like to know if there's something I need to be prepared for. I don't want to go and touch her somewhere that's going to hurt or something.

Verbal communication is certainly vital, and should probably take place before, during and after lovemaking. In our 70s, we can never be 100 per cent sure how our bodies – or our part-ners' – are going to react, so being ready to stop and change course is wise.

Since my mastectomy and the radiation treatment, I'm never quite sure how sex is going to work out for me. Sometimes I just have to ask if we can stop – then I hold him while he brings himself to orgasm. At least we have that closeness, he is satisfied – and I don't have to feel guilty about ruining everything. He will often give me a tender back massage afterwards, which is really lovely, and very comforting. It's often all I really want.

Love and relationships

People in their 70s who are searching for love and sex can still have strong, passionate feelings, and can fall in love in just the same way as they did when they were 30.

I fell deeply and crazily in love with a younger man who appeared to feel the same way. I think for a while he really did have feelings for me, and the sex was fantastic. But gradually he started expecting me to buy him expensive things, and I went along with it until one day I realised our 'love' was really just a business transaction between a gigolo and a silly old fool.

Like the measles, love is most dangerous when it comes late in life.

Lord Byron

But most seniors have had more experience with love and sex than younger people. They know it is precious and not to be taken for granted. However, one important difference between younger and older couples is that the latter may spend more time together.

Everything gets sweeter because everything ends. That is the ultimate barter.

Elizabeth Kaye

At our age we're spending a lot more time together than we did in the past. In some ways that's nice, but if he's been pole-axed on the couch in front of the TV all night without paying me any attention, why on earth would he think when we climb into bed, I'll suddenly turn into his sex kitten? All I'm in the mood for is another chapter of *Eat, Pray, Love*!

I love you for dinner but never for lunch.

Author unknown

Resolving differences prior to retiring to bed is important for people of all ages, but those in their 70s may just have a better capacity for letting go of grievances and realising that it's just not worth hanging on to things that aren't that important in the long run.

Loving whispers, touches, looks – they're all still very important to me. Sleeping in my lover's arms is just as wonderful as it was when I was 40 years younger.

It's really weird after all this time, but we're still learning about each other. She just told me that she made out with her best girlfriend after they left school. That was a hot image for me! I hope I'm still sexually curious and capable of being thrilled by her sexiness until the day I die.

Those who are still with partners at this age may receive, among other wonderful things, the benefits of regular and available sexual contact.

About two years ago I got an email from someone I'd known 20 years ago. I had been to bed with him in the late 80s. He tracked me down and emailed me – I was surprised to hear from him. I thought he was dead like everyone else I knew then. We hooked up, and we've been having sex for the last couple of years. He's 57, with a really handsome face. I've always liked faces. Since he was the only thing available, I've been doing it with him. But he's too moody – he withdraws. We don't really have much in common. We have great sex, but I can't deal with that moodiness. I saw him this past weekend, but he got pissed off after something really minor. I haven't heard from him since, and I don't give a shit. I don't feel like putting up with it. But it's been great because I realise that I love sex again, and I have discovered that I don't need Viagra. We'll probably hook up again, but I'm not in any rush. I'm a real slob and if I bring him home, he'll spend the first day or two cleaning up. I loved that.

With my husband regular sex is good ... sometimes very, very good if he hits the G-spot ...

I do feel that I have the privacy for sex that I need – but only because I am 'happily married', whatever that is!

Now the importance of sex in my life is six out of ten more important than when I was younger ...

We try and schedule sex, although that can be a bit 'formulaic'. But, if I don't, we tend to 'let it drift' and not have sex.

I still have fantasies. I saw two young boys walking down street – maybe they were in their late 20s – amazing-looking kids. I would have loved to have been with them, but I'm not stupid enough to think I'd ever be able to have sex with them. When I was their age, I would have been horrified to think of having sex with anyone even in their 40s. I once innocently and stupidly accepted an invitation to stay with a professor. I was 30 and he was 47. It was absurd – he might as well have been 87. You only fucked people your own age.

When I was young, I thought sex between older people just 'didn't happen'. Now I don't care what people do (within reason) or how old they are.

Many of the people in their 70s to whom I spoke – whether they were married, single, divorced, co-habiting, in a civil union or widowed, whether or not they had medical problems and whether or not the ageing process had affected their sexuality – disagreed with the idea that sex is only for young people. They viewed sex as a fantastic gift that enhances our quality of life at every age. We just need to find the inspiration, have the courage to overcome sexual challenges if they present themselves and seek sexual health – whatever that means to each one of us. Sexual expression – including being a little 'naughty' – is life-affirming.

> *Lead me not into temptation. I can find the way myself.*
>
> Rita Mae Brown

10

In Our 80s, 90s and Beyond

Hot, Creative Sex

Sex can be fun after 80, after 90, and after lunch.

George Burns

Unfortunately, George Burns's view is not a widespread notion. However, I have found the stereotype of older adults being disinterested in sex to be untrue. Younger people do not find it easy to imagine their grandparents as being sexually active; however, many adults in their 80s told me that they are still interested in having an active and varied sex life, and many value it enormously as a fantastic source of comfort and pleasure.

We can, without question, be sexual until the day we pass on – if we look after our sexual health. For sexual longevity, health is more the defining factor than ageing itself. But even people in ill-health – or with physical or mental disabilities – can still find creative ways to have pleasure, if they wish. But sometimes they may have to go the extra mile to work out exactly how.

Sex at 90 is like trying to shoot pool with a rope.
George Burns

George Burns was wrong about that one. As I've said in previous chapters, men do not automatically stop being capable of erections just because they are ageing – and the fact that they may not be as firm or frequent as they once were does not mean that their owners cannot give and receive immense sexual pleasure.

As a young man I used to have four supple members and one stiff one. Now I have four stiff and one supple.

Henri, Duc d'Aumale

Some healthy 80-year-olds are surprised to discover that they still maintain the ability to have erections, and that even a partial erection can help its owner achieve ejaculation, or even intercourse. Due to the common mythology about sex and ageing, they had previously been convinced that this was impossible – or even wrong.

I am 82 and enjoying intercourse with a woman three years older than me. Should we be doing this?

Some people in their 80s still hold on to the beliefs of the Victorian era, thinking that sex is purely for procreation. Such people probably retired their genitals many years ago and, of course, it was their right to do so.

My husband and I were married until shortly after our ruby wedding anniversary. When I was maybe 43 – 40 years ago – sex died out totally. Well, our sleeping arrangements were not agreeable to my husband, with me tossing around so much.

In our 40s, sex totally faded out. We lived just like brother and sister, and I had no notion to go outside my marriage. Nor did he – he was too engrossed in TV and cigarettes, which might have been the thing that ended him. He went to local pubs and drank quite a lot of beer.

I think we both had low libidos. It's probably a good thing. Otherwise, if he'd protested when I decided he wasn't going to share my bed anymore, I would have said, 'Get lost. Go and find somebody else! Find an outlet elsewhere – I'll still live agreeably with you ...'

Changing times

A number of people I spoke to who were in their 80s had strong opinions about what they saw as an unnecessarily open climate of sexual discussion, as seen and heard in the media and in the behaviour of the younger people they see around them.

A lot of things people get up to nowadays are just unnatural. The television programmes are all about unmarried people having sex, and I even heard a doctor saying masturbation was not sinful. That's not how I was brought up.

Girls are so free and easy now, but in my time you weren't drinking at all. I played around before I got married, to be honest, but a lot of my friends got pregnant. I knew of condoms, but nobody really had money to invest in those. Now the girls have better ways.

Men are more towards sexuality; I don't think women are really that interested in sex.

Girls have freedom now, but I think they have it too early, too young. In my time, if you were out later than ten or 11 pm, you'd be in trouble. In my mid-teens there were very few dances or places to socialise. During the war, most people were away in the army – all we had were just fundraisers for the troops.

The Victorians were not prudes – they just kept it all under cover. I've heard plenty of stories about maids who worked in big houses. At night you would hear the blokes scuttling along to the girls' bedrooms. It was the done thing but, unlike today, it was secret. Now things have totally swung around.

I think sex on TV is made too much of – it doesn't seem to help for girls getting pregnant. Some do, of course, get contraceptive advice but I think it takes away something of the romance. It's common, run of the mill. In my day we'd go out for walk and a cuddle, and a kiss or a film, and sit with our arms round each other. That was it. Nobody could afford cars. There were local dances, that was it. We didn't call it 'snogging' then. Lots were having sex when they didn't want to – many women were just a breeding machine. After my children, I used condoms. I wrote to a chemist in the city and got them by post. I read about it in a magazine.

Today it's all too 'easy come, easy go'. That's what is expected ...

Others I spoke to were more accepting of current mores.

I think masturbation is an automatic, harmless release. Better that than they go out and rape somebody, for God's sake – that's my attitude. It's probably an uncontrollable urge.

Sexual learning

People in their 80s did not have sex education at school; in fact, their introduction to sex was often vastly different than it is for young people today.

I had been brought up with animals. What they did to produce their young was not called sex. It just happened.

Then, mothers would say to their daughters, 'Now watch what you're doing – come straight home!' Today, mum is often not there to see. Apart from the fact that sex has become so open with TV and so on, the young are much more enlightened. They have sex education in schools now. But sex was never mentioned in my time; only, 'Good girls don't!' If somebody found out that one or two girls had loose standards, they'd say, 'Well, you'd never be like her!' It was a threat. You didn't want to get into trouble and ruin your reputation. There were local girls who did, though.

When I was about 17, there was a young lad lived in the next farm down the road. He worked for a couple of old ladies (when I say old, they were probably a lot younger than I am now, though). He used to come up in the evenings and play whist and other games. I remember a friend of mine came over, too, and I walked her home and this lad came along. After we left her, he wanted to do a bit of that. I said, 'No, no.' It wasn't in the cards. I didn't feel that way. I knew about unwanted pregnancy. I'd have been ruined.

Sex was banned from being spoken about in the house, and we had no books. But I knew that you took the cow to the bull and I knew what went on – and I was there helping at the birth. It was so open in the field.

As I've mentioned early on in this book, the social and political landscape of a society can change the nature of a population's sexuality. Here's another illustration from a woman in her 80s.

During the war, having the troops in the area changed the whole scene. There was an acceptance about sexuality that was far greater than before. These incoming soldiers made it far more acceptable that local girls fell for them. The men coming in from outside were more slick. Local lads in country areas hadn't the right approach – they'd say, 'Just come in among these trees!' It was too rustic. But the soldiers – they'd been out and around, maybe back from Dunkirk, maybe been in France. Plus some of the girls had been away in the land army and so on. As far as women are concerned, at 17 they were called up for the forces. The country girls were away then in the towns, and that brought them out of themselves. That's the way I see it. They came back far wiser, if you know what I mean. Whereas I – who didn't go away – would have been listening to their conversations in ignorant bliss.

Still sexy

Instead of 'ageing person', I prefer the term 'chronologically advantaged' – especially when it applies to sex. But chronologically advantaged people frequently have to deal with the negative perceptions and judgements of society and families about their sexuality. I recommend that anyone who gets that kind of treatment from a family member – or anyone else for that matter – simply puts them in their place. I have met some thoroughly sexy octogenarians. They deserve our admiration, not judgement.

For me it seemed normal to be interested in both men and women. I enjoyed sex equally with men and women. I had someone practically every day. At one point, I had four men and one women. I was inventive – inclined to using imagination just as I do in other ways. There was a period of my life in my 30s when I was involved with two men and two women. That was exhausting. I was tired all the time.

Sex is like having breakfast, lunch or dinner – or it can be just a snack – and it's very nice, too. Or like having a salad – very tasty....

For 17 years I was married to a homosexual and I was a lesbian. He was older than me. We had an open relationship.

I had a very active sex life with Jean. She was really imaginative and full of beans. She was older than me. I never knew how old she was, but she was easily 100. She told her lawyer she was 91. She had a male partner, too. I never asked one question of her and I think that's why we lasted. Our 40s, 50s, 60s – those are good years. I had an extra ten years. I think it's because I just enjoyed it and didn't fight or censor it or anything.

I've been on my own for a long time – my husband died 20 years ago – but I would still have a heart to love someone if the right person came on. Yes, I'm 85, but if my heart was stirred by someone, I would quite happily sleep with them.

Everything to do with sex, I've enjoyed. For me it was not hush-hush, but originally I wasn't taught about anything. I went to the library. For me sex was just like having breakfast. You get hungry, you eat something. Anyone who makes it nasty or unusual is not on to the reality.

Through sex I've met some wonderful people.

Some people in their 80s say they don't do it as often as they used to, and that even masturbation is very infrequent.

My life is so full I never even think about intercourse. I love the love that I get, but then everybody's different. We never talk about sex here (in the residence), unless there are three or so together in the lounge – they will sort of chat together and say, 'You know what I heard?', then mention somebody, 'I heard so-and-so was meeting up with so and so ... well we know what they'll be doing!'

It's been so long since I made love, I can't even remember who gets tied up.

Joan Rivers

Others have fairly regular sexual experiences – either alone or with a partner.

My sexual desire is still the same. My orgasms can be dependent on how much time and effort I give them. But I have pleasure one way or another.

I find lovemaking a serious and delightful occupation.

Winston Churchill

The loss of a partner

People in their 80s are not without their problems. Many, for example, suffer the loss of a sexual partner.

> He started having mini-strokes and breathing difficulties, and now he has heart problems and crippling arthritis. He can barely walk, so sex is out of the question, I think. But I'm just glad he's here.

> I really wanted to have sex with Gerald, but first of all he was in his 60s – 20 years younger than me – and secondly I couldn't stop feeling that I was being unfaithful to Burt, even though he passed away 15 years ago. But eventually I wanted him so much I just gave in.

> My long-term lesbian partner is no longer living, and my son died in 2002 from AIDS-related pneumonia. I miss them terribly. It was just one big party after another.

> My husband died from having a bad heart and lungs, and I've not had a partner since my lover died in 2001. I hesitate to search for another, because I'm not that young. I'm hesitant to start something I can't continue.

> I fell in love when I was a soldier in the Second World War. We were all barely men, and I didn't understand my sexuality until I met Tom. We had very little time together – he was killed in France a year after we met. I still regard him as the love of my life – even though it was 60-odd years

ago. Last year I took a trip back to Europe to visit his grave. I wanted to say 'goodbye' to him for the last time.

In our 80s, grief about losing loved ones and also sadness about losing the physical pleasure that was once shared is often profound, and may even lead to depression.

I don't have many surviving friends who are also gay from the 70s or 80s. I had a whole network – they were my world – and they all disappeared. Many of us are devoid of our friends. I'm lucky my roommate survived it all. He's very interested in having sex, but his chances are diminished, too. When gay men are over 45 or 50, their problem is similar to many single women – they become invisible.

The last time I had an orgasm with someone else was 40 years ago. We don't have sex now. He's quite ill. Just after he retired, our sex life was very good because we had time, and the house was empty, but now we haven't had sex for 25 years. He was very embarrassed because he couldn't get erections. He said, 'Oh well, that's it. I can't do it anymore.' I didn't like that, but it didn't occur to me to object. I lost myself in work. I never wanted to have sex with anyone else. It just wasn't in me to ask my husband to do anything about it.

We're in our 80s now, but my husband stopped having erections at 59. He just didn't want to attempt it anymore. I think what makes me sad is that some affection would be nice. He wouldn't hold hands or put arm around me – he never liked displays of affection. I would put my arms around him, but he didn't like that. He's the kindest, nicest man you'd ever want to meet, but I think his upbringing was a bit strange.

She's never been one to show affection, so I've given up. She's here, and that's all I ask for. We're terrific friends. We laugh and enjoy each other's company. I don't know what the heck I'd do without her. But I do see people of about my age (just 80) who have a lot more.

I have a live-in person. We've been together for 30 years. We had sex a couple of times when we met in '78, but we're not sexually compatible. But we stayed living together – as roommates. I guess we're pretty close – there for each other.

In fact, staying socially connected apparently increases longevity, and being in a happy relationship helps a person live longer. Alternatively, being lonely may shorten our lives.

I get as many hugs and kisses from my pals as I would from a lover. I have great mates – to me that's just as important as a partner who would sleep with me. I don't think of them as sexual, just very close. Being at one with people means a lot to me.

Sexual intercourse is kicking death in the ass while singing.

Charles Bukowski

Negotiating the effects of ageing

The natural effects of ageing – particularly pervasive symptoms such as fatigue – will certainly influence sexuality for someone in their ninth or tenth decades.

I started feeling physical changes at 75. Around about 74 – at the end of that year – I started feeling older and more tired.

I get sexual feelings when I'm reading a book where someone is having passionate sex. But I've not been interested in masturbation. I don't have as much energy for anything anymore – including sex. That's hard for me. After ten hours' sleep, I'm still tired. I'm tired of being tired.

Three minutes of serious sex and I need eight hours of sleep and a bowl of Wheaties.

Richard Pryor

As I outlined earlier, many illnesses and disabilities – as well as the impact of medication, surgery and other treatments – can cause sexual problems, often more so than ageing itself. There can be psychological challenges, such as depression or anxiety, that may affect sexual responses. Nevertheless, many older adults want to have the opportunity to be sexual throughout their lives – even if it requires making accommodations. They want help figuring out how to work around their health problems so that they can enjoy the comfort, pleasure and life-affirming joy that lovemaking or self-pleasuring can bring.

The sexual embrace can only be compared with music and a prayer.

Havelock Ellis

Life expectancies are increasing for both men and women, so it is my belief that we need to pay attention to supporting sexuality among elders, banish the stereotype of older people as asexual and recognise that, for them – just as it is earlier in life – sexual expression is an important 'quality of life' issue. Not only that, but sex is healthy.

An orgasm a day keeps the doctor away.
Mae West

Of course, even for healthy people in their 80s, there may be normal, age-related physical changes that may affect their sexual response.

Is it not strange that desire should so many years outlive performance?
William Shakespeare

The natural, age-related changes in men include gradual changes to the angle and hardness of their erections and less-forceful ejaculation, while women gradually produce less and less vaginal lubrication and may experience vaginal atrophy if they do not continue with penetration of some kind. For both men and women, orgasm and desire may become less intense over time. However, as I've shown in earlier chapters, many people in their later years consider sex to be just as good – if not better – than it was earlier in life, and many say that there are special benefits, such as having more spare time to enjoy it.

Only last night I had a fantastic orgasm!

Early influences

Early environment and circumstances strongly influence the sexuality of people of any age. For those I spoke to in their 80s, the specific social environment of their childhood had profoundly affected each of them in different ways.

At 12, I had rheumatic fever, so I was lying in bed for 18 months. I lost all my school mates. My pals left school at 14, and were sent out to work at the merchant houses at 15. So girls I had been at school with before my illness were out in the world meeting chaps – but I never went through that because I was too limited. I was not even allowed to cycle.

My environment was a male upbringing – there were all boys in my class and I only had uncles.

My company was always animals. I was brought up on a farm and so I grew up with sex happening in the animal world. My brother would come and help on the farm and he spoke to me as though I was a bloke. We worked side by side on the land, harvesting. He spoke to me as just one of the lads. He never thought of me as a girl who had laid on her back for them all.

When I think about one of my grandmothers – she had 11 children – she must have been producing every second year. Oh, my God – that's a sentence! I mean she didn't have a life, and was slaving on a farm – but then it was accepted. Her oldest daughter was away working by the time her youngest was born. My grandfather was a 'man of the moment' – away socialising and playing the pipes while she was at home with all those little ones. When her oldest daughter was in her 20s and could understand, she heard him pressing her mother for sex and her weeping. Can you blame her? Resisting his urges and weeping. It's a sentence. It was a man's prerogative in those days. I can visualise her now – no modern conveniences – walking to the well and carrying buckets of water. Now I can see her when she was elderly, with a walking stick – deformed on one side from all that childbearing and heavy work. She lived a full life, though – lived into her 70s. And there were many more like her. Neighbours or even a district nurse would have helped her give birth. But many died in childbirth and babies died as well. That's how life was in the country areas.

Seasoned lovers

Understandably, some 80-year-olds to whom I spoke were unimpressed with contemporary methods of sexual enhancement.

> Sex toys are a waste of time. Some people probably need it, but I never got into it.

Physical closeness and intimate gestures, such as cuddling and non-genital stroking, seem to become more important in later life. They can be a real source of comfort, as well as an expression of love.

'Use it or lose it' is undoubtedly the mantra for sexuality in later life. If we continue to exercise our sexual response – either with a partner or without – we should be able to engage in lovemaking and/or masturbation throughout our entire life span. Then, of course, there is the matter of our lifelong erotic imagination.

I'm finished with men, but I have a very full memory.
Ursula Andress

Communicating needs

Couples in their 80s are prone to certain problems that occur frequently in younger couples – such as one partner having more desire than the other. They may find it hard to talk about sex or ask for what they need, and – in my opinion – some would benefit from learning better sexual communication. Several people in their 90s – both heterosexual and otherwise – told me that they would welcome having some help with this. They were also keen to learn new techniques in order to both give and receive more pleasure and less discomfort from lovemaking.

We lie together and cuddle, which sometimes progresses to touching each other's genitals, if one or both of us feel like it. Sometimes Harry gets an erection and sometimes he doesn't. We don't have intercourse anymore – it's too tiring. But other things are just as nice and not as likely to put your back out!

Many older adults are more interested in petting, stroking and mutual masturbation than intercourse.

We hadn't had intercourse for 15 years or so, until my husband came home one day with a prescription for

Cialis. A few hours later, he had his first erection for ages, but I was terrified. 'What exactly are you planning to do with that?' I asked him. We tried, but we couldn't get it in. I had to go to my gynaecologist and get some help. See, it's not just men who have issues.

Some people in their 80s and 90s were relieved to hear that most sexual professionals consider masturbation to be a healthy activity that can be enjoyed throughout a person's life span (some had thought it was an 'immature' thing to do). Some were eager to meet new partners and had similar fears about desirability that younger people frequently express. Homosexual men and lesbians complained about their youth-orientated communities, said that they had less sex now than they used to have – and worried more about their level of attractiveness; however they also said that there was still a fair level of support and social connected-ness in their lives.

John and I have nearly separated a number of times over the years, but I think we're both very glad we stuck it out. Our group of friends has dwindled – first during the early AIDS years, and now many have passed on due to other reasons. But whatever happens, we still have each other …

I don't miss sex as such; I miss the affection. I never really had it, but I still miss it.

I'm in my 80s, but I still go out with younger blokes. It's usually just dinner – they tell me their problems. There's one in particular – we meet regularly for a meal. They chat about sex sometimes. One says, 'What would I do without you?' I like the fact that I'm useful to them.

New tricks

The openness and interest displayed by most of the senior people I interviewed indicated that they were interested and willing to learn new techniques to enhance and enrich their sex lives, even if that meant having to learn computer skills so that they could participate in chatroom discussions and join online social networks. For them, sex was precious, and their erotic potential remained exciting and viable.

> *The real fountain of youth is to have a dirty mind.*
> Jerry Hall

Even people in their 90s can have fabulous orgasms – either alone or with someone else. Some rebels find themselves exciting younger partners, and even marry them, which is really very brave, because it is pretty well guaranteed to arouse the wrath and judgement of their families.

> *The older one grows, the more one likes indecency.*
> Virginia Woolf

Take the highly publicised case of oil tycoon J. Howard Marshall II, who, in 1994 – his 90th year – married 26-year-old model Anna Nicole Smith. Marshall died in 1995, setting off an inheritance feud over whether she had a right to the $400 million family estate, but it was probably the accentuated sexuality of Smith (who died suddenly at age 39) – and the age difference between her and her husband – that caused the headlines. Unfortunately, the truth is that Marshall was atypical; many people in their 90s find that sex is a solo experience, due to the lack of available partners.

> Why beat myself up? I'm not going to find some 30-year-old boy – I'm not going to bust myself trawling the internet looking for some kid who wants a sugar daddy.

> In some ways I'm lucky – at least I still have an 18-year-old mind!

If we can retain a sense of humour about our sexuality we'll be able to deal with it best. One wonderfully horny 93-year-old I met quipped:

> I know I had the wildest sex imaginable last night. Next morning, I had to see my doctor. Not because it hurt – but with my Alzheimer's I needed help remembering it!

> *A terrible thing happened to me again last night – nothing.*
>
> Phyllis Diller

Some things never change

Despite the mileage comedians get out of it, sex at 90 – or even 100 – is not just a joke. People in their 90s have told me that their fantasy lives have outperformed their bodies, but that there was an extremely active sex life going on between their ears.

The details of my fantasy sex life are quite similar to what they were many years ago. In my mental pictures, I haven't aged – that would be a turn-off!

The brain is viewed as an appendage of the genital glands.

Carl Jung

Some people in their 90s have told me that they still have the same sexual feelings as they did when they were younger. Others say they think about sex even more, look back on their sexual encounters with appreciation and longing – and even wish they'd been more sexual when they'd had more opportunities.

The mistakes you regret the most in your life are the ones you didn't commit when you had the chance.

Helen Rowland

When we reach 90, we have the advantage of hindsight. We can look back on decisions we made to avoid pleasure, and clearly recognise futile fears and hang-ups that may have unnecessarily influenced us.

I was a good young man and I'm glad to say it's enabled me to be a wicked old one.

W. Somerset Maugham

But at the end of the day, sex is part of our life force. Some of us can do without it, but for others it plays a huge part in defining who we are.

My doctor has forbidden me to do the three things I love most in the world – fight bulls, ride horses and mount women. It's time to go.

Juan Belmonte's final words

Conclusion

like the Buddhist notion of the 'wheel of life'. Not only does it illustrate the different realms a person might inhabit throughout her life as she strives to be a better person, but it is also designed to be interpreted as a progressive journey on which one might travel within a very short period – one minute feeling carnal and therefore inhabiting the realm of the beasts, and the next being elevated via meditation, prayer or chanting to the spiritually rich plane of the gods. Similarly, as sexuality unfolds throughout our life span, it also fluctuates – even radically – over short or longer periods as it is influenced by changing life events, thoughts and experiences.

The danger in setting out a book in sections dedicated to each human decade of the wheel of life is that a reader might be left with the impression that the development and progression of our sexuality through each decade are rigidly set – and, of course, they are not. Sex is a learned experience and each individual acquires unique learning – especially in a society like ours, where accurate sexual information can be difficult to come by.

What's more, significant life experiences – such as becoming a parent, being bereaved or getting a new job – can fundamentally change a person's sexual path. And just as people differ in the timing of their lifelong psychosocial development, the same is true of their sexuality. I trust I have already made it clear enough that our sexuality is created via a myriad of influences, including our family experiences, our society, religion, education, physical state, psychology, sexual orientation, gender, body image, health, race and ethnicity, the messages we have received about sex from media and other sources, and all earlier sexual experiences. Thus the state of our sexuality is as prone to change as our lives are generally – being predictable to most people only as far as they could ever gauge the result of a surge of certain sex hormones, the sexual impact of divorce or the sexual side-effects of a prescribed medication.

But enough about sex. I want to focus on pleasure, because I'm not sure enough of us do. Most of us have been brought up thinking that it's not altogether right to enjoy pure pleasure. The words 'guilty' and 'pleasure' are very often used together, as if it would be wrong to discuss pleasure on its own. But unless we can let go of the notion that suffering is always noble – and taking pleasure is a vice – we will never achieve our sexual potential. We have all been given the ability to experience truly intense pleasure, but many of us are simply scared of it. Not only that, but we are afraid of it in others, as if the ability thoroughly to enjoy sensual pleasures in a way we can't is an evil contagion.

Surely we would benefit by being accepting of ourselves and everyone else – no matter how different they may seem – as sexual beings simply led to seek pleasure in a natural way. Being able to focus on pleasure when it is occurring in our bodies – especially during lovemaking – is not as easy as it sounds. Many of us are focused elsewhere – on our body's imperfection, our partner's inadequacies, or what we have to do in the next hour. You see, if we do less, we can allow something important to happen, but while we are so invested in controlling our feelings, sensuality is lost. If we could let go of our need to achieve, to perfect, to try, to be good, to reach a climax or help someone else reach it, we might find that we can allow pleasure to be experienced in its most intense form, and that satisfaction would naturally follow. Of course, achieving this requires finding the time for sensual experience in the first place and, for many in today's frantic world, that's a rare commodity.

At the end of the day we're just human animals struggling to survive and thrive, to live at peace and to procreate. But given the world's current over-population, sex purely as a means of procreation doesn't really make much sense, does it? And what about the fact that – as we've already seen through the testimonies of people who are outside a procreative age, who do not wish to have children, or whose sexual orientation or style cannot lead to conception – the sexual drive is present, no matter what. We cannot entirely control our sexual urges, and it's a mistake to try.

I believe our best option is to try to understand our own individual sexuality, to be accepting of who we are as sexual beings and to seek and allow ourselves sexual pleasure in safe, sane and consensual ways. If we so wish – no matter how old we become – continuing to enjoy sexuality will enhance our quality of life. Highly pleasurable sex is not only for the young, the able or the healthy among us. It can be part of who we are for as long as we live.

Appendix

Sexual rights are fundamental and universal human rights. A Declaration of Sexual Rights was developed at the 13th World Congress of Sexology in Valencia in 1997. In 1999 the version below was adopted at the 14th World Congress of Sexology in Hong Kong.

Declaration of Sexual Rights

Sexuality is an integral part of the personality of every human being. Its full development depends upon the satisfaction of basic human needs such as the desire for contact, intimacy, emotional expression, pleasure, tenderness and love. Sexuality is constructed through the interaction between the individual and social structures. Full development of sexuality is essential for individual, interpersonal and societal well-being. Sexual rights are universal human rights based on the inherent freedom, dignity and equality of all human beings. Since health is a fundamental human right, so must sexual health be a basic human right.

In order to assure that human beings and societies develop healthy sexuality, the following sexual rights must be recognised, promoted, respected and defended by all societies through all means. Sexual health is the result of an environment that recognises, respects and exercises these sexual rights.

1. The right to sexual freedom. Sexual freedom encompasses the possibility for individuals to express their full sexual potential. However, this excludes all forms of sexual coercion, exploitation and abuse at any time and situations in life.

2. The right to sexual autonomy, sexual integrity and safety of the sexual body. This right involves the ability to make autonomous decisions about one's sexual life within a context of one's own personal and social ethics. It also encompasses control and enjoyment of our own bodies free from torture, mutilation and violence of any sort.

3. The right to sexual privacy. This involves the right for individual decisions and behaviours about intimacy as long as they do not intrude on the sexual rights of others.

   The right to sexual equity. This refers to freedom from all forms of discrimination regardless of sex, gender, sexual orientation, age, race, social class, religion or physical and emotional disability.

4. The right to sexual pleasure. Sexual pleasure, including auto-eroticism, is a source of physical, psychological, intellectual and spiritual well-being.

5. The right to emotional sexual expression. Sexual expression is more than erotic pleasure or sexual acts. Individuals have a right to express their sexuality through communication, touch, emotional expression and love.

6. The right to sexually associate freely. This means the possibility to marry or not, to divorce and to establish other types of responsible sexual associations.

7. The right to make free and responsible reproductive choices. This encompasses the right to decide whether or

not to have children, the number and spacing of children, and the right to full access to the means of fertility regulation.

8. The right to sexual information based upon scientific inquiry. This right implies that sexual information should be generated through the process of unencumbered and yet scientifically ethical inquiry, and disseminated in appropriate ways at all societal levels.

9. The right to comprehensive sexuality education. This is a lifelong process from birth throughout the life cycle and should involve all social institutions.

10. The right to sexual health care. Sexual health care should be available for prevention and treatment of all sexual concerns, problems and disorders.

Acknowledgements

The chronology of my thank-you list follows the shape of some human sexual experiences. At the *desire* stage, my agent Ed Victor and Dame Gail Rebuck, Chairman and Chief Executive of The Random House Group, enjoyed a little foreplay. Miranda West gave me the opportunity to publish this book by commissioning it, thus moving the project forward into the *arousal* stage. Susanna Abbott climbed aboard as editor and stroked me throughout the exciting *plateau* stage, when the book was actually being written. At the frustrating *pre-orgasmic* stage, Karen Sullivan edited the manuscript, and Toby Clarke designed the cover and end papers. The *post-orgasmic* stage involves the PR skills of Caroline Newbury, and the marketing expertise of Louise McKee – plus the sales and development brilliance of Hannah Telfer in the UK and David Parrish internationally. I am also grateful to Ebury MD Fiona McIntyre, and to the entire Ebury team; at all stages of this *affaire,* I have been wonderfully satisfied and extend to all my sincere thanks.

I am also most thankful to my colleague and friend Dr Dennis Sugrue, past president of the American Association of Sex Educators, Counselors and Therapists, and co-author of the excellent book *Sex Matters for Women* (Guildford Press), for so kindly reading the manuscript and offering notes and suggestions.

Finally, I owe very special thanks to the hundreds of people who generously gave me their time to talk to me about their sex lives or to complete written interviews. It's not easy to be open about such deeply personal matters as one's sexuality, and I am extremely grateful to everyone who was trusting enough to do so. Without their candid testimonies, this book could not have been written.

References

Alexander, D.A., Naji, A.A., Pinion, S.B., Mollison, J., Kitchener, H.C., Parkin, D.E., Abramovich, D.R. & Russell, I.T. (1996) 'Randomized trial comparing hysterectomy with endometrial ablation for dysfunctional abdominal bleeding: Psychiatric and psychosocial aspects', *British Medical Journal*, 312 (7026).

Allen, E. & Rhoades, G. (2008) 'Not all affairs are created equal: Emotional involvement with an extradyadic partner', *Journal of Sex and Marital Therapy*, 34.

Allgeier, E. & Allgeier, A. (2000) *Sexual Interactions*, 5th edn. Boston, MA: Houghton Mifflin Company.

Aponte, R. & Machado, M. (2006) 'Marital aspects associated with sexual satisfaction', *Journal of Sexual Medicine*, 3.

Archibald, A., Graber, J. & Brooks-Gunn, J. (2003) 'Pubertal processes and physiological growth in adolescence', in G.R. Adams & M.D. Berzonsky (eds) *Blackwell Handbook of Adolescence*. Malden, MA: Blackwell Publishing.

Atkins, D., Yi, J., Baucom, D. & Christensen, A. (2005) 'Infidelity in couples seeking marital therapy', *Journal of Family Psychology*, 19.

Baker, J. (1990) 'Coming out', *Newsweek*.

Bakwin, H. (1973) 'Erotic feelings in infants and young children', *American Journal of Diseases of Childhood*, 126.

Bancroft, J. (2009) *Human Sexuality and Its Problems*, 3rd edn, New York: Churchill Livingstone.

Bancroft, J., Herbenick, D. & Reynolds, M. (2003)

'Masturbation as a marker of sexual development', in J. Bancroft (ed.) *Sexual Development in Childhood.* Bloomington, IN: Indiana University Press.

Beckman, N., Waern, M. & Skoog, I. (2006) 'Determinants of sexuality in 70-year-olds', *Journal of Sex Research,* 43.

Berends, M.M. & Caron, S.L. (1994) 'Children's understanding and knowledge of conception and birth: A developmental approach', *Journal of Sex Education and Therapy,* 20(1).

Blackwell, D. & Lichter, D. (2000) 'Mate selection among married and co-habitating couples', *Journal of Family Issues,* 21.

Blake, S., Simkin, L., Ledsky, R., Perkins, C. & Calebrase, J. (2001) 'Effects of a parent-child communications intervention on young adolescents' risk for early onset of sexual intercourse', *Family Planning Perspectives,* 33.

Block, J. (1999) *Sex Over Fifty.* New York: Perigee.

Blumstein, P. & Schwartz, P. (1983) *American Couples.* New York: Morrow.

Boonstra, H. (2002) 'Legislators craft alternative vision of sex education to counter abstinence-only drive', *The Guttmacher Report,* 5.

Borneman, E. (1983). 'Progress in empirical research on children's sexuality', *SIECUS Report,* 1–5.

Borneman, E. (1994) *Childhood Phases of Maturity: Sexual Development Psychology.* New York: Prometheus Books.

Brecher, E. (1984) *Love, Sex and Aging: A Consumer's Union Survey.* Boston, MA: Little Brown.

Brezinka, V. & Kittel, F. (1996) 'Psychosocial factors of coronary heart disease in women: A review', *Social Science and Medicine,* 42.

Broderick, C. (1966) 'Socio-sexual development in a suburban community', *Journal of Sex Research,* 2.

Brown, S. (2003) 'Relationship quality dynamics of co-habitating unions', *Journal of Family Issues,* 24.

Bumpass, L., Sweet, J. & Cherlin, A. (1991) 'The role of

co-habitation in declining rates of marriage', *Journal of Marriage and the Family*, 53.

Burton, M.V. & Parker, R.W. (1997) 'Psychological aspects of cancer surgery: Surgeons' attitudes and opinions', *Psycho-Oncology*, 6.

Byers, E. (2005) 'Relationship satisfaction and sexual satisfaction: A longitudinal study of individuals in long-term relationships', *Journal of Sex Research*, 42.

Calderone, M.S. (1983) 'Childhood sexuality: Approaching the prevention of sexual disease', in G. Albee et al. (eds) *Promoting Sexual Responsibility and Preventing Sexual Problems*. Hanover, NH: University Press of New England.

Campbell, A. (2008) 'The morning after the night before: Affective reactions to one-night stands among mated and unmated men and women', *Human Nature*, DO110.

Christopher, F. (2001) *To Dance the Dance: A Symbolic Interactional Exploration of Premarital Sexuality*. Mahwah, NJ: Erlbaum.

Clements, M. (1994) 'Sex in America today', *Parade*, 7 August.

Colditz, G.A. (1997) 'Estrogen replacement therapy for breast cancer patients', *Oncology*, 11.

Coleman, L. & Cater, S. (2005) 'A qualitative study of the relationship between alcohol consumption and risky sex in adolescents', *Archives of Sexual Behavior*, 34.

Coles, R. & Stokes, G. (1985) *Sex and the American Teenager*. New York: Harper & Row.

Comfort, A. (1976) *A Good Age*. New York: Simon & Schuster.

Coontz, S. (2006) 'Three "rules" that don't apply', *Newsweek*, 5 June.

Cozzens, J. (2006) 'Assessing the awareness of adolescent sexual health among teachers-in-training', *American Journal of Sexuality Education*, 1.

Crawford, E.D., Bennett, C.L., Stone, N.N., Knight, S.J., DeAntoni, E., Sharp, L., Garnick, M.B. & Porterfield, H.A.

(1997) 'Comparison of perspectives on prostate cancer: Analyses of survey data', *Urology*, 50.

Crawford, M. & Popp, D. (2003) 'Sexual double standards: A review and methodological critique of two decades of research', *Journal of Sex Research*, 40.

Crockett, L., Raffaelli, M. & Moilanen, K. (2003) 'Adolescent sexuality: Behavior and meaning', in G.R. Adams & M.D. Berzonsky (eds) *Blackwell Handbook of Adolescence*. Malden, MA: Blackwell Publishing.

Crooks, R. & Baur, K. (2008) *Our Sexuality*, 11 edn., Belmont, CA: Wadsworth.

Dale, K.G. (1996) 'Intimacy and rheumatic diseases', *Rehabilitation Nursing*, 21.

Davidson, J., Moore, N., Earle, J. & Davis, J. (2008) 'Sexual attitudes and behaviors at four universities: Do region, race and/or religion matter?', *Adolescence*, 43.

DeKeseredy, W. & Kelly, K. (1995) 'Sexual abuse in Canadian university and college dating relationships: The contribution of male peer support', *Journal of Family Violence*, 10.

DeLamater, J. & Friedrich, W. (2002) 'Human sexual development', *Journal of Sex Research*, 39.

DeLamater, J. & Sill, M. (2005) 'Sexual desire in later life', *Journal of Sex Research*, 42.

Donnelly, D. (1993) 'Sexually inactive marriages', *Journal of Sex Research*, 30.

Dunn, M. & Cutler, N. (2000) 'Sexual issues in older adults', *AIDS Patient Care and STDs*, 14.

Eastman, K., Corona, R., Ryan, G., Warsfsky, A. & Schuster, M. (2005) 'Work-site-based parenting programs to promote healthy adolescent sexual development: A qualitative study of feasibility and potential content', *Perspectives on Sexual and Reproductive Health*, 37.

Elias, J. & Gebhard, P. (1969) 'Sexuality and sexual learning in childhood', *Phi Delta Kappan*, 50.

Ellis, H. (1912) *Studies in the Psychology of Sex*, Vol. 3. Philadelphia, PA: F.A. Davis Company.

Ellison, C. (2000) *Women's Sexualities: Generations of Women Share Intimate Secrets of Sexual Self-Acceptance.* Oakland, CA: New Harbinger.

Else-Quest, N., Hyde, J. & DeLamater, J. (2005) 'Context counts: Long-term sequelae of premarital intercourse or abstinence', *Journal of Sex Research*, 42.

Feldman, H.A., Goldstein, L., Hatzi Christou, D.G., Krane, R.J. & McKinlay, J.B. (1994) 'Impotence and its medical and psychosocial correlates: Result of the Massachusetts Male Aging Study', *Journal of Urology*, 151.

Finkelhor, D. (1980) 'Sex among siblings: A survey on prevalence, variety and effects', *Archives of Sexual Behavior*, 9.

Fishel, E. (1992) 'Raising sexually healthy kids', *Parents*, 67.

Foley, S., Kope, S. & Sugrue, D. (2002) *Sex Matters for Women: A Complete Guide to Taking Care of Your Sexual Self.* New York: Guilford Press.

Ford, C.S. & Beach, F.A. (1951) *Patterns of Sexual Behavior.* New York: Harper & Row.

Fossa, S.D., Woehre, H., Kurth, K.H., Hetherington, J., Bakke, H., Tustad, D.A. & Skanvik, R. (1997) 'Influence of urological morbidity on quality of life in patients with prostate cancer', *European Journal of Urology*, 31.

Fraley, M., Nelson, E., Wolf, A. & Lozoff, B. (1991) 'Early genital naming', *Developmental and Behavioral Pediatrics*, 12.

Frayser, S. (1994) 'Defining normal childhood sexuality: An anthropological approach', *Annual Review of Sex Research*, 5.

Friedrich, W., Grambsch, P., Broughton, D., Kuiper, J. & Beilke, R. (1991) 'Normative sexual behavior in children', *Pediatrics*, 88.

Friedrich, W. et al. (1998) 'Normative sexual behavior in children: A contemporary sample', *Pediatrics*, 101.

Gaylis, F.D., Friedel, W.E. & Armas, O. A. (1998) 'Radical

retropubic prostatectomy outcomes at a community hospital', *Journal of Urology*, 159.

Gecas, V. & Seff, M. (1991) 'Families and adolescents', in A. Booth (ed.) *Contemporary Families: Looking Forward, Looking Back*. Minneapolis, MN: National Council on Family Relations.

Goldfarb, E. (2005) 'What is comprehensive sexuality education really all about? Perceptions of students enrolled in an undergraduate human sexuality course', *American Journal of Sexuality Education*, 1.

Gordon, B.N. & Schroeder, C.S. (1995) *Sexuality: A Developmental Approach to Problems*. Chapel Hill, NC: Clinical Child Psychology Library.

Greene, K. & Faulkner, S. (2005) 'Gender, belief in the sexual double standard and sexual talk in heterosexual dating relationships', *Sex Roles: A Journal of Research*, 53.

Greenwald, E. & Leitenberg, H. (1989) 'Long-term effects of sexual experiences with siblings and non-siblings during childhood', *Archives of Sexual Behavior*, 18.

Gunderson, B.H., Melas, P.S. & Skar, J.E. (1981) 'Sexual behavior of preschool children: Teachers' observations', in L.L. Constantine & F.M. Martinson (eds) *Children and Sex: New Findings, New Perspectives*. Boston, MA: Little Brown.

Harlow, H. & Harlow, M. (1962) 'The effects of rearing conditions on behavior', *Bulletin of the Menninger Clinic*, 26.

Harmon, M.J. & Johnson, J.A. (1993) 'Sex education: Piagetian stages and children's perceptions of sexuality', *TCA Journal*, 22 (2).

Hatfield, E., Schmitz, E., Cornelius, J. & Rapson, R. (1988) 'Passionate love: How early does it begin?', *Journal of Psychology and Human Sexuality*, 1.

Hatfield, R. (1994) 'Touch and sexuality', in V. Bullough & B.B. Bullough (eds) *Human Sexuality: An Encyclopedia*. New York: Garland.

Hechtman, L. (1989) 'Teenage mothers and their children: Risks and problems: A review', *Canadian Journal of Psychiatry*, 34.

Helstrom, L., Lundberg, P.O., Sorbom, D. & Backstrom, T. (1993) 'Sexuality after hysterectomy', *Obstetrics & Gynecology*, 81.

Hill, C. (2008) *Human sexuality: Personality and Social Psychological Perspectives*. Los Angeles, CA: Sage Publications.

Hulter, B.M. & Lundberg, P.O. (1995) 'Sexual function in women with advanced multiple sclerosis', *Journal of Neurology, Neurosurgery and Psychiatry*, 59.

Hutchins, L. & Kaahumanu, L. (eds) (1991) *Bi Any Other Name: Bisexual People Speak Out*. Los Angeles, CA: Alyson Books.

Hyde, J. & DeLamater, J. (2008) *Understanding Human Sexuality*, 10th edn, New York: McGraw-Hill.

Impett, E., Schooler, D. & Tolman, D. (2006) 'To be seen and not heard: Feminine ideology and adolescent girls' sexual health', *Archives of Sexual Behavior*, 35.

Janssen, D. (2007) 'First stirrings: Cultural notes on orgasm, ejaculation and wet dreams', *Journal of Sex Research*, 44.

Janus, S. & Janus, C. (1993) *The Janus Report on Sexual Behavior*. New York: Wiley.

Johnson, B. et al (2003) 'Interventions to reduce sexual risk for the human immunodeficiency virus in adolescents', *Archives of Pediatrics and Adolescent Medicine*, 157.

Kanin, E. (1970) 'Sexual aggression by college men', *Medical Aspects of Human Sexuality*, 4.

Kaplan, H. (1979) *Disorders of Sexual Desire*. New York: Brunner/Mazel.

Kaye, E. (1997) *Mid-Life: Notes from the Halfway Mark*. London: Fourth Estate.

Kellet, J. (2000) 'Older adult sexuality', in L. Szuchman & F.

Muscarella (eds) *Psychological Perspectives on Human Sexuality*. New York: Wiley.

Kelly, G. (2008) *Sexuality Today*, 9th edn., Boston: McGraw-Hill.

Kempner, M. (2003) 'True integration of prevention programs requires broad focus on sexual health', *SIECUS Report*, 31.

Kimmel, M. & Mahler, M. (2003) 'Adolescent masculinity, homophobia and violence', *American Behavioral Scientist*, 46.

Kingsberg, S. (2002) 'The impact of aging on sexual function in women and their partners', *Archives of Sexual Behavior*, 31.

Kinsey, A., Pomeroy, W. & Martin, C. (1948) *Sexual Behavior in the Human Male*. Philadelphia, PA: Saunders.

Kinsey, A., Pomeroy, W., Martin, C. & Gebhard, P. (1953) *Sexual Behavior in the Human Female*. Philadelphia, PA: Saunders.

Kirby, D. (2002) 'Effective approaches to reducing adolescent unprotected sex, pregnancy and childbearing', *Journal of Sex Research*, 39.

Kirby, D. (2002) 'The impact of schools and school programs upon adolescent sexual behavior', *Journal of Sex Research*, 39.

Kirkpatrick, Lee & Davis, Keith. (1994) 'Attachment style, gender and relationship stability: A longitudinal analysis', *Journal of Personality and Social Psychology*, 66.

Knox, D., Zusman, M. & McNeely, A. (2008) 'University students' beliefs about sex: Men vs women', *College Student Journal*, 42.

Kontula, O. & Haavio-Mannila, E. (2002) 'Masturbation in a generational perspective', *Journal of Psychology and Human Sexuality*, 14.

Koss, M. & Dinero, T. (1988) 'Predictors of sexual aggression among a national sample of male college students', in R.A.

Prentky & V.I. Quinsey (eds) *Human Sexual Aggression: Current Perspectives*, Annals of the New York Academy of Sciences Vol. 528. New York: New York Academy of Sciences.

Lammers, C., Ireland, M., Resnick, M. & Blum, R. (2000) 'Influences on adolescents' decisions to postpone onset of sexual intercourse: A survival analysis of virginity among youths ages 13 to 18 years', *Journal of Adolescent Health*, 26.

Langfeldt, T. (1981) 'Childhood masturbation', in L.L. Constantine & F. M. Martinson (eds) *Children and Sex*. Boston, MA: Little Brown.

Laumann, E., Gagnon, J., Michael, R. & Michaels, S. (1994) *The Social Organization of Sexuality.* Chicago, IL: University of Chicago Press.

Leiblum, S. & Seagraves, R. (2000) 'Sex therapy with aging adults', in S. Leiblum & R. Rosen (eds) *Principles and Practice of Sex Therapy*, 3rd edn., New York: Guilford Press.

Lemoire, S. & Chen, C. (2005) 'Applying person-centered counseling to sexual minority adolescents', *Journal of Counseling and Development*, 83.

Levin, R. (2002) 'The physiology of sexual arousal in the human female: A recreational and procreational synthesis', *Archives of Sexual Behavior*, 31.

Levine, J. (2002) 'Promoting pleasure: What's the problem?', *SIECUS Report*, 30.

Levine, J. (2002) *Harmful to Minors: The Perils of Protecting Children from Sex*. Minneapolis, MN: University of Minnesota Press.

Lieber, L., Plumb, M.M., Gerstenzang, M.L. & Holland, J. (1976) 'The communication of affection between cancer patients and their spouses', *Psychosomatic Medicine*, 38.

Liu, C. (2003) 'Does quality of marital sex decline with duration?', *Archives of Sexual Behavior*, 32.

Mannino, D., Klevens, R. & Flanders, W. (1994) 'Cigarette smoking: An independent risk factor for impotence?', *American Journal of Epidemiology*, 140.

Mansfield, P., Voda, A. & Koch, P. (1995) 'Predictors of sexual response changes in heterosexual midlife women', *Health Values: The Journal of Health Behavior, Education and Promotion*, 19.

Martin, Carol & Ruble, Diane (2004) 'Children's search for gender cues: Cognitive perspectives on gender development', *Current Directions in Psychological Science*.

Martinson, Floyd M. (1994) *The Sexual Life of Children*, Westport, CT: Bergin & Garvey.

Masters, W.H. & Johnson, V.E. (1966) *Human Sexual Response*. Boston, MA: Little Brown.

Masters, W.H., Johnson, V.E. & Kolodny, R.C. (1982) *Human Sexuality*. Boston, MA: Little Brown.

Maurer, H. (1994) *Sex: Real People Talk about What They Really Do*. New York: Penguin Books.

Megan, K. (2008) 'Head of polyamory group discusses multiple partners', *Hartford Courant*, 8 May.

Miller, B., Benson, B. & Galbraith, K. (2001) 'Family relationships and adolescent pregnancy risk: A research synthesis', *Developmental Review*, 21.

Money, J. (1980) *Love and Lovesickness*. Baltimore, MD: Johns Hopkins University Press.

Moore, J. & Kendall, D. (1971) 'Children's concepts of reproduction', *Journal of Sex Research*, 7.

Mundy, L. (2000) 'Sex and sensibility', *The Washington Post* online, 15 July.

Newcomer, S. & Udry, R. (1985) 'Oral sex in an adolescent population', *Archives of Sexual Behavior*, 14.

Newman, R. (2008) 'It starts in the womb: Helping parents understand infant sexuality', *Electronic Journal of Human Sexuality*, 11.

Nusbaum, M., Lenahan, P. & Sadovsky, R. (2005) 'Sexual health in aging men and women: Addressing the physiologic and psychological sexual changes that occur with age', *Geriatrics*, 60.

O'Donnell, L., Stueve, A., Wilson-Simmons, R., Dash, K., Agronick, G. & Jean Baptiste, V. (2006) 'Heterosexual risk behaviors among suburban adolescents', *Journal of Early Adolescence*, 26.

O'Sullivan, L., Cheng, M., Harris, K & Brookes-Gunn, J. (2007) 'I wanna hold your hand: The progression of social, romantic and sexual events in adolescent relationships', *Perspectives on Sexual and Reproductive Health*, 39.

O'Donnell, L. et al (2005) 'Saving sex for later: An evauation of a parent education intervention', *Perspectives on Sexual and Reproductive Health*, 37.

Ogletree, S.M. & Ginsberg, H.J. (2000) 'Kept under the hood: Neglect of the clitoris in common vernacular', *Sex Roles*, 43(11/12).

Ott, M., Millstein, S., Ofner, S. & Halpern-Felsher, B. (2006) 'Greater expectations: Adolescents' positive motivations for sex', *Perspectives on Sexual and Reproductive Health*, 38.

Overbeck, G., Vollebergh, W., Engels, R. & Meeus, W. (2003) 'Parental attachment and romantic relationships: Associations with emotional disturbance during late adolescence', *Journal of Counseling Psychology*, 50.

Partington, A. (ed.) (1996) *The Oxford Dictionary of Quotations*, 4th edn., Oxford: Oxford University Press.

Pipher, M. (1994) *Reviving Ophelia: Saving the Selves of Adolescent Girls.* New York: Ballantine.

Plummer, K. (1991) 'Understanding childhood sexualities', *Journal of Homosexuality*, 20.

Pogrebin, L.C. (1983) *Family Politics.* New York: McGraw-Hill.

Puentes, J., Knox, D. & Zusman, M. (2008) 'Participants in

"friends with benefits" relationships', *College Student Journal*, 42.

Rathus, A., Nevid, J. & Fichner-Rathus, L. (2002) *Human Sexuality in a World of Diversity*, 5th edn., Boston, MA: Allyn & Bacon.

Reinisch, J. (1991) *The Kinsey Institute New Report on Sex*. New York: St Martin's Press.

Renshaw, D.C. (1988) 'Young children's sex play: Counseling the parents', *Medical Aspects of Human Sexuality*, 22(12).

Renshaw, T. (1988) 'Sexuality in the later years', *Geriatric Sexual Counselling Mediguide to Aging*, 3(1).

Rickert, V., Sanghvi, R. & Weimann, C. (2002) 'Is lack of sexual assertiveness among adolescent and young adult women a cause for concern?', *Perspectives on Sexual and Reproductive Health*, 34.

Roberts, E. (1983) 'Childhood sexual learning: The unwritten curriculum', in C. Davis (ed.) *Challenges in Sexual Science*. Philadelphia, PA: Society for the Scientific Study of Sex.

Rosenthal, D., Smith, A. & de Visser, R. (1999) 'Personal and social factors influencing age at first intercourse', *Archives of Sexual Behavior*, 28.

Rowe, J. & Kahn, R. (1998) *Successful Aging*. New York: Pantheon Books.

Russell, S. (2001) 'LGBTQ youth are at risk in US school environment', *SIECUS Report*, 29.

Ryan, G. (2000) 'Childhood sexuality: A decade of study, Part 1: Research and curriculum development', *Child Abuse and Neglect*, 24.

Sandnabba, N., Santtila, P., Wannas, M. & Krook, K. (2003) 'Age and gender-specific sexual behaviors in children', *Child Abuse and Neglect*, 27.

Sarrel, L.& Sarrel, P. (1984) *Sexual Turning Points: The Seven Stages of Adult Sexuality*. New York: Macmillan.

Schachner, D., Shaver, P. & Gillath, O. (2008) 'Attachment style and long-term singlehood', *Personal Relationships*, 15.

Schiavi, R.C. (1992) 'Normal aging and the evaluation of sexual dysfunction', *Psychiatric Medicine*, 10.

Schover, L.R. (1987) 'Sexuality and fertility in urologic cancer patients', *Cancer*, 60.

Schover, L.R. (1993) 'Sexual rehabilitation after treatment for prostate cancer', *Cancer*, 71.

Schover, L.R. (1998) 'Some perspectives on Viagramania', *Cleveland Clinic Medical Journal*, 65.

Schover, L.R. & Jensen, S.B. (1988) *Sexuality and Chronic Illness: A Comprehensive Approach*. New York: Guilford Press.

Schover, L.R., Fife, M. & Gershenson, D.M. (1989) 'Sexual function and treatment for early stage cervical cancer', *Cancer*, 63.

Schover, L.R., Montague, D.K. & Lakin, M. (1997) 'Supportive care and the quality of life of the cancer patient: Sexual problems', in V.T. DeVita, S. Hellman & S.A. Rosenberg (eds) *Cancer: Principles and Practice of Oncology*, 5th edn. Philadelphia, PA: Lippencott.

Schover, L.R., Evans, R.B. & von Eschenbach, A.C. (1987) 'Sexual rehabilitation in a cancer center: Diagnosis and outcome in 384 consultations', *Archives of Sexual Behavior*, 16.

Schover, S. (2000) 'Sexual problems in chronic illness', in S. Leiblum & R. Rosen (eds) *Principles and Practice of Sex Therapy*, 3rd edn. New York: Guilford Press.

Schreiner-Engel, P., Schiavi, R.C., Vietorisz, D. & Smith, H. (1987) 'The differential impact of diabetes type on female sexuality', *Journal of Psychosomatic Research*, 31.

Segraves, R & Segraves, K. (1995) 'Human sexuality and aging', *Journal of Sex Education and Therapy*, 21.

SIECUS (2003) *The Truth about Adolescent Sexuality*. New York: Sex Information and Education Council of the US.

Sieving, R., Eisenberg, M., Pettingell, S. & Skay, C. (2006) 'Friends' influence on adolescents' first sexual intercourse', *Perspectives on Sexual and Reproductive Health*, 38.

Spica, M.M. & Schwab, M.D. (1996) 'Sexual expression after total joint replacement', *Orthopaedic Nursing*, 15.

Starr, B. & Weiner, M. (1981) *The Starr Weiner Report on Sex and Sexuality in the Mature Years*. New York: Stein & Day.

Steinke, E. & Petteron-Midgley, P. (1996) 'Sexual counseling following acute myocardial infarction', *Clinical Nursing Research*, 5.

Strong, B., De Vault, C. & Sayad, B. (1999) *Human Sexuality: Diversity in Contemporary America*, 3rd edn., Mountain View, CA: Mayfield Publishing Company.

Talcott, J.A., Rieker, P., Clark, J.A., Propert, K.J., Weeks, J.C., Beard, C.J., Wishnow, K.I., Kaplan, I., Loughlin, K.R., Richie, J.P. & Kantoff, P.W. (1998) 'Patient-reported symptoms after primary therapy for early prostate cancer: Results of a prospective cohort study', *Journal of Clinical Oncology*, 16.

Taverner, B. (2003) 'All together now: Combining pregnancy and STI prevention programs', *SIECUS Report*, 31.

Thanasiu, P. (2004) 'Childhood sexuality: Discerning healthy from abnormal sexual behaviors', *Journal of Mental Health Counseling*, 26.

Tolman, D., Streipe, M. & Harmon, T. (2003) 'Gender matters: Constructing a model of adolescent sexual health', *Journal of Sex Research*, 40.

Treas, J. & Giesen, D. (2000) 'Sexual infidelity among married and cohabitating Americans', *Journal of Marriage and Family*, 62.

Treboux, D. & Busch-Rossnagel, N. (1990) 'Social network influences on adolescent sexual attitudes and behaviors', *Journal of Adolescent Research*, 5.

Trudel, G., Boyer, R., Villeneuve, V., Anderson, A., Pilon, G. & Bounader, J. (2008) 'The Marital Life and Aging Well

Program: Effects of a group preventative intervention on the marital and sexual functioning of retired couples', *Sexual and Relationship Therapy*, 23.

Virtanen, H., Makinen, J., Tenho, T., Kiilholma, P., Pirkanen, Y. & Hirvonen, T. (1993) 'Effects of abdominal hysterectomy on urinary and sexual symptoms', *British Journal of Urology*, 72.

Weijmar Schultz, W.C., van de Wiel, H.B., Bouma, J., Janssens, J. & Littlewood, J. (1990) 'Psychosexual functioning after treatment of cancer of the vulva: A longitudinal study', *Cancer*, 66.

Whitbeck, L., Chen, X., Hoyt, D., Tyler, K. & Johnson, K. (2004) 'Mental disorder, subsistence strategies and victimization among gay, lesbian and bisexual homeless and runaway adolescents', *Journal of Sex Research*, 41.

Whitbeck, L., Simons, R. & Kao, M. (1994) 'The effects of divorced mothers' dating behavior and sexual attitudes on the sexual attitudes and behavior of their adolescent children', *Journal of Marriage and the Family*, 56.

Willetts, M. (2006) 'Union quality comparisons between long-term heterosexual co-habitation and legal marriage', *Journal of Family Issues*, 27.

Williams, A. (2008) 'Hopelessly devoted to you, you and you', *New York Times*, 5 October.

Wilson, S. and Medora, N. (1990) 'Gender comparisons of college students' attitudes towards sexual behavior', *Adolescence*, 25.

Wincze, J.P. & Carey, M.P. (1991) *Sexual Dysfunction: A Guide for Assessment and Treatment*. New York: Guilford Press.

Woody, J., Russel, R., D'Souza, H. & Woody, J. (2000) 'Adolescent non-coital sexual activity: Comparisons of virgins and non-virgins', *Journal of Sex Education and Therapy*, 25.

Yalla, S.V. (1982) 'Sexual dysfunction in the paraplegic and quadriplegic', in A.H. Bennet (ed.) *Management of Male Impotence*. Baltimore, MD: Williams & Wilkins.

Index